GOOD-BYE FOR EVER

GOOD-BYE FOR EVER

EVER

The victim of a system

By

JOHN PUGH

BARRY ROSE (PUBLISHERS) LTD.

London and Chichester

PRINTED IN GREAT BRITAIN
BY EBENEZER BAYLIS AND SON LTD
THE TRINITY PRESS, WORCESTER, AND LONDON

FOR
JONATHAN

AUTHOR'S NOTE

The name of the lady who gave birth to the baby, the subject of the charge of Murder, does not appear; nor does that of her son. For narrative purposes I have referred to her as Maisie ———— and her son as Michael ————. I have also amended all other reference to them, both in the transcript of the trial, newspaper reports and personal recollections.

J.P.

CONTENTS

ILLUSTRATIONS

ACKNOWLEDGMENTS

I gratefully wish to acknowledge the assistance that I have received from the Home Office; and in particular the help, advice and guidance constantly given to me by Mr. H. G. Pearson, the Departmental Record Officer.

My thanks go to the Honourable Mr. Justice Kilner Brown; the Honourable Mr. Justice Michael Davies; the Honourable Mr. Justice Croom-Johnson; Mr. J. F. Milward J.P.; Mr. J. A. Alderson; Mr. Inspector Michael Balmer, of the West Midlands Police Force; Miss Helen Beattie; Mr. James Black; the late Mr. George Blackborow; Mr. H. G. Blenkinsop; Mr. Roy Brown, of C. S. Bailey (Bromsgrove) Ltd.; Miss Beverley Dunn; Mr. Charles Elworthy; the late Mrs. N. Fearnley-Whittingstall; Mr. Charles Harvey, formerly of the *Sunday Mercury*; Mrs. Hazel Hubball; Mr. Frank Jordan, formerly Assistant Chief Constable (Crime), of the West Midlands Police Force, but now Deputy Chief Constable of Kent Constabulary; Sir Philip Knights, Chief Constable of the West Midlands Police Force; Mr. W. E. Lovsey; Mrs. Pauline Lyon; Mr. Honorary Alderman J. S. Meadows, a former Lord Mayor of the City of Birmingham; Mr. Frank Mountford, Clerk to the City of Birmingham Justices; Mr. J. Newbould, the Deputy Superintendent Registrar for the City of Birmingham; Mr. F. B. Normansell; Lord Paget of Northampton; Mr. Albert Pierrepoint; Dr. Vera Pugh; Mr. Walter Rose; Miss Sue Smith; Miss Jean Startin; Mr. Clive Taylor; Miss Pam Thompson; Señor Javier Villa; Mr. D. Valentine; Mr. Dave Walsh and Mr. Woodrow Wyatt.

I am particularly grateful to Mr. T. D. Morris, the Managing Director of the Birmingham Post & Mail Ltd., who has allowed me the freedom of his files and to the Editor of the *Evening Post*, published in Reading, for permission to quote from his newspaper. Thanks go to the British Newspaper Library; in particular Mr. T. P. Kay; and the Birmingham Reference Library; in particular Mr. Michael Young, for all the help and support that they have given to me. My thanks also go to Mr. Roger Calvert for permission to reproduce part of his splendid painting; and to the Universal Pictorial Press and Agency Ltd.; and others for photographs. Each individual photograph is acknowledged where appropriate.

I acknowledge, with thanks, permission from Messrs. Martin Meredith & Co., and Messrs. Walsh, Cherer & Co., official shorthand writers to the Birmingham Assizes in 1951, to reproduce the transcript of the trial, and Thames and Hudson Ltd. for permission to refresh my memory of the year 1951 from their book *A Tonic to the Nation*—the story of the Festival of Britain Year 1951.

Thanks, too, go to Mr. P. Ashley, press officer of the City of Birmingham publicity section, for permission to quote from the City's *Official Guide* to the Festival year of 1951. Many others, too numerous to mention individually have helped me and I wish to record my appreciation of their help.

This book could not have been written without the support of many who cannot be named. My thanks go to each of them; individually they know the part that they have played.

JOHN PUGH

Bromsgrove

PREFACE

This is a true story. One day in the spring of 1977, I was walking along a beach in Gran Canaria when I saw a man—a deck chair attendant; he reminded me of someone. At the time I could not think who. Then, suddenly, perhaps mellowed by a glass of my favourite Fundador, it all came flowing back: March 1951; William Arthur Watkins. The similarity was uncanny to the point of being unnerving; from that moment I could not let rest what I had experienced, so many years before.

This book is the result; every fact has been authenticated, everyone who remembered has reflected and now with the passage of time all that is available can be revealed. The story is emotive, though I have tried not to make it so; but no story of any human life can fail to be full of happiness and sorrow. No person lives without laughter or tears; no person who lives to maturity can fail to make some impression upon someone else. Bill Watkins, whom I shall see in my mind to my dying day, made such an impression upon me in March 1951: I, then a young man; inexperienced in life, in emotion and in death.

William Arthur Watkins found his God, and when he knew that mortals would not save his life, and helpers failed him and all comfort fled, turned to Him, the helper of the helpless, and went happily to meet Him.

I wrote this book in a part of Spain, so beautiful that even the Devil could never destroy it; so tranquil, that even the sound of the sea will never deafen the chirping of the birds. Each day that I was there the morning broke and earth's vain shadow fled, leaving me with pen, paper and memories.

JOHN PUGH

Spain

INTRODUCTION

Neville Chamberlain was a Birmingham man; it was he who promised "peace in our time". In 1951 Great Britain was still recovering from the aftermath of victory; Chamberlain was dead and the peace that he never lived to see became a phoney peace. Winston Churchill had declared: in war: resolution; in defeat: defiance; in victory: magnanimity; in peace: goodwill. There was little magnanimity and even less goodwill for the under-dog in the years that immediately followed the war; the slums remained; England did not change for the better and the victorious people became discontented. The euphoria of victory soon faded and nothing that Churchill could do would alter the syndrome that he himself had helped create. "Peace in our time" became forgotten and the long uphill struggle for a better world had begun. 1951 was Festival Year and Great Britain put on a bold face, for whilst much jollity was planned, certain commodities were still rationed.

It was in this atmosphere, in the slums of Birmingham's Balsall Heath that William Arthur Watkins, a humble, if then an unfriendly man, sought to make a new life for himself and his common law wife, Maisie. They started living together on 26th January, 1946, after Watkins had left his wife and family. Later Maisie gave birth to a son, Michael, who in 1951 was to be 4. Shortly before Christmas 1949, the couple and their little son returned to Birmingham, from Sunderland, where they had lived since 1948, and moved into No. 6 back of 79 Clifton Road. On 28th May, 1946, an order was made against Watkins by the Birmingham Magistrates, whereby he had to pay £1 a week maintenance to his wife, Doris, and 10 shillings a week for their youngest child. Of their four children, who lived, two had grown up and so Doris was granted custody of the two youngest. The order was made on the grounds of desertion.

Life was not easy for Bill and Maisie, and money was desperately short. Watkins still had to maintain his wife in accordance with the court order: to do this and keep himself, Maisie and little Michael, Watkins earned £9 a week; he was a labourer, working nights, at the Hercules cycle factory in Birmingham. In January 1951 his difficulties were further burdened by the fact that he had become very deaf. Maisie and he had one secret: since July the previous year they knew that she was pregnant and as a result they had become very frightened.

Birmingham had suffered a certain amount of war damage, but the brunt of the Luftwaffe's fury had fallen on neighbouring Coventry. Balsall Heath survived and the pre-war slums became the post-war slums: the same old houses slowly and at times wilfully fell apart. The city fathers in 1945 began a period of reconstruction for England's second city. Balsall Heath was not one of the priorities: many years were to pass before the planners turned their attention to this small locality just south west of the city centre, knocking down the terraced slums and replacing them not only with modern houses but with blocks of tower flats. It was the centre of the city's vice, and gangs controlled the girls with a viciousness that was their own. Nearby stands the headquarters of the Warwickshire County Cricket Club, significantly called Edgbaston. From the top of the pavilion roof in 1951, rows upon rows of tiny roofs could be seen; these were the roofs of much of Balsall Heath, although Clifton Road itself could not be seen from this vantage point. Professor A. E. Richardson, writing "An Impression of Birmingham" which was printed in the first edition of *The Birmingham Post Year Book and Who's Who* published in 1949, stated that the "most remarkable feature of the city's growth was the jealous care given to Edgbaston, where the houses and gardens are a delight". He went on to write "From the sashed windows of the Golf Club one looks across the silhouette of the new hospital buildings and recalls the lines of a near eastern town. In the other direction there is the diminutive Parish Church of Edgbaston, and nearby are the beautiful Botanic Gardens. It is difficult to realize that the chromium plate facias of New Street are only a mile distant". No mention is made of the squalor that still then existed only a mile distant; but in 1949 one did not talk of such things, let alone write about them. Clifton Road was one of the better roads in Balsall Heath and most of the residents took pride in their homes. No. 6 back of 79 was the exception rather than the rule; it was cold, simple and very dirty because the occupants had neither the resources nor the energy to make it otherwise; sadly, it was a slum.

The Festival of Britain took place exactly a century after the Great Exhibition of 1851. The Royal Festival Hall in London was the only permanent building erected for the Festival. 1950 had seen the vast preparations for the on-coming year and no one was allowed to escape from the whirlwind of bureaucratic euphoria. The Labour Government, led by Clement Attlee, was in its last months and the solidarity with which the party had swept into power in 1945 was wilting. Ernest Bevin, one of the greatest politicians never to be prime minister, died shortly before the dedication service for the Festival at St. Paul's Cathedral on 3rd May, 1951. Aneuran Bevan, another of Labour's stalwarts, had resigned from the Government, and terrible fighting was taking place in Korea. The King was far from well. It was not a good time for a festival and those who were on the breadline did not appreciate the vast extravagances which were to cost the country many hundreds of thousands of pounds: to cap it all when 3rd May arrived the South Bank site in London was incomplete.

1951 was to be the year of all years; "the curtain now rises on the Festival of Britain designed to put the whole of Britain on show, both to its own people and the world" was the description given to it by Birmingham's official guide and programme which was published in March; and the writer went on to describe the part that Birmingham would play in the celebrations:—

> The Festival of Britain is intended to be nation wide and in carrying out its task to display the British contribution to civilization, past, present and future, in the arts, in science and in industry, in sport and in the British way of life, it hopes to serve as a token of thanksgiving for her past and as a testimony of faith in the future.
>
> Unhappily the international situation has worsened considerably since the Festival was first conceived. But the Festival of 1951 means something more than funfairs and fireworks, entertaining as they may be. The Festival of Britain is an act of national re-assessment and an affirmation of faith in the future, and possibly at no time is there a greater need for this kind of demonstration of a living democracy and a free people.
>
> From May to September there will be displays and demonstrations illustrating all phases of the British way of life from the skill of her craftsmen to the talent of her musicians, ranging from the British Industries Fair in London and in Birmingham to Festivals of drama and music in places as far apart as Brighton and Inverness, each preserving the distinctive character appropriate to the traditions and amenities of the places in which they are held.
>
> It is fitting, therefore, that the citizens of Britain's Second City should be given

2

every opportunity to share in this great Festival year and the wide variety of Birmingham's interests are reflected in the programme of the City's celebrations.

There is a range of events to suit the taste of every one of Birmingham's million inhabitants, and it is hoped, of many visitors from both home and overseas.

Highlight of the celebrations in Birmingham will be the visit of Her Royal Highness The Princess Elizabeth on June 9th. Her programme of engagements includes starting a Veteran Car Rally from Birmingham to Coventry, and visits to an Exhibition depicting the part women play in the City's life and to a Physical Training Display at Villa Park.

During the opening days of the Festival, Birmingham will be the host to industrialists at the British Industries Fair at Castle Bromwich and later an exhibition of aspects of industry that are more peculiar to Birmingham will be staged in the new Industrial and Science Museum.

Literature will be represented by an Exhibition of Rare and Valuable Books in the Central Library and music by a week's Festival of British Music at the end of September. The programme includes many events of sporting interest— football matches and a Festival week of County Cricket, athletic meetings, swimming galas and physical training displays. Of more particular interest is the holding of the Junior World Chess Championship, and the English Model Yacht Championships, while entertainments in the parks from drama to Punch and Judy, floodlighting and fireworks, brass bands and open air dancing all go to make a programme that should long be remembered. And among the permanent projects to mark the great year, improvements to the interior of Birmingham's famous Town Hall, a new layout for Victoria Square and improvements to Chamberlain Place will serve in the years to come to remind us that in 1951 Birmingham shared with the rest of the land in this great demonstration of our pride in the past and of our confidence in the future.

The programme listed so many activities that there was something for everyone—if they wanted to participate. Birmingham itself was given a clean-up, and in the same guide more details were given:

In several ways the amenities of Birmingham will be added to in order to commemorate the Festival of Britain. In Victoria Square an improvement scheme has been carried out, in which the new bronze replica of the original statue of Queen Victoria now stands on a pedestal of reconstructed Cornish Granite surrounded by flower beds and turf.

Considerable alterations have also been made in Chamberlain Place with a view to opening up what was previously a somewhat cramped and sombre area. A number of the old statues has been removed and the one remaining, that of Joseph Priestley, has been cast in bronze. The fountain has been relined, the jets illuminated and the addition of new flower beds should give a new emphasis to the fine architecture of the Town Hall, where, also to mark Festival year, several improvements are to be carried out during the summer. These will include the redecoration of the interior, the provision of a new lighting system and alterations to the stage, all of which should improve considerably the amenities of the building.

In Colmore Row, Bull Street and High Street, the Festival year has been marked by the provision of specially designed lamp standards equipped with vertical fluorescent fittings. In Cannon Hill Park, the Golden Lion, believed to have been the Clergy House and School of the Guild of Deritend, has been repaired and in the immediate surroundings a cobbled frontage and gravel terrace, coupled with a small intimate garden, Elizabethan in character, has been introduced.

In Lightwoods Park 1951 will be marked by the restoration of the Shakespearean garden.

At Bartley Green Reservoir a new viewing point is to be provided and trees are to be planted near Frankley Beeches.

R. C. Yates, a Birmingham solicitor, was Lord Mayor, and *ex-officio* presided over the city's Festival Committee which included representatives from many associations; Leslie Deakins (then secretary of the Warwickshire County Cricket Club) represented the club in what was to be their championship year: the county had made the almost unheard of appointment—a professional captain. H. E. (Tom) Dollery was one of the most respected players of his time and his captaincy was superb. Other notable representatives on the committee were Alderman J. Crump, J.P.; Percy Eames, the city treasurer; Ted Dodd, the chief constable; Harry Coleman, the chief fire brigade officer; Alderman J. C. Burman; Trenchard Cox, the director of the museum and art gallery and Derek Salburg and Sir Barry Jackson represented the Alexandra Theatre and Repertory Theatre respectively. Bert Manzoni, the city surveyor, and Birmingham worthies such as Sir Wilfred Martineau and Norman Leaker, were also included. Later in life many were to be honoured for services in their particular fields and knighthoods went to four of them: Sir Edward Dodd, Sir John Burman, Sir Herbert Manzoni and Sir Trenchard Cox.

Yes, indeed; 1951 was going to be a great year—but one event cast its shadow over all else for a handful of Birmingham people. Yet no one knew why; it was no one's fault except Bill Watkins' and for some extraordinary reason known only to himself he would not tell those, whose task it was to help him, any information that they could use to assist him. He found his God and died for it.

Birmingham has produced many High Court Judges; but few so illustrious in their time as Mr. Justice Finnemore. In 1951 he was in his 62nd year and had been a High Court Judge since 1947; he died in 1974. A tall, angular man with a prominent nose, he was well known in the city of his birth not only for his standing in the law but for his untiring work for the Boys' Brigade. Sir Donald Leslie

Finnemore, a bachelor, lived in Handsworth, a suburb to the north of the centre of Birmingham. After a distinguished career at the Bar, he was made a County Court Judge in 1940. He was a man of considerable warmth, yet a stern Judge who would stand no nonsense and when the occasion merited it, his warmth left him and he could become icily cold. It is probable that before the Winter Assizes held at the Victoria Courts in Corporation Street, Birmingham, on 15th March, 1951, William Arthur Watkins had heard of him; for in his youth Watkins had been a member of the Boys' Brigade. When the two were face to face, it was the icy Finnemore that Watkins was to be confronted with.

Theodore Beal Pritchett, M.C., solicitor, and Alderman of the City, was a distinguished looking man. He had been Lord Mayor at the outbreak of the Second World War and was later to be knighted for his services to the City. His personality and standing in his profession made him much sought after. Tall, with prematurely white hair, he sported the most magnificent eyebrows, and with a throaty voice of considerable charm, fitted the part of a leading city solicitor to a tee. He was a general practitioner dealing with a considerable company practice, yet still found time for criminal work. Since 1923 he had been part-time clerk to the Redditch and Wythall Petty Sessional Divisions and made not infrequent forays into the Victoria Courts. In 1951, he was just 60, and whilst others of that age were often tempted to ease off, Pritchett was the exception to the rule. His name in Birmingham was a household word and whilst Watkins undoubtedly would have heard of the name of Pritchett, that is as far as his knowledge would have gone. He little knew that Maisie's forthcoming pregnancy was going to result in Pritchett's firm, Hatwell Pritchett & Co., undertaking his defence on a charge of murder. Whilst Pritchett kept an eye on the case, its conduct was left to Tony Alderson, a solicitor who though then a young man, had already made his mark in legal circles as an advocate of no mean ability. It was left to him to see Watkins and prepare the case for the defence. Alderson found it difficult to communicate with Watkins because of the latter's deafness and now, with the passing of time, one wonders whether Watkins had then just given up. Life for him since he deserted Doris had been a terrible struggle in which all the standards that he had set himself in life were abandoned, one by one. The events of the night 20th/21st January were the final straws. To prepare a defence when the accused will not help is an impossible task and Alderson, try as he did to discover, was told very little of Watkins' past. He briefed one of the most brilliant advocates of his time, William Fearnley-Whittingstall, and even the great K.C. could glean virtually nothing from Watkins of his past.

"Mr. M. P. Pugh, prosecuting, said . . ." was the preface practically every night in the Birmingham evening papers (there were two in 1951, *The Birmingham Mail* and the *Evening Despatch*) to some story of woe. Pugh had been prosecuting solicitor in Birmingham since 1924; he had succeeded Mr. J. E. Hill, a former Warwickshire county cricketer. In 1951 he was into his last decade of office, for he had planned his retirement to coincide with his 65th birthday. Now 58, he was still the undisputed *tour-de-force* in the courts that his earlier reputation had earned him. Every prosecution brought by the police within the city boundary went through his department, and he was the only agent of the Director of Public Prosecutions outside London: a position he cherished, for it meant that every D.P.P. case was dealt with by him personally—these cases, of course, included murder. Stockily built with thinning hair, a large double chin and piercing blue grey eyes, always immaculately dressed, Pugh dominated every court appearance in which he was concerned. Half-moon glasses with a heavy frame perched on the end of his nose made him look even more formidable. The First World War, in which he was highly decorated, had brought to him a horror of unnatural death. Whilst he was in favour of capital punishment, he firmly believed in the prerogative of mercy. He publicly stated that Bentley would not be hanged, and when the ultimate fate was decreed for Watkins, was heard to say "he won't swing".

Pugh had many friends, and two men within the inner sanctum of the Victoria Courts were particularly close to him: Edward James Dodd, Chief Constable at the age of 36, and James Mathewson Webster, Professor of Forensic Science at Birmingham University and head of the West Midland Forensic Science Laboratory. All three were to be concerned with the happenings at No. 6 back of 79 Clifton Road, Balsall Heath, on the night of 20th/21st January, 1951. About 3.00 a.m. on the morning of 21st January, Maisie Watkins, as she was known, gave birth to a male child. Within 15 minutes the baby was dead: within 48 hours William Arthur Watkins was charged with murder.

The wheels of justice started to turn against him with righteousness and the law to support them, and help them on their way to the ultimate, yet at the time, not inevitable, end. Webster conducted the *post-mortem* and then with Pugh, Dodd and Dodd's senior officers, discussed his findings: the child had lived and was not stillborn.

Edward Dodd (later to become Sir Edward Dodd, H.M. Chief Inspector of Constabulary, before his untimely death) was a handsome man, rather like a youthful Jack Hawkins. He wore his uniform well and looked the part of Chief Constable. He was 42 in 1951; ten years' earlier he had been appointed Assistant Chief Constable, coming to the City from the Metropolitan Police. Like Pugh, he was born in Reading and from their first meeting there was an affinity which grew into a great personal friendship. All major crimes went personally through the Chief's office in Newton Street, and as that was only two rooms away from the office of the prosecuting solicitor, there was ample opportunity each day for the two to meet and discuss the preparation of cases. They both lunched in the senior officers' mess just along the corridor, although there, except in times of crisis, talk rarely touched the work of the day; more often than not the subjects bantered around the table were, in the winter, National Hunt racing and in the summer, cricket.

Newton Street links Steelhouse Lane and Corporation Street; it housed the County Court and the Coroner's court. In 1951 Professor Webster with his small retinue conducted his *post-mortems* in the mortuary which was almost opposite the private entrance to the office complex of the Victoria Courts, proudly guarded during the day time by Police Constable Leslie Syrell and his colleagues. Syrell was a well-built man, symbolic of Jack Warner's portrayal of P.C. George Dixon. All the giants of the day knew and liked the officer, and as they came and went, Syrell touched his helmet in the form of a salute. There had been difficulties in the early days between Pugh and Webster. Each thought that the other should visit the other's office if one had a point to discuss. Pugh had the upper hand as not only did he possess a vastly superior office into which no unwanted visitor could penetrate, but also it was near to Dodd. Webster's office was small, cold and unprotected. Ultimately, Webster having made his point, and in so doing earned the respect of Pugh and Dodd, would make his way across Newton Street; be saluted by P.C. Syrell, turn right up the stairs to the first floor and proceed along the wide polished corridor. There were two conditions attached to these visits: Webster would go at a time convenient to himself and he would not have to wait.

James Mathewson Webster was a large balding Scot. He had a glass eye and wore a monocle to enhance the vision of the surviving eye. He loved to perpetuate the Scottish misnomer of meanness: "Och, a pair of glasses is no damn good to a man with a glass eye", he would declare. He was untidy in his dress, generally wearing baggy trousers with an old brown Harris tweed jacket: his tie would be half round his neck; there, with the outward appearance, the untidiness ceased. His case notes were immaculate, his forensic skills unparalleled, though often disputed. He was frequently referred to as "The Home Office Pathologist", a title which he thoroughly enjoyed even though no such appointment existed. Stories of him are legion. Once he was called in by a Welsh force to carry out a *post-mortem* upon a murder victim. He lived in Beacon Hill, Rubery, to the south of Birmingham, and at that time part of the then Urban District of Bromsgrove. By the time he arrived at the scene of the crime it was dark and the weather was atrocious. The tent hastily erected around the body billowed in the wind. A young policeman who had been deputed to greet the pathologist waited, holding a torch. Webster drove a black, 1½ litre 1948 model Riley, and, on recognizing the car, the officer stepped forward. "I think I know who's done it, sir," he whispered in a lilting Welsh accent. "Aye," replied Webster, "do you laddie, then tell me." "Well, sir," said the officer, "there's been a strange fellow round these parts, he's got a glass eye and wears a monocle; very suspicious he is." In the dark of the night Webster grabbed the officer's hand. "Flash your torch on my face, laddie"; by the time this had been done Webster's monocle was firmly fixed in place. The Prof. smiled, and whilst the policeman was beginning to realize what a fool he had made of himself, Webster was already saying "Come on laddie, we've got work to do: now I'll show you what to do. . . ."

Former Mr. Chief Superintendent Walter Parsons, ex-City of Birmingham Police, known to all his friends as "Wally", was a great friend of both Pugh and Webster. After leaving the Force he became head of the Works Police at the then Austin Works at Longbridge. One summer Saturday around 1950, the three decided to go to Nottingham to see Worcestershire play the home team. Pugh and

Parsons were fanatical cricket followers, Webster could not abide the game. The trio set off with Pugh at the wheel; they had not gone far when Webster called a halt, "the cheapest and best beer in the Midlands is in that pub" he declared in his rich Scottish accent. Pugh pulled on to the car park, got out of the car and made for the lounge bar. "Not there," shouted Webster, "the public bar." Eventually they arrived at Trent Bridge only to find that rain had stopped play for the day. "So much for your cricket, told you it was a daft game," said Webster with a chuckle. "Now, what shall we do?" Parsons and Pugh studied the paper, then the map. To their delight Leicestershire were playing Kent at Loughborough. When they arrived, play was in progress with Kent fielding. To his amazement, the Prof. found that the game was not so bad after all, and he delighted in the way Godfrey Evans kept wicket. It was perhaps as well that they ended up in Lough-borough, for Pugh supported Worcestershire and Parsons Warwick-shire—here there were no binding loyalties; but had the trio seen play at Nottingham, Parsons would immediately have supported the home team just to annoy Pugh, and Webster would have thought the game sillier than he already did. On the return journey they stopped again at the pub with the cheapest beer, passing the evening away in friend-ship. Webster had the last say as Pugh pulled up outside his home, "A good day, M.P., and now you know where to find the cheapest beer south of the border!"

Oliver Quinton, known to his friends as "Olly", was a Detective Chief Inspector in January 1951, stationed at the headquarters of "E" Division of the City of Birmingham Police Force at Acocks Green; heavily built and every inch a policeman, he was a good humoured member of the Force who was particularly respected for the way that he managed those beneath him. His relationship with all junior officers was first class. James Black was a good natured Scot who had had to come south of the border to become a policeman, for he was only 5′ 9½″. In Scotland you had to be 5′ 10″, so that he knew that any application by him to join the Ayrshire Constabulary would be rejected. Black, 37 at the time, known as Jock, was the Detective Sergeant stationed at Edward Road police station, Balsall Heath, a sub-station in "E" Division. James Mitchell, another Scot, was the Detective Inspector at Moseley Street police station, another sub-station in "E" Division. Aged about 45, nearly 6′ tall and weighing some 14½ stone, Mitchell was still nimble on his feet. He was a dour Scot, and a very keen policeman. Helen Anne Beattie, a Detective Inspector, and another Scot, was stationed at the C.I.D. Headquarters in Newton Street. She was known particularly for her kindness and sympathetic approach to those in trouble or in need of help. Her cheerful approach to everything was a tonic to all who had the fortune to serve with her in the City Force. Ultimately, after 30 years' service, she retired in 1971 with the rank of Chief Inspector, taking with her the good wishes of everyone. Quinton and Black, like Helen Beattie, have retired from the Force and all are still active, but in different fields. Mitchell is dead. Christina Coutts was a young policewoman in January 1951; at that time she and Helen Beattie worked as a team. Now, in the West Midlands Police Force, she is a Detective Sergeant.

The City of Birmingham Police Force is no longer in existence; all serving officers on 1st April, 1974, together with those of the neighbouring Force of the West Midlands Constabulary; and officers from part of the Staffordshire, Warwickshire and West Mercia Forces joined together to form The West Midlands Police Force.

George Blackborow, then Detective Chief Superintendent, was an extraordinarily smart officer. Not only did he wear his uniform well but it was often suggested, in a kindly way, that in civilian dress he had just walked out of a Montague Burton's window. He was one of Pugh's greatest friends, and it was he, in 1961, who led a contingent of the City Force which headed the cortège at Pugh's funeral. He ultimately retired from the City of Birmingham Police Force as Deputy Chief Constable and he was a senior executive with a security firm, which is nationally known, until his death.

These six officers were all to be concerned with the happenings at 6 back of 79 Clifton Road, although ultimately only Quinton, Mitchell, Black and Miss Beattie gave evidence.

In November 1950, 82-year-old Balthazar Stephen Sargant Foster 2nd Baron Ilkeston, the only peer ever to be a stipendiary magistrate, retired from Birmingham, an appointment that he had held since 1910. He lived in Warwick and was punctilious to the minute, he travelled by train arriving each morning in time to enter the "number one" court dead on 10.30 a.m. As he walked past the ticket collector at Snow Hill Station he would raise his bowler hat, season ticket secure inside: to him this ritual served three purposes; he could raise his hat in morning greeting, show his ticket and he never had to fumble in his wallet. In the evening the same ritual was repeated. He was succeeded by John Frederic Milward, aged 42, a barrister, who took office on 6th January, 1951: 28 years' later with a reputation equal to, if not exceeding, that of his predecessor, Mr. Milward can still be seen dispensing justice with a fairness that over the years has become the mark of the Birmingham Magistrates' Court. During the early days of January 1951, Milward was gently finding his feet; he had already altered the commencement time to 10.00 a.m. and the regular advocates realized that the new Stipendiary was not only a gentleman but a lawyer of great ability. Before his appointment to Birmingham he was the Associate on the Oxford Circuit and also had been a J.P. for the County of Worcester since 1940: he was greatly experienced in the way of the courts, though he had yet to preside at committal proceedings relating to a charge of murder.

Ralph Kilner Brown was a year younger than John Milward; he was called to the Bar in 1934 in which same year he crowned a career as an International athlete by winning the British hurdles championship. In 1945 and 1950 he had contested the parliamentary division of Oldbury and Hales Owen as a Liberal, but was not to turn to politics again, rather preferring to enhance his reputation as a barrister. In 1945, following a distinguished army career, he was awarded an O.B.E. He was also awarded the Territorial Decoration. His chambers were No. 41 Temple Row which he shared with, amongst others, Arthur Evan James and A. P. Marshall both of whom, like Ralph Brown, were ultimately to become High Court Judges. In 1951 he had the reputation for thoroughness in the preparation of his cases, and when asked to be led by a K.C. would give as much attention to the case as would the silk himself. This, probably, was the result of his academic education which he completed in triumph by being made a Harmsworth Scholar.

Previously these chambers had two other barristers who were to become famous Judges, Norman Birkett and Donald Finnemore. Now in 1950 the Chambers at No. 41 Temple Row had recently been joined by an up and coming young man for whom many could foresee a great legal career: Alfred William Michael Davies was 29, he had been called to the Bar two years earlier. He hailed from Stourbridge, a Worcestershire town which bordered the Black Country. In 1973 he became Mr. Justice Michael Davies: six High Court Judges from one set of chambers, out of London, since 1941 when Norman Birkett was appointed, must be a record.

Both R. K. Brown (as Mr. Justice Kilner Brown was then known) and Michael Davies were to have briefs delivered to No. 41 in February of 1951. For Brown the brief was for the prosecution in a case of murder; leading him would be Mr. R. T. Paget, K.C.; and for Davies the brief was for the defence; in the same case, and leading him, would be Mr. W. A. Fearnley-Whittingstall, K.C.: both briefs concerned the happenings at No. 6 back of 79 Clifton Street, Balsall Heath, on the night of 20th/21st January: the name of the accused was William Arthur Watkins.

Reginald Thomas Paget (now Baron, Lord Paget of Northampton) was in 1951 not only a K.C. but an M.P. He was one of the post war political lawyers who were able to make a success of both careers. He became Labour M.P. for Northampton in the Labour landslide of 1945, and a K.C. in 1947. In 1951 he was 42, and at that age one of the youngest silks. In 1953, jointly with the late Mr. Sidney Silverman, he wrote a book entitled *Hanged—and Innocent?* Educated at Eton and Trinity College, Cambridge, he was both eloquent and learned.

William Arthur Fearnley-Whittingstall, K.C., was a fighter; brought up in the courts in the same era as Gilbert Beyfus, who was known as "The Old Fox". Not only was he a fighter, but a character too. My first recollection of him, though I am sure I saw him in court before, was when he clashed with the late Mr. Justice Croom-Johnson, the father of the present Mr. Justice Croom-Johnson. The clash came whilst the jury were being sworn in and Fearnley-Whittingstall rose to make a challenge: on seeing him rise, the cross-fire started:

Mr. Justice Croom-Johnson: "I cannot see you, Mr. Fearnley-Whittingstall."

Mr. Fearnley-Whittingstall: "My lord, I am before you wigged and gowned."

Mr. Justice Croom-Johnson: "I still cannot see you, Mr. Fearnley-Whittingstall."

Mr. Fearnley-Whittingstall: "My lord, is it my yellow waistcoat that you cannot see?"

Mr. Justice Croom-Johnson: "Yes, it is."

Mr. Fearnley-Whittingstall: "Well, my lord, you can see me."

Mr. Justice Croom-Johnson: "Oh, very well, let's get on with the case."

On his day he was brilliant. In 1951 he was a fashionable silk: on paper he was the better advocate matched against Paget but as it turned out for William Arthur Watkins, Fearnley-Whittingstall was not at his best. Part of his brief was to challenge a statement alleged to have been made by Watkins and in so doing persuade Mr. Justice Finnemore to eliminate it from the trial; then it would not go before the jury as evidence. In this he failed and from that moment never again, in this case, save perhaps in his address to the jury, captured the brilliance of which he was so often the master.

Each defence case that came to him was prepared with great thoroughness and he literally lived the case putting himself into the defendant's shoes, in so doing convincing himself that his client was innocent.

He was tall and thin, with appalling eyesight: his glasses were so thick that they lay heavily on his nose and a frequent touch of the glasses was necessary to hold them in place. He, as Pugh, was highly sensitive and easily hurt if a decision taken was not the right one. He could be incredibly rude and was thought by some to be the most fearlessly outspoken silk since F. E. Smith; yet behind his verbal attacks there was never any malice. He was a volatile character much loved and sadly missed. Stories about him are legion; some perhaps apocryphal with the passing of time. He and Ryder-Richardson were the last of the fashionable silks who never reached the High Court bench; both dying at the height of their powers at an all too early age. In January 1951 he was 48. Like Kilner Brown he first aspired to a political life and was the son of a clergyman; he would frequently refer to their common vicarage upbringing. His first judicial appointment came in 1946 when he was appointed a Deputy Chairman of the Bedfordshire Quarter Sessions. His two unsuccessful political forays were in 1929 and 1950 when as a Conservative he contested Seaham and South Bedfordshire respectively.

Even Fearnley-Whittingstall was unable to break the barrier of silence that Bill Watkins had spun around himself. If only he had known that for 30 years Watkins had been an active member of the Aston Division Unionist Association and that he had driven each Conservative candidate throughout each election campaign, he would have made much of it; if only he had known that Watkins had been a member of the Boys' Brigade he would surely have made that point to Finnemore. There was so much that Watkins could have told him; Watkins appreciated his counsel and solicitor and later from the condemned cell was to write "I had one of the best K.C.'s in the country". But for reasons that he, and only he, knew Watkins remained mute as to his previous life; maybe because of his deafness Watkins found it difficult to communicate, but by way of compensation he was a good letter writer and he so easily could have put pen to paper.

Fearnley-Whittingstall was to worry more about Watkins than he would care to admit except to those who were near and dear to him.

James Chuter Ede was Home Secretary in 1951. Starting adult life after an elementary education, he became a schoolmaster for a while, before taking up politics. He was Charter Mayor of Epsom and Ewell in 1937. He was widowed in 1948. In 1964 he was created a Baron having changed his name by deed poll from Ede to Chuter-Ede thus linking his middle name to his surname by adding a hyphen. It was, however, as Chuter Ede that he was always referred to so it was a natural, though unusual, course that he took. The Home Secretary has the power to recommend to the Monarch that a condemned person be reprieved. It is a terrible burden to place on anyone and if at heart, kind, all the more onerous. Chuter Ede was a kind and gentle man: the agony that must have been his was unbearable. The power in 1951, behind the Home Secretary, was Sir Frank Aubrey Newsam who had held office as Permanent Under Secretary of State at the Home Office since 1948: he retired in 1957 and died on 25th April, 1964. He it was who advised the Home Secretary against a reprieve and he it was who advised the same Home Secretary, later in 1951, to recommend a reprieve in two further separate cases of murder, where the death sentence had been pronounced, within the City of Birmingham. Newsam was not universally a popular man, Webster detested him and when talking about him almost spat the name out. Nevertheless, Newsam was a devoted civil servant, and if Fearnley-Whittingstall did not know all that there was to know about Watkins, how possibly could Newsam?

John W. Brown was the Governor of Winson Green Prison, Birmingham and a kinder and more considerate Governor it would be hard to find. H. M. Blenkinsop was Under-Sheriff, a position now held by his son, and the Reverend F. Thompson was the prison chaplain. In the last three weeks of his life, Watkins was to know Brown and Thompson so well; so much so that he looked upon them as his friends and his last words were for the Chaplain.

Albert Pierrepoint, like his uncle and father before him, was the official executioner. Well dressed and a quietly spoken Lancastrian, 5' 7" in height, he was known as a perfectionist. To him it was a duty, for it to be anything else would have been disastrous. A publican by trade, he and his wife Anne, in 1951, kept a house known as "Help The Poor Struggler"—an extraordinary name for a public house and all the more so for the part-time profession of its occupant. To talk to Pierrepoint is fascinating; but what comes out most of all is the wholesome respect that he had for those about to die. Having been concerned with so many executions, many he cannot recall, he can still to this day remember Bill Watkins.

Dr. William Henderson Davison, O.B.E., M.B., Ch.B., D.P.H., J.P., was the city coroner, a man of quiet charm who like nearly all of his brethren could bring respect, kindness and understanding to all who came in contact with him; his office was at No. 50 Newton Street. Now he is dead but his son, His Honour Judge William N. Davison, brings to his court the same attributes as did his father.

Percy Lionel Edward Shurmer was 61; he was the Labour Member of Parliament for the Sparkbrook Division. Sparkbrook, whilst being an area in its own right, included Balsall Heath when the time came for elections. His home was "St. Ives", in Belgrave Road. Though born in Cheltenham, he was to become a "Brummie" through and through. He became an apprentice in the Merchant Navy when he was 12; but after 10 years at sea joined the staff of the Post Office and came to live in his adopted city. He was a good man and a dedicated politician. Elected to the City Council in 1921, he became an alderman in 1934 and a magistrate in 1943. One of his proudest moments was when he was arrested during the General Strike of 1926 for obstruction: he listed his recreations simply as "Social Work". In the Labour landslide of 1945 he won the seat for his party, and was to represent Sparkbrook until his early death.

So it was that on Thursday, 15th March, 1951 William Arthur Watkins stood in the dock in number 5 court at the Victoria Law

Courts to answer a charge of murder, and all those that I have mentioned became concerned with Watkins and the little dead baby, which although prematurely born, was normal in every way, yet was only to live for barely fifteen minutes.

On Friday, 16th March, 1951, having sat throughout the entire case, I left the Victoria Courts, dejected at the verdict, but with the words "he won't swing" ringing comfort in my ears.

The case of William Arthur Watkins has worried me ever since, and to this day I can still see him; the prematurely old man, standing in the dock flanked by three warders, his steel grey hair brushed straight back, glazed eyes and drooping chin, straining because of his deafness to listen to the final words of Mr. Justice Finnemore "And may the Lord have mercy on your soul".

PROLOGUE

Part I

"Murder! Murder! Fetch the police." One October evening in 1932 Harry Thompson was walking along Willows Crescent, so near to Edgbaston Cricket Ground, when he heard those words as a young girl ran from a house followed by another girl; they ran to Thompson saying "come here and get this strange man out of the house." He went, asking "who is it" and the elder of the two girls replied "I have never seen him in my life before. He hit me in the mouth. There was a ten shilling note on the table, and when we came down it had gone." Thompson, followed by the two girls, went into the house and he saw a man by the wall in the passage beyond the front door. Believing the girls, Thompson grabbed his wrist, saying "What's your game." "I've done nothing," the man answered in a meek voice. Thompson began to drag him towards the front door and as he did so he slumped to the floor. "He's only shamming, he's done that before," said the elder of the two girls, contradicting her statement made only moments earlier, "I have never seen him in my life before". The man was dead: he had a massive stab wound and strangely the blade of a knife was in his pocket as was a crumpled ten shilling note. The dead man was Sidney Marston and the girls were Marjorie Kathleen Yellow and her youngest sister Emily Eleanor Thay. Talk, today, to anyone in Balsall Heath about murder and if they know of one; then it will be the Yellow case; I could find no-one who could remember the 1951 murder in Clifton Road. The girls aged 19 and 16 were duly charged with murder. They were fortunate; for their defence counsel was the legendary Norman Birkett. The case for the prosecution had been prepared by M. P. Pugh and the junior counsel whom the D.P.P. chose was Donald Finnemore. He was led by Maurice Healy, K.C. The girls were acquitted; even now the mystery is unsolved and people still speculate as to what Marston was doing at No. 63 Willows Crescent. It was a slum. Marjorie Yellow had married a coloured man from whom she was separated and moved into No. 63 with a man named Gwinnell. Emily had come to spend the weekend with her sister. Marston knew Marjorie, for in the little note book he carried was the name Miss Gwinnell, and at the inquest, Marjorie told the Coroner that she had met a young man, called Sid, a few weeks earlier, and that she had given him her name and he had asked her and her sister to go dancing with him and a friend.

Two months after the acquittal, Marjorie was fined in Manchester for disorderly conduct and assaulting a policeman. After the trial, both Marjorie and Emily had left Birmingham: Mr. Gwinnell too. Two months later Marjorie was sent to prison for ten weeks for assisting in the management of a disorderly house and two years later she again found herself in the dock when she was charged with stabbing the coloured man with whom she was then living. Her defence was that intending to leave him, she stood on a chair holding a knife with which she meant to cut down the curtain; he caught her hand and in so doing slipped to the floor: the knife was pulled down on to him. She was found guilty and sentenced to eighteen months' imprisonment.

Donald Finnemore was never to forget that case nor the descriptions of the squalor in which Marjorie lived. Occasionally he would talk of it, and once at a legal dinner in Birmingham, finding himself next to his old friend Pugh, passed away the evening in reminiscence. Balsall Heath has always been associated with slums and crime; an unfair association because whilst there were slums and there was crime; neither were endemic to the area.

At the turn of the century William and Louise Watkins lived in Nechells Park Road, Aston; at No. 2 back of 107, and there on 23rd January, 1902, Louise gave birth to a baby boy—they called him William Arthur; they already had another son Charles. The house was next door to the slaughterhouse, and the cries of the baby were frequently overshadowed by the death cries of the beasts, for in those days a slaughterman lived up to his title. Louise died shortly after William's birth and William senior stayed on at No. 2, but left the factory where he worked, as a labourer, and went into business on his own account as a wood merchant; giving himself the title "Circular Sawyer". He re-married, and in so doing, made a terrible mistake— for she was mad. William took to drink and his wife was taken to an asylum. The Watkins' boys were left to fend very much for themselves, and in so doing vowed one to the other to do well in the world.

William was Bill and Charles was Charlie. Bill worked for his father after leaving the Elliott Street School in Nechells at the age of 12. Life with father became impossible and Bill sought escape. He had many friends, made mainly through the Boys' Brigade. He attended Christ Church, which was the Baptist church in Aston Park. He never knew a time when life was not a struggle and in his youth it was particularly so. The Church, the Boys' Brigade and later the Aston Unionist Association occupied all his free time. Working for his father was difficult, and living with him even more so.

Fortunately, the date of Bill's birth was never officially recorded. He looked more than 18 in 1920 and was mature. His teenage days were spent in the knowledge that he might be called up. The horrors of the 1914–18 war were relayed, and Bill often wished that his father would be called up, but it was not to be because he suffered from congenital deafness. So it was that Bill decided to give himself three years and masquerade as 21. This one lie was to benefit him twofold, first, he could obtain a driving licence enabling him to drive a charabanc and secondly he could get married: two events in life for which in those days one had to be 21.

The driving licence was first obtained and then he applied to Mr. Reuben Lowe, a charabanc and lorry proprietor, in Victoria Road, for a position as a driver. Mr. Lowe liked the look of this clean cut young man of whom he had heard through his own connection with the Aston Unionist Association. So Bill became a charabanc driver.

Marriage was now possible: Bill had already met a Handsworth girl, Doris Morley. Doris was a year older than Bill, and was smart and very attractive; she too had a drunken father. When Bill proposed there was no doubt in Doris's mind that he was the man for her.

It was a quiet wedding with no fathers present: they had not been told, nor invited. Notice was duly given to the registrar that a marriage was to take place between William Arthur Watkins, a bachelor aged 21, a motor bus driver, and Doris Morley, a spinster, aged 21. On 1st August, 1920, in the presence of two strangers, Samuel and Rose Guise, who acted as witnesses, the marriage was solemnized at the Aston Register office by Mr. E. Hastings, the Registrar. Doris was born in West Hartlepool, on 17th July, 1901, and later came with her parents to live in Birmingham. The Morley home was at 40 Arthur Place, Argyle Street. Her father, George Henry, was a metal turner by trade.

There was no honeymoon; the happy couple had found a house and they went straight to it: No. 7 Matlock Place, Holdford Road, Handsworth: it was not a palace but it was a home, although it was small and untidy. Doris immediately started to smarten the house up and Bill put in many hours overtime to earn more money. The furniture they had was second hand and cheap. Before her marriage Doris had worked in a factory as a press operator but Bill did not approve of ladies working; he felt her place was in the home and in any event she was quickly pregnant. She became very ill for a while and there was concern for her: when the baby arrived, prematurely, it was to live for only two hours. The birth which took place at the Hallam Hospital, West Bromwich, drained her physically and mentally. She was young and resilient and soon fought back only to find that she was pregnant yet again. The birth was normal and the child, a boy, healthy. Bill continued with his driving but Mr. Lowe's business was not prospering. The post-war depression affected everyone, culminating in the General Strike of 1926. Bill lost his job with Mr. Lowe and joined the Army as a driver. This meant a regular pay packet, and with employment difficult to come by, Bill and Doris were at least secure. The rent for their home was never in arrears, both were thrifty and Bill was a worker. Meanwhile Doris had given birth to a girl—she was born in 1923. Then tragedy struck, when their then five-year-old son had acute pains in the stomach; his appendix had burst and the little lad died in the Hallam Hospital. It was August 1927, and on the last day of the month the small coffin was buried in the common grave at Witton Cemetery. Frank Flight had taken over Mr. Lowe's business and was making a great success of it, so Bill approached him about becoming a driver. His Army contract was due to expire, and he felt no desire to renew it; to the contrary, he wanted to return to civilian life and to live at home again. Frank Flight was only too pleased to employ Bill, whose record as a driver was first class. In the Army he had driven lorries and coaches (as charabancs were beginning to be called) and as he had previously worked and driven for Reuben Lowe, Frank Flight knew he had a good man. Flights' garage was in Victoria Road, Aston, on the left hand side going down from Six Ways.

After Matlock Place Bill and Doris moved about; it was not that they were restless—it was a question of bettering themselves. In Holborn Hill they lived for a while at No. 7 back of No. 58. In Slade

Road they lived at No. 272 and, strangely, for a while returned next door to Bill's childhood home, No. 2 back of No. 107 Nechells Park Road, living for a short while at No. 4 back of No. 107 Nechells Park Road. The slaughter house was still there and No. 107 had become a shoe repairer's. It was from this house that they moved to No. 123 Victoria Road, opposite Flights' Garage and almost on the corner of the junction of Victoria Road with Potters Hill. Aston was, in the twenties and thirties, very much the same as it had been in 1900 except that the gas lights had become electric lights and the tramway had been built; up and down the long road, the No. 5 tram trundled along. Named after the Queen, the road contained terraced houses of considerable quality. It was a good address. Nearby was Albert Road which had been developed at the same time as Victoria Road. During her long reign many roads were named after Victoria, the Queen, and her Consort. Nearby in Erdington there is also a Victoria Road and an Albert Road.

To own a camera was in 1930, quite exceptional. A family portrait was something rather special and Bill and Doris thought they had earned the privilege, so with their two children, the boy and the girl, (the second son was born soon after their daughter, the younger ones were not born then) they put on their best clothes and went to the photographers: it was the only time they ever did so.

Bill was pleased to be back in Aston, the Unionist Association of which he had remained a member had its headquarters in Victoria Road. Whilst Bill was an ardent Tory, Doris was not; she fell for the persuasive charm of Ramsay MacDonald and always voted Labour after he had become the party's first Prime Minister. It was always a joke within the family that their votes cancelled each other out and at election times posters for both parties would appear in the windows of their home. As the years passed by the family increased and when they lived at No. 123 Victoria Road, Bill and Doris had two sons and two daughters. The eldest girl was always "the dad's favourite", the youngest girl was very shy, and the baby of the family, a boy, was a bright young spark, and a promising artist. The eldest son and daughter helped Doris a great deal in the house: they were then a happy united family.

Bill was a popular fellow in Aston; he seemed to know everyone and often people would specifically ask Mr. Flight for Bill to be the driver; Flight's garage now owned a fleet of hire-cars specializing in taxi work and weddings. 123 Victoria Road was a happy home for the Watkins family during the early months of the Second World War. The depression had passed them by, whilst of course they were affected as was everyone else, though Bill's regular employment thankfully kept the household ticking over. When on charabanc duty he would wear a smart white coat and he had a peaked cap, which he rarely wore, but it came in most useful for collecting his tips. At the end of the day, after an outing, he would tip all the coins he had received on to the kitchen table and Doris would count them out. As to his earnings, they were never very high, but they were able to manage. Bill was generous to the family, giving all to them; so much so that Doris would give him his pocket money each week, Bill having first given her his unopened wage packet.

Bill owned a motor cycle and sidecar: originally he only bought the cycle but Doris refused to go on the back so they saved up and bought a sidecar so that Doris could go with him. Doris' brother lived with them for a while and one day he brought home a new girl friend who was very smart. The family always washed up for Doris, and visitors to the house were expected to help. After high tea an opportunity arose for Bill's humour to make the children laugh. Bill was washing and Uncle and girl friend were drying. They dried up staring into each other's eyes, and as they put the clean crocks down Bill would pick them up and wash them again and again. The elder children started to titter, and Doris wondering what was happening and why it was taking so long, came in. Then the starry-eyed pair realized the trick that had been played upon them and roared with laughter. Bill kept chuckling about it for days afterwards.

The Lovsey's of Birmingham were a well-respected family: William Edward Lovsey, senior, was for a time chairman of the City Magistrates and an alderman on the City Council. William Edward, junior, was the agent for the Aston Divisional Unionist Association and as such knew Bill Watkins well, not only as a member, but as a driver, for between the wars the Association had frequent outings and Bill was the popular driver; Flight's charabancs were always hired for these trips which would take Bill many miles from Birmingham.

Life at 123 Victoria Road was good, but there was forever a shortage of money; Bill, remembering how he was ignored by his own father and resenting his mother's early death, was determined that his children would not suffer. He began to sacrifice everything for their happiness, which meant more and more driving and it followed that he was away from his home more often than not. Sometimes, in the school holidays, Mr. Flight would allow him to take one of the children on his trips; they loved to be with their father and rivalled each other as to who would be the lucky one. Bill was scrupulously fair, and made certain that they each took it in turn to accompany him. Very occasionally Doris would go with him, but this was all too rare, for her hands were full in keeping the home clean and tidy, cooking, and being a good mother.

In the summertime many of the charabanc parties would choose to go to Evesham, Broadway, Stow-on-the-Wold, Moreton-in-Marsh, and Bourton-on-the-Water, stopping on the way back to Birmingham at roadside stalls to purchase the fruit that was in season. Doris was a splendid cook and loved making jam; Bill would bring her strawberries and plums which were her favourites. Once neighbouring children came into the kitchen, whilst Doris was stirring her jam, and fooling around, they knocked the cauldron off the stove, spilling its contents. Doris, quite rightly, was furious—but Bill, who did not like trouble, eased the situation by saying how lucky the children were not to have been scalded and in any event jam was supposed to be put in jars, not on the floor. At this, the tension passed and everyone laughed. This action was typical of Bill Watkins; he was not a strong character and would always try and find an easy solution to problems that arose within the house. To someone who did not know him it might well have been seen as a weakness, but it was his way of making a happy home. In the mid-thirties he found that he was going slightly deaf. It was hereditary, but his determination was such as to not let it overtake him and dominate his personality. He could be firm with the children; when he looked at them with a stern face and raised eyebrows, the look was sufficient to register his disapproval. Never once did he lay a hand on any of his children.

Bill Watkins was an avid reader, and as his deafness took a greater hold upon him, he would rarely be without a book. Some he would buy, but mostly he walked round to the public library in Albert Road. At the library he was well known, his favourite author was Edgar Wallace—and often new thrillers would be put on one side for him.

Newspapers too, were quickly read, and here he was fortunate because many people on a day's outing would take with them a paper, and when read, leave it in the charabanc, so when Bill returned home it was often with an armful of newspapers. He would scan the papers for the crime stories and never missed a murder case. With Doris and the elder children, he would talk about the cases and more than once told them how he admired Albert Pierrepoint. He would say, "It's a horrible job, but he is a good man".

Besides his books, he loved going to the pictures; it was the only real treat that he ever gave Doris. There was no particular type of film that he enjoyed more than any other—it was the thrill of moving pictures that enabled him to relax and to see how the other half of the world lived: in particular, he enjoyed the Gaumont British News. He was a Royalist at heart, and was saddened in 1937 when Edward VIII renounced the throne for the woman he loved. For hours he would discuss the pros and the cons with Doris and in so doing remembered when they themselves had been madly in love; and realizing that for them so much of their once "eternal" love had now passed by and that like so many others; their's was but an existence to provide for one's children. Yet—neither at this time, admitted to the other, their innermost thoughts. The gradual dawning of this was not seen by either of them in the first instance; but was to break with a crescendo a few years hence.

Meanwhile, Doris continued to look after her family, despite the fact that her health was beginning to cause her concern. She knitted for the children and made as many of their clothes as she could. She was forever sewing and knitting; that is one of the happy memories of her that remain with those that knew her, then. Bill eventually bought her a secondhand, treadle type, Singer sewing machine. At the back of the houses on this side of the road was a yard and behind No. 123 an old greenhouse which Bill quickly made use of. One of the first things she did with her machine was to make some aprons out of old potato bags: she called them "Washing Aprons".

In the home, when he was there, Bill would play games with the children, ludo, snakes and ladders and especially draughts. They loved to play with him and very occasionally he would, unknown to them, let them win.

Not far from Flights was the Aston Hippodrome, where six nights a week, twice nightly, a variety show was the bill of fare. It was the only theatre where naked girls occasionally posed motionless on the stage, and for miles around people, especially men, would travel to see the "naughty show". Not all the shows had a nude; in fact they were very few and far between, and in any event a G string had to be worn. Flights had an agency for the theatre and sold tickets which included a charabanc trip from all parts of Birmingham. There were two coaches in the cream, and blue line, livery of Flights (they bore the motif of a blue-bird and were known as the "Blue-Bird Coaches") and most nights Bill and another driver worked. On Thursdays came the reward, a pair of complimentary tickets, and Bill and Doris took advantage of them. The famous stars did not appear at Aston, but as in all professions, there was a ladder to be climbed and many who were later to become "stars" trod the boards of the Aston Hippodrome in their early days. There was no television, before and during the Second World War for the masses, but the wireless brought voices to the fans. Sometimes between the shows Bill would go home, but as most of the shows were often less than two hours he would sit in the charabanc with a book or drive one of the hire cars, and sometimes he would go into the theatre by the stage door, by invitation, because Bill, through the passage of time, knew many theatrical personalities. Later, when the family had moved across the road to No. 136, Bill often brought some of the artists home. The family can remember Donald Peers, Jane of the *Daily Mirror* fame, and a harp player by the name of Carlos Ames sitting in the family room having tea before the first house. Bill knew them because he would meet them at Snow Hill or New Street Station and drive them to their theatrical digs: some were more friendly than others—Donald Peers and Carlos Ames became family friends, though they lost touch when real stardom came their way and no longer were they on the bill at the Aston Hippodrome.

On Saturdays, Bill would walk to Six Ways and visit Skidmore's the newsagents and, with the money Doris had given him, buy comics for the children and sometimes a book or two. Bill always encouraged the children to read.

One of the Watkins' girls was a member of St. John Ambulance Brigade—Bill, remembering the happiness that he derived from his childhood days, passed on the enthusiasm to the children, and the boys, too, followed in his footsteps. Knowing that Bill drove for Flights, the lady who was the leader spoke to the little girl to ask her dad if an outing could be arranged. When the day came, with the children clutching their precious pennies, Bill would not take them and gave them all a free trip. When they returned the children gave him three hearty cheers, and some even hugged him. Later that night he saw Mr. Flight and offered to pay for the petrol used, and said that he did not want any pay for that day. Frank Flight was a generous man and refused the petrol money, patting Bill on the back as a gesture of approval for what he had done.

In the early days at No. 123 Doris was very poorly; she suffered from rheumatoid arthritis in her knees and was unable to climb the stairs, so she had a bed downstairs. Doris, as the elder children grew up and made their own way and their own entertainment, became lonely, with Bill away so much: she had also just lost a baby who died aged three months, just after the Second World War began. This was just before they moved into No. 123 Victoria Road; so the new home was more than welcome. The child, a boy, was born prematurely and suffered from gastric intestinal catarrh, which were the causes of death diagnosed by Dr. G. R. Cooper, the family doctor. The family remembers life at No. 123 as some of the happiest days of their lives.

In April 1939, the Unionist member of Parliament, Captain the Hon. A. O. J. Hope, was unexpectedly appointed Governor of Madras, which meant that a by-election must follow and the writ issued for Wednesday, 17th May. There had not been an election since 1935, and little did the people of Aston then realize that there would not be another until after the war, which was looming ahead in those dangerous, treacherous days of 1939.

James Crump, J.P., was then the Labour Lord Mayor of Birmingham and as such was the returning officer. Crump was a popular leader of the City Council, widely respected by all parties; his greatest enjoyment was to smoke huge cigars. Bill Watkins was asked, through Mr. Flight, by Mr. W. E. Lovsey the Unionist Agent, to chauffeur the Conservative Candidate throughout the campaign. Mr. Flight put one of his cars and Bill Watkins at the disposal of Major Edward Orlando Kellett—known as "Flash Kellett"; for he was always so immaculately dressed.

Neville Chamberlain had more things on his mind than the Aston

By-Election but he knew that the votes cast in that Division and two other by-elections that were to go to the polls the same day, would show whether he still had the confidence of the electorate. Sir Frederick Smith was Chairman of the local Unionist Association. He, with Kellett and the local Unionist hierarchy consisting of Alderman and Mrs. Lovsey and Mr. Lovsey, Jnr., went to the Council House to hand in Kellett's nomination papers. Bill Watkins drove the Major, his wife, and Sir Frederick. There, they met the Labour candidate and his retinue; the Aston Labour Party had chosen a genial London doctor, Samuel Segal, as their candidate; he was accompanied by his wife and young daughter, Maureen. The papers were handed in and Jim Crump said that he hoped the contest would be cleanly fought and that personalities would be avoided. The candidates and their wives posed for a photograph, and to add to the picture Mrs. Segal held up Maureen, who was dressed in her party best and wore a huge ribbon in her hair. The Kelletts and the Segals shook hands and there was no fear of a difficult campaign; both were gentlemen and vowed each to the other so to remain. Major Kellett was in the Territorial Army and lived at 5 Clifton Place, London W.C.2, and Dr. Segal, described as a physician and surgeon, lived at 222 Walm Lane, London, N.W.2. Both wore huge rosettes of appropriate colours, pinned to the left-hand lapels of their suits.

Major Kellett later stressed to the electorate that the election was not only important to Aston, but to England and Europe; for from the result, would be judged the measure of support given by the country to the Prime Minister, in his efforts to bring about a peaceful solution of the problems of the world. Luckily, the papers were handed in in the morning, for in *The Birmingham Mail* of that evening it was reported that reconstruction work was to begin in Victoria Square at 2.00 p.m. that day, and it would present problems for drivers. Wages were soaring as a result of rearmament orders: some munition workers were earning as much as £8 a week compared to £3 6s. that had been the standard wage for a 47-hour week. Mrs. Kellett issued a message to the electorate and in referring to Chamberlain as "the peacemaker" showed her full support for her husband.

The weather outlook was one of thundery showers as the campaign started. Kellett was defending a majority of 10,355. At the previous election only 27,000 voters went to the polls. If Dr. Segal was going to upturn that majority it would indeed be a vote of no-confidence in "the Peacemaker".

There were to be three by-elections on 17th May, the other Divisions being the Abbey Division of Westminster and North Southwark. The Abbey majority was a Unionist one of 12,862, out of total votes of just over 23,500. At North Southwark it was a different situation, the previous election had shown a majority of only 79 to the Liberal-National candidate. These two by-elections had each resulted from the death of the previous Member.

In Aston itself there was little excitement until the last day, as *The Birmingham Mail* reported.

Bill Watkins drove Major Kellett to all his meetings, and he thoroughly enjoyed it. He and the Major got on well together and Watkins' quiet sense of humour, and even temper were an asset, especially in the last hours when election fever pitch was reached. At the meetings Bill would get out of the car and stand to the fore; a press photographer, on election day, took only the second photograph known to be in existence of Bill; standing smartly, near to Kellett, in his blue mackintosh. It rained throughout 17th May and when the results were announced it was obvious that many voters had stayed at home. Nevertheless the results were interesting: Major Kellett was duly elected with a majority of 5,901. The Unionist vote had dropped by just under 6,000, and the Labour vote by just over 2,000. Bill, of course, voted for the Major and Doris for the doctor. There were never any political arguments within the Watkins' family and Doris was secretly proud of the part Bill played, but she would never admit it to him. In the Abbey Division, the Unionist majority was cut to 5,004 and at North Southwark, Labour gained the seat from the Liberal-National Party, by a majority of 1,493. Hardly the support anywhere that Chamberlain so desperately needed. Sir Harold Webbe was the victor in London and Mr. George Isaacs in North Southwark.

The Birmingham Mail of Thursday, 18th May carried the following report:

"After the Lord Mayor had declared the result in the Aston contest, Major Kellett proposed a vote of thanks to him and to the staff. He said it had been a great pleasure to take part in a contest in which the best traditions of political controversy had been maintained, and both sides had attempted 'to go for the ball and not for the man.' Councillor Normansell had given him the badge of Aston Villa F.C., and he had tried to preserve a good sporting spirit. The same thing could be said of Dr. and Mrs. Segal, and of all his opponents in the contest. Naturally, he had nothing but the highest praise for his supporters. He came to Aston as a stranger, but they had helped him in a truly noble way.

Dr. Segal, seconding, said he wished to offer Major Kellett warmest congratulations on his victory. On both sides they could take pride in the fact that the election had been conducted with friendly warmth and mutual self-respect and in accordance with the highest traditions of public life in this country. The Labour party in Aston had no reason to be discouraged by the result. When he entered the contest a machine had to be improvised. Major Kellett had won, and it would be churlish not to extend him congratulations. He looked forward to a return contest, and when that contest came it would be with the same friendly feeling.

Major Kellett, in an interview afterwards, said: 'The result of the election is an endorsement of the Prime Minister's policy. It shows that Aston is true to the principles of the National Government and of Mr. Neville Chamberlain. It is true that there is a reduction in the poll, but the reduction is as evident in the figures of my Labour opponent as of my own. It should not be overlooked also that the total electorate in the division is smaller than it was in 1935. The majority secured for the National Government shows that people in the division have appreciated the issue. I should like to express my thanks to all those who have worked so hard for me, and especially the agent (Mr. W. E. Lovsey), who most efficiently organized the campaign on my behalf.'

Dr. Segal said: 'These figures show that Chamberlain's tradition in Birmingham is being smashed. The Premier himself, by his foreign policy blundering and his broken pledges, has broken faith with his home town, and the people of Aston realize it. The day is nearer when Aston will be no longer be a Tory stronghold, but a safe seat for Labour, and safe for progress and political honesty.

'I have enjoyed this campaign, and have had the satisfaction of seeing whole streets of Unionists taking an interest in Labour's prepared plans for peace and real security. Many Aston electors, clinging to the Chamberlain tradition for years, started realizing the dangers of Tory government for the first time. But the Tories poured all their resources into the fight. What they lacked in policy they made up with money and organization. Nevertheless, the number of their supporters has diminished.

'Aston Labour, by carrying on a campaign from now to the next election, can smash down Toryism until the seat is ours.'

In an interview after the declaration in the Abbey Division, Sir Harold Webbe said: 'The primary reason why I won is that the people of Westminster support the Government in foreign policy, and are convinced that compulsory military training is necessary both for national and international reasons. Had it not been for the weather, I am convinced that the poll would have been very much higher and that my majority would have been higher accordingly. Having regard to the fact that the election was fought on an old register and that there were many removals unaccounted for, I consider the result can be regarded as highly satisfactory.'

Sir Harold, a Birmingham man, was invited to fight the Aston election, but the invitation was received after he had allowed his name to go forward for consideration by the Abbey Division officials. For that reason he declined. He was born in Birmingham, and graduated from King Edward's School to Queens' College, Cambridge.

Speaking at North Southwark, Mr. Isaacs said: 'I won this election because of the profound dissatisfaction of the people of North Southwark with the conduct of the Government. I base my conclusions on the questions put to me while canvassing at public meetings. People resented the Government's handling of international affairs—not only the failure to adhere to the pledge given by Earl Baldwin while Prime Minister that this country would stand firm to the principles of the League of Nations, but also the continued betrayal of the system of collective security.' "

The *Birmingham Gazette* of the same day printed the photograph of Bill Watkins standing near to Major Kellett.

Practically 40 years later, one still ponders on whether a snap election, after these by-elections, would have made any difference to the course of world events. It is so easy to look back with hindsight but perhaps if Churchill had been at the helm before 3rd September, 1939, things may have been different: we shall never know.

In 1939, Bill Watkins was 37, and that is how the family remember him: the black hair brushed back, no stoop; he was 5' 7" then, but the stoop that came to him later, made him look that much smaller.

The war brought more work to Flights, for petrol was only available to essential users; coaches were in constant demand, taking and fetching the workers to the factories. The Hercules Cycle and Motor Co. Ltd. were hard pressed for workers, and advertised all over the country. Bicycles were needed not only for the public with the gradual withdrawal of private motor cars from the roads, but the army needed them too. Girls from all over England came to Birmingham and Flights were given the contract to transport them to and from their premises in Rocky Lane. On Mondays, during the wartime, Bill would have to find lodgings for the girls and sometimes when they were impossible Bill would bring them to No. 123 to stay on a temporary basis. Bill was always concerned that they contacted their homes to say that they were safe.

With so many factories in the area, Birmingham was vulnerable to the war and the sirens were sounded most nights. No. 125 Victoria Road was on the corner of Potters Hill, and beneath that house (the Watkins' home at 123 and the adjoining house No. 121) were cellars: they were converted into an air raid shelter to take as many as 100 people. There was a public entrance just beyond the corner in Potters Hill and a private entrance in No. 121 for the residents of the three houses. Bill became an A.R.P. warden and was delighted when he was officially put in charge of the shelter with the title of Section Warden. Spirits at times in Victoria Road were low. The relationship between the people being so similar to that of the characters in R. F. Delderfield's splendid story of "the Avenue". One Tuesday night Bill suggested a whist drive in the shelter. So successful was it, that Tuesday night became "Whist Drive Night" and for the first four weeks Bill himself provided small prizes at his own expense. He was (according to someone who was there) "very popular and had many friends—not close friends but he was very much a respected member of the community and as such liked."

Bill arranged for some old coach seats from Flights to be taken down and in the family's private section he constructed a huge bed with a curtain all the way around so that the children could sleep. Hot cocoa was always available and good neighbourly relationships made it "just like home from home". Bonds grew between the families and then it happened—a bomb dropped by a German pilot to ease his load, landed right next to the garage and exploded with a tremendous burst of noise, and another fell just along the road, but did not explode. Bill rushed to the unexploded bomb and thankfully, it was only an incendiary bomb—he was quickly able to defuse it. As however, he was working on it he suddenly realized that the explosion from the bomb was enormous and could even be catastrophic so he ran to the shelter where so many people were huddled together in fright. Of the houses above; No. 123 was shattered beyond repair but, as if by a miracle no one was killed; in the panic Doris was thrown down the stairs from the blast and with her went a neighbour's pet dog which was so badly injured that it had to be destroyed: it belonged to the friendly Mrs. Edwards. A rescue team was quickly on the scene and forbade anyone to go into the houses. The Watkins' family had to spend three days and three nights in the shelter, for they were homeless. Bill, defying the advice of the rescue team, went into his home to salvage what he could. This was 1940 and the war was in its infancy. Almost opposite No. 123 was No. 136, and it was then the home of a middle-aged nurse, Mrs. McDivett, and for her, she had had enough and offered Bill the tenancy of her home. It was a noble gesture of generosity and Mrs. McDivett quickly made arrangements to live in the country. The Watkins' family, three days after the tragedy, moved into their new home. They loved it, for it had a huge garden at the back, something they had never had before. The house was spacious, it was very narrow but long, its width was throughout that of one room and a passageway. The death of the baby seemed a long time ago and Bill's affection for Doris took on a new lease of life. His special name for her was Doss and the children noticed that he called her that far more often than before. Upstairs they had three large bedrooms and a bathroom, downstairs three more rooms and a large kitchen. Outside was a toilet. Doss felt better, too, and to their mutual pleasure she was pregnant again. In April of 1941 Doris gave birth to a little girl: seven weeks later the child was rushed into the Children's Hospital and on 20th June she died. Dr. A. Cavendish diagnosed three causes of death (a) Intestinal obstruction of Toxaemia (b) paralyticileus and (c) Intersusception of recent peritonitis. Bill and Doris arranged for her little body to be brought back to No. 136 where she lay in the front room. Previously in 1939 Bill had been reluctant to go into the same room as the dead body and now he just would not go in. It was a foible within him; just as some people suffer from vertigo. Ultimately, persuaded by Doris and holding her hand he went into the room. He quickly looked; turned away and his friendly eyes were suddenly filled with tears. It was the first time that the children had visibly noticed his emotion: it was not to be the last.

The little girl was the eighth child of Bill and Doris and the fourth to die by natural causes, the third to die as a baby. Bill had only once before seen a dead child. The eldest son who survived died in hospital and Bill did not see him. Although one had died at home the doctor was present and took the little body away with him. Doris was there and later registered the death, but Bill was too "full up" to wish to see the body.

This fear of death, it can now be said, was possibly to bring about his own execution, for at the time of the trial one of the major points of evidence against him was that he put the dead child in a pillow case and then heaped dirty clothes on top of the zinc bath, which was still full of water. If Bill had told Tony Alderson or Fearnley-Whittingstall, of what had happened in the past, it would have provided the key to his actions; but he remained mute, giving his lawyers nothing upon which they could say in answer to his actions. There was to be another baby's death at No. 136 and again as the story will show that same fear returned. It is hardly credible, that when charged with the murder of a new-born baby, he who had fathered, by his wife four babies, all of whom had died within months of birth and all quite naturally and each death medically attended and properly recorded could not then tell of his terrible fear—truth is often stranger than fiction.

I have evidence to substantiate that what I write is the truth and I have been satisfied, and have satisfied myself, beyond any doubt that these facts are true. When I first learnt of their deaths, a terrible thought went through my mind; and I had to research each and every death; for had I not done so this story could not have been told as I have told it. If the facts were not as I found them, it would have been better to have abandoned my research; and that I would have done. I am saddened by the fact that what I have discovered was not given in evidence; but for all this there is only one person to blame: William Arthur Watkins. Not one iota of blame (or as Pugh would say "a scintilla of evidence"), falls on those who defended him nor on any member of the family. I think I owe an explanation to the reader for placing the blame wholly on Watkins. At the time of the trial Bill Watkins was practically stone deaf, had abandoned his family and old friends and was no help to his solicitor or counsel. Maisie, with whom he was living, did know that he did not have four grown up children yet she was not in court when they were referred to and as the trial occupied so little lineage in the papers that part of the evidence went unnoticed and unchallenged. The family, from whom he was then totally estranged, knew nothing of the circumstances of the case until I told them: they were in no position to help. I have deliberately taken these points out of context for whilst they will be referred to in context I would not like the reader to feel, in any way, that Watkins was let down; save and except by himself. Nor have I, at any stage, referred to any child of Bill and Doris by name. Let me just say that these names are known to me, some I have met, but I will never publicly disclose who they are: to do so, would be for me, a terrible thing and my conscience would not allow it, in any event.

Returning now to 1941: the neighbours rallied round and gave Bill and Doris what support they could. Even though Victoria Road was a long road, the family were known to many of the residents and when shortly after the funeral Bill starting keeping pigs in the garden everyone knew him. He went to market and purchased a sow and seven piglets; they arrived, to the amazement of the neighbours, in a truck and getting them into their run at the bottom of the garden was a feat beyond many a pig farmer. There was a joint entrance to rear of No. 136 and No. 138, above which, and it can still be seen today, is a stone bearing the name "Claremont Place"; and they were herded down this entry by Bill, Doris and the children, with the neighbours standing by. The sty and run had been built by Bill; it was not an elaborate sty, nor decorative, but it was effective. To the neighbours' questions about noise and smell, Bill had a simple answer which more than satisfied them: he would, when a pig was killed, make them a gift of a joint. To keep pigs during the war was a sacrifice because not only did the keeper have to have the consent of the Ministry of Agriculture but had to surrender the families' meat and bacon ration; in addition random checks were made on all registered pig keepers to see that they were well kept and were no nuisance. Bill built his own boiler house to boil the pig food and forever kept the sty sparkling white with frequent whitewashing. After a few weeks Bill decided that he would breed from his sow so he bought a boar. It was enormous and vicious. Bill realized his mistake before he had taken the beast to the sty, for it butted an old arm chair lifting it from the ground and then charged at a sack of cement powder lifting it as if it was made of feathers; on the second toss the bag burst spilling its contents all over the garden. All this was before the sty was reached; eventually after much shouting, arm waving and prods with a strong stick the boar was pushed through the door. On arrival in the sty he did not think much of the sow and her growing off-spring. The next day it had to go and the boar's departure was almost as hazardous and dangerous as its arrival.

Bill never had any problem with the Ministry inspectors, and in fact frequently received their congratulations for his cleanliness and one described his boiler as "great".

Around Christmas time, 1941, Bill decided that one of his fast growing herd must be killed. This caused terrible problems; for by this time the family treated them as pets and cried at the decision. After the slaughter and curing which he had professionally done, the children were loath to eat any part of the animal but common sense eventually prevailed and the family and friends enjoyed the bacon, ham and pork that Bill proudly presented to them.

During the early years of the Second World War Bill excelled himself; the coach trips continued with an ever increasing rapidity;

regretfully he was away from the family too much. They missed him and he suddenly found that he was becoming estranged from those whom he loved. His rejuvenated love for Doris was slipping and she became, once again, lonely. The move to No. 136 Victoria Road had given both of them new hopes; she was tired, though, through so many pregnancies and her arthritis; and found herself now unloving and she thought unloved. The children were growing up and even the youngest was now at school. Time was on her hands and she began to find solace amongst the customers in the neighbouring "Bricklayers' Arms". Her beauty was beginning to fade, yet she still had poise. Bill was out so much, on Monday mornings there was the Hercules trip and on other mornings too, there were pre-arranged journeys which occupied his time: he was up early and back late; then he was too tired to listen to the everyday events. His pigs were there and whilst the children would feed them, it was Bill who cherished them.

Frank Flight and Bill got on well together; it was a working arrangement more than a friendship, but between them there existed considerable mutual respect. Flight did not live at the garage and found it difficult to deal with the ever increasing bookings from his home. Each morning there were callers complaining of being unable to get through; the effects of war were being felt and National pride forbade, except amongst the "spivs", the illegal use of petrol. Flight was unable to provide the personal service that he had previously given to the public. Motor coaches and hire cars were much in demand, for they were allowed petrol coupons. So it was that Flight approached Bill one night to see whether or not he would have a telephone installed at No. 136 (the entry in the directory to be that of Flights), so that his ever increasing cliental could have a 24-hour service. Bill readily agreed and Doris, too, found it very useful. The account, of course, was always paid by Flight.

The theatre tickets were no longer used by Bill and Doris and the visits to the cinema ended. Doris began drinking more and more. Their home at No. 136 was clean and tidy and over the years they had obtained some adequate comfortable furniture. Bill still thought the world of the children, and suddenly one Saturday night his excitement took the better of him for on checking his pools coupon he had won the four aways. In those days they were more popular than the "treble chance" which did not exist as we know it today. He was cock-a-hoop with joy.

(*Time plays havoc with one's memory and it has certainly done so with the family. Now, in later years: it was thought that this excitement happened at No. 123 in late 1941 or early 1942. If it did happen at No. 123 it must have been before 20th June 1941, because on that day the eighth child died and the address on the death certificate was No. 136. It would appear that the family did not live long at No. 123; because when the seventh child died on 12th October, 1939 the address given on the death certificate was back of 104 Nechells Park Road. It is of little significance but some of the happenings related may be out of context and this particular event [if it did happen at No. 123] certainly is out of context. One must not be critical of the family, who have assisted me, for they never expected at any time that they would be searching their minds into the past as they have so willingly done.*)

Early on the following Monday evening after work he rushed down Potters Hill with Doris to W. M. Taylor's shop in Potters Hill on the corner of Barton Bank Road and there he purchased four chairs with brown leather seats and four golden eiderdowns. The chairs were known as the "four away chairs". Later that week when the envelope from the pools arrived it contained a postal order for a few shillings. Bill got the four aways up in a week that was full of aways! Yet his temperament was such that he shrugged it off and laughed at himself.

(*This event in all probability did take place at No. 123 because in that house the unhappiness between Bill and Doris was not outwardly apparent.*)

Whilst Doris drank her beer Bill hardly drank at all. He told the family that he had seen what it had done to his father and to Doris's father and that drink certainly was not going to take a hold on him. Neither of the grandfathers made any significant impression on the children except that they were not very nice people. Bill's stepmother lived with Bill and Doris when they were in Holborn Hill and it was from this house that she entered an asylum, so the children with Doris's mother dying, at the early age of 47, had little to recollect from personal experience that was good, about their grandparents.

As a child Bill regularly attended church but this appears to have stopped when he married Doris, and whilst he encouraged the children to go and also to believe in God, Bill and Doris did not go to church. The main reason for this was that it was so often on Sundays, especially during the war, that the long coach trips took place. On Saturdays, too, there were outings. In the week it was contract work and at the weekends the trips. Bill was certainly working a seven-day week but he did not complain: he loved his work. There was only one day that he would not drive and that was Friday the 13th. Sometime earlier he had been caught speeding on one Friday 13th and thereafter feigned illness or had a day off, counting towards his holiday. In the end Mr. Flight realized that he was superstitious and deleted any Friday 13th from Bill's list of engagements. Stupidly the offence was one of exceeding a speed of 20 m.p.h. but it hurt Bill's pride to such an extent that he was dogmatic on the point. Later Bill was to write that "he had prayed for a house and got one". This must have related to the day of the bomb when the family were homeless and Nurse McDivett came to the rescue. The children knew of his belief in God and simply accepted the fact that he did not go to church. Doris was not so forthcoming to the children, as to her beliefs, when religion was mentioned.

Soon after the family moved into No. 136 the rubble from the bombed house next to the garage was removed and Nos. 121, 123, and 125 restored and a new occupant took over No. 123. The shelter life continued and every time the siren went the residents of Victoria Road took cover: the bomb had been a little too near for comfort and no one was going to take a chance. There were no more bombs in Victoria Road but precautions were maintained until VE Day: 8th May, 1945. The City of Birmingham had a magnificent fleet of trams which bore the same livery as now do the West Midlands 'buses. No. 5 tram travelled regularly up and down Victoria Road. The photograph of the road was taken *circa* 1900, before the trams and now of course the trams have gone and so have many of the houses on the right-hand side from Six Ways. No. 136 still stands, it is empty: waiting for the demolition team to arrive: its use done for ever.

In the early days of 1944 Doris again found that she was pregnant. The child, a girl, her ninth, was born. It was treasured by the others who were considerably older and Bill would look adoringly at the little baby: alas it was a shortlived treasure. The family doctor was called in, there was no cure within his power for the little girl had pneumonia and had not the strength to survive. She died on 17th November, 1944. Again at Doris's behest the child lay in state in the front room so that the family and the neighbours could pay their last respects. Again Bill would not go into the room alone and two of the children clearly remember that their mother insisted that he go and Doris took him in, again holding his hand, but within a split second he was out. At night, with the dead child downstairs he could not sleep. As before, as for the other children, the five who died, a little card of remembrance was printed (to this day those cards are treasured and when looked at bring back so many memories). The child, like the others, was buried in the children's common grave at Witton; where there is no stone or mark to show the exact spot. The children, except the youngest, went with Bill and Doris to the funeral and afterwards friends and neighbours joined them for tea. Bill's eyes were full and it was noticed that he had nothing really to say to anyone. For him to go into the front room thereafter was difficult, though he made himself do it. He was still smart—Doris saw to it that he had a clean shirt and handkerchief every day and even on the hottest of days he still wore a tie. Doris would talk of her dead children to the others saying they were "pretty when alive, and now they are at peace, and will suffer pain no more". Bill never spoke to the children about them.

In those days, prior to the National Health Service, a doctor was paid privately and whenever Doris had any worry about herself—for she was constantly unwell—or the children, the doctor was called and the bill always paid. The family cannot remember Bill ever being unwell save and except the usual colds and sore throats from which no one can escape.

The pigs remained and Bill had one favourite which he called Bet. They had a dog called "Bob" until it gave birth to a litter of puppies in one of the girls beds! Doris was furious but Bill just laughed it off as one of those things, saying "it went to the right place, didn't it?" In the large garden Bill grew enough vegetables to feed the family and more. He would tend the garden during the long wartime summer nights when we had double summertime, when it could be light until midnight. The children had pet rabbits and the family cat was a huge ginger neutered tom called "Sandy". Once again happiness returned to the Watkins family but the huge gap, that "the Dad" always seemed to be away, could never be filled.

For a while after the last baby died Doris had a job at a small factory in Victoria Road called Cyclo-Gear. This displeased Bill and there were terrible arguments about it. Doris needed the extra money for her beer but finally gave in to Bill and handed in her notice. This was possibly the last major disagreement between them before the final break was made.

Bill Watkins hated liars—he admitted to falsifying his age earlier in his life but would justifiably excuse himself that wrong; he would instill upon the children that it is better to be a thief than a liar and "by God he loathed, detested and abominated stealing", I was told. Later he was to lie and in such a stupid way—how, then, he must have hated himself? He strongly disapproved of Doris's drinking and made that fact well known. Shortly before the final break someone remembers seeing her in a filthy temper shouting at Bill in Victoria Road outside the garage.

From this picture of life at No. 136 comes the fact that Doris was the dominant partner: Bill undoubtedly the weaker of the two. He was a good coach driver, a kind father but a weak husband: "anything for peace" was his unsaid attitude. His deafness, of course, accounted for much and as each year passed by his hearing became worse. He would not admit to it, for fear of losing his driving work, but now with the passage of time the children with whom I spoke can remember instances when "the Dad" clearly did not hear what was being said. He enjoyed the radio and had it on too loud for the others; this, too, caused trouble between Doris and himself.

In the halcyon days before their trouble began, Bill and Doris would celebrate Christmas in their own particular way with the children. Money was never easy and presents nearly always consisted of new clothes; the children rarely had a toy as a gift from their parents. Every Christmas Eve was devoted to decorating the house and on Christmas morning Bill would be up early, rushing around the house like a two-year-old. He would make everyone a cup of tea and they could, even the youngest, if they wanted it, have a splash of whisky in the cup. Christmas Day was the only day in the year when he was with the family; to be there with them all the time and for every meal. After a traditional Christmas dinner the six of them would play games—he loved his board games and on this one day in the year everyone, including Doris, did what Bill wanted. No one was allowed out of the curtilage of the house; "Keep your feet under

your own table and enjoy the family" was his motto. He had nick-
names for the girls, Totea Fay and Totea Fluta, the origination of
which is lost to them for ever but to this day it is remembered; though
now the names are never spoken.

"The German War is therefore at an end," growled Churchill in a
speech broadcast to the nation on 8th May, 1945. Japan still had to
surrender and this did not happen until 15th August, 1945 following
the dropping of the Atom Bomb. This world war had been horrific
and when all was over many personal scars remained. And in the
world, Germany the vanquished, was divided only to rise again to
play an active part in all aspects of International affairs, and when
Churchill eventually returned to Downing Street, later in 1951, he
was an old man beyond his best. Yet in 1945 the warrior was still full
of fire and the Government, which was a National Government,
consisting of all parties, called a general election—the first for ten
years. When the votes were counted (and this was delayed so those in
the services could vote) Churchill was out of office and the Labour
landslide had arrived. During the election campaign Bill was again
asked by Bill Lovsey to ferry the Conservative candidate, Mr. F. B.
Normansell, about and this he did; but at this time the Conservative
Agent noticed a distinct change in Watkins. He had been driving
coaches for Mr. Lovsey continuously during the war years, but this
was the first time for some months that he had seen him at close
quarters; the old repartee between them was a thing of the past.
Birmingham, like nearly all the country, turned against the Conservative Party, and Labour took both Aston and Sparkbrook:
Woodrow Wyatt and Percy Shurmer being the respective victors.
This was the first time since Bill Lovsey had been agent that he did
not have an M.P. Major Orlando Kellett, M.P., was killed in the war
in 1943 and Bill Lovsey himself held the Aston Divisional Unionist
Association together throughout the long days before victory.
After Kellett's death there was a by-election in Aston. Under a pact
made between the major parties, they did not oppose the Conservative
candidate though others did. Commander Redvers Prior was duly
elected as Conservative member for Aston.

Bill and Doris were drifting rapidly apart and now they found,
and had to admit that, they had little in common except the children
and they were growing up—the eldest son had already left home.

Later, when the youngest daughter was married, Doris said to her, "When your husband asks you to go out, don't keep saying no; try and compromise with each other—please, please don't make the same mistakes as me". Here she was referring to the fact that going to the pictures with Bill was not her idea of fun nor the theatre also. She liked to go to the pub and Bill would never go with her—herein lay the beginning of incompatibility and credit to her for acknowledging the fact especially when one knows that this was before the events of 21st/22nd January, 1951; but after the day in January 1946 when Bill finally left home.

As the story unfolds Doris comes out as a woman prepared, at a time of real horror, to forgive and forget. In all marriages there are moments of great joy and bitter sadness. When all is over one tends to remember at first only the bad times, then as time heals, the memories come flowing back; as if bathed in eternal sunshine. And as such they hurt. For five long lonely years Doris lived with bitter memories struggling so hard to keep what was left protected and unharmed. All this came about as the result of Bill's contract work for the Hercules Cycle and Motor Co. Ltd. One Monday morning just after May 1945, a girl from Sunderland, by name of Maisie, came to the company to seek work. Bill, as usual, had the task of finding her digs and on this particular day he failed and so he took Maisie home. Doris then was 44, Maisie about 26. The eldest Watkins daughter suggested to her parents that perhaps Maisie could stay at No. 136 until something turned up—other girls had often done this for a few days. Doris asked Maisie if she would like to "stay a few days until she found some digs"; and the young woman quickly said "Yes". A few days became a few weeks then a few months and in the following January Bill and Maisie left No. 136 together. From 26th January, 1946 until 21st January, 1951 hardly anything is known of Bill, his movements or his work. Doris obtained a court order against Bill in the Birmingham Magistrates' Court on 28th May, 1946. The order was for £1 a week for Doris and ten shillings a week for the youngest child, a boy. Doris was also given custody of the youngest girl but no order for payment was made in respect of her. At this time she was 18 so it is strange that no financial order was made in respect of her, but I would imagine that this was because she was a wage-earner. Bill had to be found as he moved around and during this time sometimes went into arrears with his payments. At no time did he contact Doris or any of the children, yet whenever he could be found, and a summons was served on him for arrears, the court record shows that he immediately paid the sum required. Paradoxically it seems that for a while the two went back to Victoria Road and lodged with Mrs. Edwards, Bill's previous neighbour when he was at No. 123. How long this was for, I cannot say, but even then he did not attempt to talk or communicate with Doris—let alone the children. Nor did he go back to Flights.

In 1948, by which time Maisie was pregnant, Bill was in Sunderland and one can only surmise that they returned to Maisie's home. The last reference to him in the Birmingham Courts is on 19th October, 1948, when it appears that the order was transferred to Sunderland. This too is strange because in 1950 Bill and Maisie were living in Balsall Heath and one would have imagined that the order would have been transferred back to the Birmingham Magistrates' Court; but it was not. The youngest of the children was then still at school and Doris and three children still lived at No. 136. Bill Lovsey remembers receiving a telephone call from his counterpart in Sunderland saying that Bill Watkins was in his office and asking for a reference. Watkins was described to Lovsey and he was able to confirm that it was Bill. What work the reference was required for, we do not know, and that was the last Bill Lovsey heard from or of Bill Watkins until January 1951. We do know that for a time Bill and Maisie lodged in Tower Road, Aston and that Maisie stated in court that she and Bill had lived at 6 back of 79 Clifton Road, Balsall Heath for just over a year and Bill in evidence said two years. This last statement may be very relevant, for it is not the only statement that he made, which having little relevance to the trial, was inconsistent either with what someone else said or was untrue. Later he was to say he could not hear a word and perhaps herein lies the truth. So all we know is that Maisie said they had lived at that address for just over a year which would put their moving in to No. 6 back of 79 Clifton Road, around December 1950; if Bill is to be believed it was around January 1949. We also know that by January 1951 he was so deaf that he could not drive; he now worked, ironically, at the Hercules Cycle and Motor Co. Ltd. as a labourer.

Most important of all he had grown prematurely very old, his black hair was now steel grey, his face always looked as if he needed a shave and no longer did he hold his head high but walked like an old man with a drooping chin. No longer did he have a clean shirt every day, nor did he wear a tie. Within him had taken place the most unexplainable metamorphosis; unexplainable, that is, if one does not take into consideration the deafness. How any man with children whom he clearly adored, who lived a life of good standing, who ate well (for the family always ate well—Doris was such a good cook), could so lower himself to live in such a slum, as he did, and become so pathetic in character is beyond explanation to all that knew him.

The slum in which Marjorie Yellow lived in Willows Crescent in 1932 was described at her trial as most appalling; No. 6 back of 79 Clifton Road was, so a police officer who saw both told me, worse. Some time in 1947 Maisie gave birth to a little boy, Michael, of whom Bill was the father and the three of them survived in this council backwater, which ultimately in 1967 was demolished. Nothing now stands on the site so close to the "Railway Arms" and a little further away from the railway bridge. We know too how upset Doris was when Bill left home and as the story unfolds we find her behaviour most Christian; but she knew in 1950 through a neighbour, when Mrs. Edwards had told her, that he was in Clifton Road, still with Maisie. Yet she did not go to see him. We know that Bill kept in touch with the kindly Mrs. Edwards but he did not tell this to his lawyers for if anyone outside the family could have spoken of his previous good character it was Mrs. Edwards. Doris and the children also knew that living there with them was a child and that the child was Maisie's and Bill's. Bill did not approach Mr. Lovsey nor any of his mates at Flights nor other friends in Victoria Road. Previously he had imparted to the children the virtue of always speaking the truth and adding "if you tell a lie, you have to tell another, to cover that lie, and then another and so on and so on". Now he was in an era when even that attribute appeared to be lost to him. He abandoned all in life that once he held sacred: it was as if he were another person. Finally we know that in July 1950, Maisie missed her period thus confirming that she was again pregnant.

For the rest we have to look at the facts that are available and for the omissions there is no answer. There are inconsistencies; there are untrue statements from Watkins which have no bearing on the events which possibly indicate that when he said he did not hear what was said in court he was telling the truth.

The fact that he was so deaf may have given to those that did not know him the impression that he was simple or as someone who knew him said "plain daft" for at the trial that was the impression that he gave.

It is likely that none of his old friends and colleagues connected the "William Arthur Watkins" of 6 back of 79 Clifton Road with the "Bill Watkins" they once knew, who used to live in Victoria Road.

Before looking in detail at the events of the night of 20th/21st January, 1951, I find that there are some questions, the answers to which I have been unable to provide. I list them in the knowledge that no matter what the answers are you can never alter what was to some, the inevitable end. But, maybe, if the answers had been available, then perhaps, there would have been a different verdict—or at the best, following the conviction for murder, a reprieve.

The questions which immediately come to my mind are:—

1 Why was there dissent between Bill and Maisie as to how long they had lived at 6 back of 79 Clifton Road?

2 Was Watkins hit by a policeman, if so by whom?

3 How many statements did he make to the police? The evidence of Quinton and Mitchell was that there were two. Watkins said that there were three. *On reading the transcript it is now possible to understand the confusion in Watkins' mind for now we do know that Watkins, after the trial, wrote that he could not hear a word in court.*

4 Why did Watkins say he had four children, all of whom had grown up? Mr. Justice Finnemore commented adversely on this point.

5 Why did Watkins remain practically mute to his solicitor and counsel as to his background?

6 Why did one of the police officers in the case say to me "I looked for friends but couldn't find a single one: I could find no one who could say a good word for him." If that officer had been given the information I have discovered, surely someone would have come forward? Why were no inquiries made by any one from Doris who was living openly at No. 136 Victoria Road, Aston? Is it conceivable that Watkins was now so ashamed of his life style that he did not allow Doris to be contacted?

7 Why did Doris nor the family never know the details of the offence with which Watkins was charged? When I told certain members of the family in 1978, even then, they did not know.

8 Was the leaving of the baby in the bath consistent with his foible

as to his reactions upon the death of a baby: namely that he would not go into the room where the body lay, unaccompanied?

9 If Watkins did murder the baby, as the jury found, why did Watkins show no concern at Mrs. Revell going to see Maisie alone and with the dead baby in the next room? One's immediate thought would be—that Watkins would go upstairs with her to make certain (a) that she didn't go into the other room and (b) that he could hear what Maisie had to say to Mrs. Revell?

10 Why did Watkins tell deliberate lies to Mrs. Revell about a miscarriage and then immediately tell the truth to the police officer? When Black and Miss Beattie arrived there was no suggestion of telling untruths.

11 What did Mrs. Revell learn from Maisie? (which evidence would have been inadmissible).

12 Why when Watkins knew Maisie was pregnant did he not insist that she see a doctor? or attend a clinic?

13 Why on the Sunday morning of 22nd January when he knew that the baby was dead, when he knew that he had buried the after-birth, would he not admit that Maisie had had a child to Mrs. Revell? Why did he not go to her first thing in the morning or even in the night; if the baby died as he said it did? Or was the fact that the baby was dead to him so frightening that all his past fears and dreads returned; to the extent that he panicked? If Fearnley-Whittingstall had had this knowledge his powers of advocacy would have spelt it out to the jury.

14 What did he plan to do with the baby after it had drowned?

15 Why was he so changed? Was it just his deafness or was there some underlying reason for not wanting to help himself?

16 Why when sentenced to death did he smile?

17 Why did he revert in character to his old self in the condemned cell?

18 Why is Pugh reported in *The Birmingham Mail* as saying that Watkins had made a statement saying "I've done it, the baby is dead" when no evidence was brought of such a statement at his trial? Did Maisie make a statement to the police indicating that Watkins had said this to her? If so, what happened to it?

19 In 1951 in the slums when you had no money, was it reasonable to expect that preparations would be made 5–6 weeks before the expected birth? We now know it was 5–6 weeks because Professor

Webster said that the child was born 5–6 weeks prematurely; but did Maisie know the expected date of birth? She had at no time during this pregnancy seen a doctor: all she says is that "I missed my periods at the end of July". No attempt appears to have been made by anyone to determine what "The end of July" means.

20 The prosecution made much of the fact that Watkins had left the dead baby in the water: forgetting the argument about how the baby was drowned we now have the knowledge that he suffered from the terrible fear of dead babies. No one within the court room except Watkins and possibly, Maisie, had that knowledge. Does this provide an answer to two questions? First, does it give sense to the verbal statement Watkins made to Black "It's quite all right officer, I'm not frightened of it"? If it does then the fact that he was able to go into the room and lift the baby out of the water indicates (or does it?) that the company of Black provided the courage to go into the room, thus immediately eliminating his foible?

22 We know that Watkins lied to Mrs. Revell but as soon as the police officer arrived there was no suggestion of a miscarriage. With the knowledge we now have of Watkins is it possible to put his conversation with Mrs. Revell into the "white lie" category? especially as he did not accompany Mrs. Revell when she went to see Maisie?

23 Was the tying of the door anything other than making the room safe, so that under no circumstances could Michael gain entry?

24 Maisie was so ill after the birth that she was taken immediately to hospital. If she had not been so ill would the baby have been so left? or would it even have died? "The wife was shouting out, I must have panicked" Watkins told Black. If there had been no shout from Maisie: what then? and did he bury the afterbirth so that Maisie would not see it? Maisie knew that he had cleaned up the bed.

25 If Watkins was going to murder the baby why should he take such care about the temperature of the water in the tub?

26 If the baby was murdered, as the court found, then any pre-meditation by Watkins to murder must have been almost instantaneous. Did he know when he went to sleep on the night of Saturday, 21st January that Maisie was so near her time?

27 Why were there so many variations on the extent of the deafness of Watkins? The following list gives some indication of the variance amongst those concerned.

Could one man have appeared so different to so many? Black said (to the author): "He was obviously a bit deaf as he cupped his hand over an ear as I spoke to him. I have a quiet voice so I had to speak loudly close to his ear."

Miss Beattie said (to the author): "He appeared to be of low mentality and rather stupid. I did not know, at that time, that he was so deaf."

Mitchell said (on oath) in answer to a question by Fearnley-Whittingstall: "I should say he was below average intelligence."

Quinton said (on oath) in answer to the question from Fearnley-Whittingstall: "He must have been a very irritating man to take a statement from, with his deafness?" replied "Not particularly so"; Fearnley-Whittingstall then asked "Was he also distressed, crying at some portion of time?" and Quinton said "Not crying, he was distressed, but he looks that way naturally."

Did Quinton know Watkins prior to 22nd January?

Alderson said (to the author): "He was very deaf. I had to shout but I could get through to him."

A prison officer said (to the author): "He was hard of hearing, to the point of deafness, but if he was watching you when you were talking to him you could actually see him making sense to himself of what he was seeing from the speaker's lips and what he was obviously faintly hearing. And then he would understand. You could carry on a reasonable and rational conversation with him, provided that when speaking to him, you looked him in the face and you were prepared to be patient: which we were."

Fearnley-Whittingstall said (to Mr. Justice Finnemore in the presence of the jury): "Your Lordship will appreciate that I am in some difficulty because he is very deaf."

His family said: "He gradually did go deafer and deafer . . . when we saw him in prison he was much deafer than he had been when we had last seen him in 1946."

28 Was Watkins born on 23rd January, 1902, as he said he was? and it therefore follows did Watkins really give a false age when he married?

29 Why did not Fearnley-Whittingstall put to Quinton before the jury the two questions which are referred to in question number 27 that he put to him before the Judge alone when he was challenging the statement?

As I say the answers to these, or even some, may hold the clue to what motivated him. The jury clearly did not believe that he panicked and Sir Frank Newsam clearly thought that the murder was premeditated. And finally:

30 What would have been the verdict of a jury faced with the same evidence in 1981?

BILL WATKINS
CIRCA 1930
"A POPULAR FELLOW IN ASTON"

CLIFTON ROAD, BALSALL HEATH

CIRCA 1900

THERE WAS LITTLE CHANGE IN 1951

VICTORIA ROAD, ASTON

CIRCA 1900

THE ONLY CHANGE IN 1951 BEING THE TRAMWAY

TED DODD
"RATHER LIKE A
YOUTHFUL
JACK HAWKINS"

—: Reproduced by courtesy of the Evening Mail, Birmingham

M. P. PUGH
"MR. M. P. PUGH
PROSECUTING SAID . . .
'I'VE DONE IT, THE
BABY IS DEAD' "

J. F. MILWARD J.P.
"NOT ONLY A GENTLE-
MAN BUT A LAWYER OF
GREAT ABILITY"

PROFESSOR
J. M. WEBSTER
"OCH A PAIR OF GLASSES
IS NO DAMN GOOD TO A
MAN WITH A GLASS
EYE"

JOCK BLACK
TO WHOM WATKINS SAID
"IT'S QUITE ALRIGHT
OFFICER, I'M NOT
FRIGHTENED OF IT"

MISS
HELEN BEATTIE
"PARTICULARLY KNOWN
FOR HER KINDNESS AND
SYMPATHETIC
APPROACH"

J. A. ALDERSON
"AN ADVOCATE OF NO
MEAN ABILITY"

GEORGE
BLACKBOROW
"AN EXTRAORDINARILY
SMART OFFICER"

PROLOGUE

Part II

So far as the witnesses who gave evidence, including William Arthur Watkins are concerned, their part was told on oath to the Judge and Jury and is reproduced in full; but happily former Inspector Miss Beattie and former Detective Sergeant Black can fill in some of the facts which were not necessary for the trial and these facts together with their own thoughts give colour to the picture and in parts take from the transcript the coldness that lies within any such document.

On the morning of Monday, 22nd January, 1951, the residents around No. 79 Clifton Road were murmuring one to the other that a doctor must go to poor Mrs. Watkins: they all knew she was pregnant and now they learnt that she had had a "miss", yet still they knew no doctor or nurse had called. No. 6 back of No. 79 was one of those terraced houses that no one could go in or out of without someone knowing. A telephone call was made to the surgery of Dr. Albert Salmon whom it was thought was the Watkins' doctor. Following this a call was made to Central 5000 and a voice asked to be put through to the C.I.D. On duty was Detective Inspector Helen Beattie; she took the call: it was then about 1.45 p.m. Miss Beattie was told that it was thought that Mrs. Watkins was pregnant and near her delivery time but neither the doctor nor the midwife had been called. There was, Miss Beattie heard, no sign of a baby nor news of Mrs. Watkins. Helen Beattie said she would look into it straight away. Christine Coutts, a policewoman, was nearby. Helen spoke to her and then telephoned Edward Road police station. At about 2.00 p.m. Jock Black, Detective Sergeant, was having a conversation with Sergeant Joe Phillips. This is what Jock remembers:

"I was at Edward Road police station as Detective Sergeant, I think the time was around 2.00 p.m. and late going to lunch as usual! Sergeant Joe Phillips, the Second Watch Sergeant, casually mentioned that he had to go down to Clifton Road as 'there was a bit of talk' amongst neighbours about Mr. Watkins and his wife. It was believed

5

by the neighbours that they were not married, but they had a little boy about 4 years old, and Mrs. Watkins had been expecting a baby any minute. On that morning Watkins had told the neighbours that she had had the baby during the night, and that the local Doctor and District Midwife had been in attendance. The neighbours were suspicious as there had been no commotion in the night and despite very obvious attempts to get invited in to see Mrs. Watkins and the baby, Mr. Watkins had not asked anyone in at all to see either. The neighbours had been in touch with the Doctor and Midwife but neither knew anything about Mrs. Watkins or a birth at that address. Joe Phillips said that he was going to take a walk down to see what it was all about. 'Probably nothing in it but rumour,' Joe said.

I asked Joe if he had arranged for a policewoman to be with him and he said that he had not at that stage. I felt a bit wary about the matter and suggested to Joe that he leave the matter to me and I would get Inspector Helen Beattie out from Town to go with me to which he agreed," and at that moment the telephone rang on his desk. He picked it up, "Inspector Beattie for you," said the telephonist—thus their minds were working identically. Helen said she would be over as soon as possible. She came quickly and as Jock Black said:

"That was lunch missed once again, and I was quickly joined by Inspector Miss Beattie. We walked down to the Watkins' address in Clifton Road. We went to the door and, after a lot of knocking, Mr. Watkins came to us. A tall, slightly stooping man, a bit grey and needing a shave. He was obviously a bit deaf as he cupped a hand over an ear as I spoke to him. I have a quiet voice so I had to speak loudly close to his ear."

Helen Beattie remembers what happened on arrival at the house, and in her own words said:

"On arrival at the house Watkins answered the door. I told him who we were and asked if I could see his wife. He said she wasn't very well. I asked 'What's the matter with her?' or words to that effect. He said she had a baby . . . I asked 'Where is she?' He said 'She's in bed upstairs'. I said 'Could we see the baby?' He said 'Well, I was sort of washing it over like and something happened'. I asked if he would take us to see his wife and he took us to a bedroom upstairs where she was in bed. She had not had any medical attention, her face was ashen white and she looked very ill. After speaking to the woman I said 'Could we see the baby?' Watkins then took us to the room next door, but first he had to untie the wire with which he had secured the door. When he opened the door, it was a small room completely filled with junk and old clothes, and general rubbish. In the centre of the room on the floor was a zinc wash-boiler. On top of the lid of the boiler was a heap of dirty clothes, which he removed and then took the lid off the wash-boiler. Inside was a pillow-case immersed in deep water and inside that was the body of a lovely little curly headed baby-boy, which had been inserted into the pillow-case head first.

I have no recollection of what I said then.

I sent P.W. Coutts to telephone the senior C.I.D. officers on the Division, Detective Chief Inspector Oliver Quinton and Detective Inspector James Mitchell and Mr. George Blackborow, who was then Head of the C.I.D.

In the meantime, as the house was very cold and there was no other means of heating, I told Watkins to light a fire (coal) and make a cup of tea, just to humour him and keep him occupied until the senior officers arrived. He appeared to be of low mentality and rather stupid. I don't think he ever succeeded in making a fire or making tea.

Detective Chief Inspector Quinton and Detective Inspector Mitchell then arrived and I then took a statement from the woman, who was not the wife of Watkins, although they already had one child, and they did not want another one. Not being the 'wife' she was a competent witness and eligible to give evidence, which she did.

Arrangements were made for her admission to hospital, and I have a vague recollection that P.W. Coutts and I went with her in the ambulance.

Watkins was taken to Edward Road police station, where he was interviewed by the senior officers.

There had to be a *post-mortem* examination on the body and after that was completed Watkins was charged with the murder of the baby and taken to the lock-up.

At Edward Road police station I hurriedly wrote, in shorthand, on a piece of paper the man's answers to me after my arrival at the scene. This I later attached to my official pocket book, which, of course, was submitted as an exhibit."

The official police note-book of Detective Sergeant James Black has in it the following entry:

(This is reproduced word for word save and except the names of "Mrs. Watkins" and the little boy have been altered in accordance with the whole story.)

"*3 pm. Monday, 22nd January, 1951.*

With Miss Beattie and Miss Coutts to 6/79 Clifton Road. Saw Wm. Arthur Watkins. Told who we were, asked into house.

Black. 'Who lives here?'

Watkins. 'Me and the woman I live with and the boy.'

Black. 'How old is the boy?'

Watkins. 'He's three.'

Black. 'Is everything all right?'

Watkins. 'No.'

Black. 'What's the matter. Where is your wife?'

Watkins. 'She's ill; she had a baby on Saturday night.'

Black. 'What happened?'

Watkins. 'I was helping her, I got a bowl with water and was bathing the baby. It slipped and I let it drop in the water. The wife was screaming and shouting.'

Black. 'Is the baby dead?'

Watkins. 'Yes.'

Black. 'Where is it now?'

Watkins. 'Upstairs. I put it in the back room.'

Cautioned. Watkins made statement; I took it down and read it to him. He read it and signed it.

Then with Miss Beattie, Miss Coutts and Watkins, went upstairs into front bedroom. Saw Maisie —— sitting up in bed and small boy Michael asleep by her side.

Watkins (to Maisie). 'It's the Police about the baby. Don't worry, I've told them everything about it.'

I told Maisie who we were and I then left Miss Beattie and Miss Coutts with her.

I took Watkins out of the room then on to the stair landing. He pointed to door leading to back bedroom and said, 'It's in there.'

Saw that door handle was fastened to a cup hook on door jamb with copper wire and string.

Watkins undid the wire and string and we went into the room. Just inside behind the door near the wall saw a pile of clothing;

a pillow.   a lady's vest.

a blanket.   a lady's dress.

a bed sheet.   a small hand towel.

part of a blanket.

Some of these articles were stained.

Watkins pulled these articles away and I saw a small zinc tub with a lid about 16″ × 10″. Watkins lifted the lid off. I saw that the tub was $\frac{1}{2}$ full of water with a pillow case in it and a baby's leg protruding from the open end. The baby was in the pillow case head first in the water. Watkins lifted the body out, placed it on the pile of bed linen etc., which had been covering it and pulled the pillow case off. Watkins then said to me, 'It's quite all right officer, I'm not frightened of it'. I saw that it was a male child. Watkins was crying and distressed.

Black.   'Who cut the cord?'

Watkins.   'I did, with a pair of scissors.'

He was upset and crying.

Watkins.   'We hadn't made any arrangements for it. I didn't know what to do. The wife was shouting out. I must have panicked.'

I then took him downstairs into the front room and stayed with him there. Whilst in the front room, Watkins said, 'I buried the afterbirth in the garden up by the hutch. I did it after dark.'

About 5.00 p.m. the same day, was joined by Miss Beattie and Miss Coutts. In their presence I cautioned Watkins and said to him, 'You needn't answer this question unless you wish to do so, also what you say will be written down and may be given in evidence.'

'You say you were bathing the baby and it slipped and fell into the water; did you pick the baby out of the water again at any time after it fell in?' Watkins said, 'I couldn't have done.' I said, 'How do you account for it being inside the pillow slip?' Watkins did not reply for a moment then said, 'I got the pillow slip and put the baby into it, and then I was washing it over the top of the pillow slip like.' He then cried and said no more. I said to Watkins, 'You say you cut the cord with the scissors, can you find them for me?' Watkins did not reply but took me upstairs into the room at the front occupied by Maisie. He took a pair of scissors off a bed adjoining that occupied by Maisie and handed them to me. We then left the room, I was in front of

Watkins. We were half way down stairs, when Watkins turned back and put his head round the bedroom door and said to Maisie, 'What have you said?' Maisie replied, 'It's all right, I've told them the same as you have.' Watkins looked round, and saw that I had stopped on the stairs too and was listening, and came away from the room and downstairs with me.

At about 5.30 p.m. Doctor Sandilands arrived with Detective Inspector Jim Mitchell and examined the body of the child. He also went to see Miss Maisie with Miss Beattie. I was present when the Police photographer Det. Sgt. Pountney arrived and took photographs.

Later, with D.I. Mitchell and with Watkins present I dug in the front garden of the house near the small rabbit hutch and about $1\frac{1}{2}'$ down I found what appeared to be an afterbirth wrapped in newspapers.

I took possession of

1) the piece of wire and string from the back bedroom door.
2) a pillow, blanket, bed sheet, part of a blanket, a lady's dress, a lady's vest, a small hand towel.
3) the small zinc tub containing water and the lid.
4) the pillow case in which the body was found.
5) a stained bed sheet from the corner of the back bedroom.
6) a suitcase containing a gents shirt, a lady's cardigan, lady's knickers, some brown paper (all stained).
7) the body of a male child.

I conveyed them all to the Central Mortuary at Newton Street.

At 11.00 p.m. Monday, 22nd January, 1951, at the Central Mortuary, Newton Street. Present were Professor J. M. Webster, Doctor Sandilands, Detective Chief Superintendent George Blackborow, Detective Chief Inspector Oliver Quinton, Detective Inspector Jim Mitchell.

I identified the body of the male child to Professor Webster as that of the child found by me at 6/79, Clifton Road at 3.00 p.m. on Monday, 22/1/1951. Professor Webster then conducted a Post Mortem on the body of the child.

At 11.55 p.m. Monday, 22/1/1951 I was present at Edward Road police station when Watkins was charged by Chief Inspector Quinton with the murder of a male child at 6/79 Clifton Road on Sunday,

21st January, 1951. Watkins was cautioned by Chief Inspector Quinton. He did not make any reply."

From this note of what actually happened a number of points come quickly to mind and the answers to them set up more questions than they actually answer.

From the moment the officers arrived until Watkins left with them he appears in every way to have told the truth. There was no evasion, no attempt not to answer and no question of him being violent in any way. He told the Detective Sergeant where the afterbirth was, quite voluntarily without any prompting from Jock Black. He took him to where the baby was and had been for nearly 36 hours and then he made what then appeared to be the most extraordinary remark. But when one remembers the past it immediately becomes the most natural thing for him to say and to do: he was never afraid of being in a room with one of his dead babies when he was with someone. Now with Black there all his fears vanished for he had company: he could not have gone into that room on his own; he just could not. The early untimely deaths of his own children and his memories of the little open coffins provided the barrier over which he could never climb unaccompanied. Again quite unnecessarily and unprompted he said "it's quite all right officer, I'm not frightened of it." Throughout all this he was crying and distressed. His behaviour could not have been otherwise.

That night Maisie was in hospital, Michael in care and Watkins in custody. They gave him a number: 7122. On the morning of his 49th birthday William Arthur Watkins, wearing an old grey suit with a knotted neckscarf around his neck, looking unshaven, with his steel grey hair untidily brushed back, walked up the stairs into No. 1 court of the Victoria Law Courts to face the learned Magistrate, Mr. John Milward. The charge of murder was put to him and he was told he need not say anything in reply, he cupped his right ear, kept his chin low and smiled. The charge was re-read by the clerk in a louder voice and Watkins lifting, momentarily, his drooping chin, nodded in assent. Mervyn Pugh addressed the Magistrate briefly upon the facts and asked for a remand in custody for seven days. The learned Magistrate granted what was then known as a Poor Persons Defence Certificate so that Watkins could have legal assistance. Watkins had never had need of a solicitor and did not know of one. Unknown to

Watkins Mr. Lovsey's son had qualified as a solicitor and was then in practice in the City. Watkins left it to the court to assign one to him. Later that day Mr. J. A. Alderson of Messrs. Hatwell, Pritchett & Co. received a telephone call from the office of the Magistrates' Clerk asking if he would undertake the defence. Alderson readily agreed and on that night there appeared in *The Birmingham Mail* under the heading "Accused of Baby Murder—Man put child in bath court told":

> The discovery of the body of a newly-born male child inside a pillow slip in a bath of water led to the appearance at Birmingham today of William Arthur Watkins (aged 49), a labourer, of 6/79 Clifton Road, Balsall Heath, charged with murdering the child.
>
> Watkins, shabbily dressed, without collar or tie, was remanded in custody for eight days and granted legal aid.
>
> Mr. M. P. Pugh (prosecuting) said Watkins was a married man, but for the last five years had been associating with Maisie ———. She gave birth to a child when there was no one in the house except Watkins and another child. No help was sought from anyone.
>
> According to Watkins, said Mr. Pugh, he put the child in a pillow-case and then placed it head downwards in a bath of water and covered it with old clothes. He told the woman the child was dead.
>
> The next day Detective-Sergeant Black found the body in the same position. Watkins had made a statement.

In another court, on the same day, in the same building, Pugh's first senior solicitor, Charles Smallwood (Roy Dunstan was Pugh's deputy) prosecuted a man who lived at No. 58 Willows Crescent on a charge relating to embezzling caravan deposits from a Bromsgrove firm known as Becketts. On that night Watkins was placed in the hospital wing: how ironic that on his 49th birthday, never having been in trouble before, he should find himself under the same roof, on a charge of murder as a man from Willows Crescent; where nineteen years earlier the shout "Murder! Murder! Fetch the police" had been made.

A woman who lived in Victoria Road worked at Winson Green prison, to which Bill was taken. She saw his name and was horrified; she made inquiries and when she knew the charge she cried. That night, his 49th birthday, Doris was told: "I had to come," she said "and tell you before you heard from someone else or saw it in the papers." Doris thanked her and an air of utter despair and helplessness enveloped those who knew and remembered the Bill Watkins of old. "It's impossible"; "It can't be true"; "Not our Bill", they said, and someone rushed to the newsagents and bought *The Birmingham Mail* and the *Evening Despatch*: then and only then did they realize what had happened. There was sadness throughout that section of Victoria Road around No. 136; all the wrong that Bill had done was suddenly forgiven and people said one to another, "What can we do?" And no one knew what to do.

A dispute between two doctors which Mr. Justice Vaisey called "a sordid story" took the headlines that night on page 5 of the *Evening Despatch*. A licensee whose re-trial, on motoring charges, at the Lichfield Quarter Sessions, had been ordered after the jury failed to agree, obtained more lineage than the "murder" in Balsall Heath. On the same day, an M.P. asked Mr. Herbert Morrison in the House of Commons if he would postpone the Festival of Britain in view of the international situation. Mr. Morrison replied to the effect that such a move would be a heavy discouragement to those who believed in Britain. There were avalanches along the 10,000 feet high mountain barrier between Italy and Austria and many people were killed. Twenty members of the Priory Lawn Tennis Club from Edgbaston were marooned at Klosters as a result. There was talk of war with Russia and Sir Hartley Shawcross made a stirring speech condemning their policies. "Why," he asked "in the name of humanity do they go out of their way to make enemies?"

Newspapers were bought the following day and avidly studied for reports of the "murder". There was mention, but nothing new. There was no new news that day except that the licensee had been acquitted and that did not really interest them. The lawyers noted that it was yet another success for Mr. Kenneth Mynett, a rising star in the Midlands courts. Strikes were in abundance. Bill Watkins who until the day he walked out of No. 136 Victoria Road had always worked so hard, would nevertheless have smiled at a small news item that night:

> "A letter received by a Birmingham firm from a customer in Eire reads as follows:
> 'With reference to your application for November account. I wish to state that these goods have not arrived here yet as they were held up by the rail strike. Even if they had arrived we have no cheques to pay you as we cannot get them owing to the bank strike. Further, even if we could send cheque, you could not cash it on account of strike, so I think it is better to let the matter lie for the moment'."

Alderson telephoned Pugh and arranged for the information that he required to be sent to him. Pugh had already been in touch with the office of the Director of Public Prosecutions, whose agent he was, and agreed for the committal proceedings to take place on the 15th February: this date was convenient to Alderson.

On 31st January Bill Watkins appeared once more on remand. He wore the same clothes but this time his shabby jacket was unbuttoned and one could see his shirt was collarless and striped; the same neck scarf was tied around his neck. Alderson had seen him previously at Winson Green and having read his statement knew that the plea must be one of "Not Guilty". When Alderson first saw Watkins his eyes were full of tears and he just seemed to nod at everything; Alderson found him deaf; but that by shouting he could get through to him. The remand was again for eight days and merited a few lines in the evening papers. The next remand went by unnoticed by the press.

On Thursday, 15th February the committal proceedings took place. The following is the extract from the note-book of J. F. Milward, Esq. J.P., Stipendiary Magistrate for Birmingham. [*These appear exactly as Mr. Milward wrote them with the exception of the pseudonym, which is consistent throughout the book.*]

William Arthur *Watkins* (49)
> Murder (of new born child by drowning in basin)
> Pugh pros. (D.P.P.)
> Alderson (Hatwell Pritchett) def. (PPD)

Ian Macrae *Sandilands* Dr.

Sgt. *Pountney* Photographer Ex. 1 (negatives)

Ex. 2 (photographs. 2)

P.C. Stanley *Miller*	E.276 Plan Ex.3
Maisie ———	Baby born 3.30 a.m. 21.1.51
D.Sgt. *Black*	Ex.9. Statement of deft.
	Ex.7. Clothing
	Ex.4. Zinc tub and lid
	Ex.5. Pillow Case
	Ex.8. Scissors
	Ex.6. Shirt.
Dr. Albert *Salmon*	Panel Dr.
Prof. *Webster*	
Mrs. Lilian May *Revell*	Neighbour

Insp. Helen Anne *Beattie*
Insp. James *Mitchell* Ex.10. Statement
D.Ch.Insp. Oliver *Quinton*
  Committed to Birmingham Assizes
  Def. Cert. 2 Counsel
  Form B   15 Quns.

The proceedings again only merited a few lines. Webster was quickly busy in the coroner's court and there were far more exciting pieces of news than the single appearance of a down and out man on a charge of murder. Churchill took the headlines moving a vote of no confidence in the Government. Ernest Bevin was recovering, so it said, from the pneumonia that shortly was to kill him; Z notices were sent out to former Anti-Aircraft men warning them of a possible call up. There was chaos at the Smethwick Magistrates' court and in heavy black print the *Evening Despatch* under the heading "Solicitor acts as J.P.'s Clerk" reported:

> "Smethwick court proceedings were delayed ten minutes today while hurried efforts were made to find a magistrates' clerk to act in place of Mr. T. Craddock, who has flu.
>
> An SOS to West Bromwich drew the reply: 'Sorry we are running two courts of our own.'
>
> Finally, Mr. Geoffrey H. Piddock, a local solicitor appearing in a matrimonial case on the list, agreed to deputize. He took all the cases, leaving his own till last.
>
> Then he conducted his case from the solicitors' table, while Mrs. M. Telichowska, chief assistant to Mr. Craddock, acted as clerk."

This gained far more lineage than the committal proceedings but *The Birmingham Mail* did report the case under the heading "Newly-born baby in bath: Man sent for trial." The report read:

> The discovery by Birmingham detectives of the body of a newly-born baby boy, head downwards in a pillowcase in a tub of water in a house at Balsall Heath, led to a charge of murder being heard at Birmingham Magistrates' Court today.
>
> William Arthur Watkins (aged 49), of 6/79, Clifton Road, Balsall Heath, was committed for trial at Birmingham Assizes charged with the murder of the child in the early hours of January 21.
>
> Mr. M. P. Pugh, prosecuting, said Watkins, a married man separated from his wife, had been living with Maisie —— for the past five years and they already had one child, a boy three years old. The woman gave birth to another male child, and she saw Watkins take the child into the back bedroom. He returned in a short time and, Mr. Pugh alleged, told her: "I've done it. The baby is dead."

Earlier, Watkins had told a neighbour that a doctor had been booked but Watkins had in fact made no arrangements. Mr. Pugh continued. The matter came to the notice of the police who visited the house on January 22 and found the body.

Watkins, he alleged, made a statement in which he said: "We had made no arrangements. I lost my head and did not know what to do. I went to bathe it and it slipped and dropped into the water. I have not slept since. If I drowned the baby I did it in a panic."

Professor J. M. Webster made an examination of the body and found the child, born a month prematurely, had had a separate existence and had died from asphyxia, due to drowning.

Watkins, who was represented by Mr. J. A. Alderson, pleaded not guilty and reserved his defence. He was committed for trial in custody, and granted a defence certificate for two counsel at his trial.

The statement "I've done it. The baby is dead" did not appear in the later trial. Pugh was always meticulous in the preparation of his cases and would not have made such a comment if it were not before him: perhaps it appeared in the depositions? but if it did one of the counsel for the prosecution would have picked up the omission and pounced on it in cross examination when Watkins gave his evidence. At the trial this alleged statement was never put to Maisie.

At Stratford-upon-Avon, at the Memorial Theatre, Michael Redgrave, Harry Andrews, Hugh Griffith, Richard Burton, Heather Stannard and Anthony Quayle were rehearsing for the season's repertoire which was to begin on 24th March. When at Flights Bill had often taken parties to that same theatre and bought with the previous day's tips, which Doris had allowed him to keep as "pocket money", a ticket in the gods. That, though, was now a long time ago and he was, he knew, a different man and such trips were but memories of a life that once he had so enjoyed.

Alderson prepared his brief for the forthcoming trial and was fortunate to obtain the services of the most eminent silk, Bill Fearnley-Whittingstall and as a junior he chose Michael Davies. As Alderson prepared his brief so did Pugh; the Director nominating R. T. Paget, K.C., and R. K. Brown.

At Winson Green, Bill fitted happily into the routine, he did not talk to the others in the hospital wing preferring to sit quietly and read. Those that saw him then, still talk of the eyes being so full: all the time he cried in a curiously silent painful way and he would take no comfort from any solace offered. He did as he was told, ate well and slept well; all in a world of his own. It was as if he was shell-shocked though yet, occasionally, through the tears, he would smile in acknowledgement for some kindness done for him.

Earlier the youngest daughter of Bill and Doris had married: Bill did not know. At No. 136 the two daughters, her son-in-law and the younger son, who was 13, supported Doris. They did not go to Winson Green: rather they strengthened themselves in readiness for the impossible. In Doris the family saw flickers of emotion but in front of them she did not allow herself to break; keeping her sorrows, her memories, her silences, to herself: in particular her weaknesses, and at this time she brought back from the hidden depths of her mind all that was good in Bill. The newspaper report said that he "was shabbily dressed, without collar or tie": "not her Bill, it couldn't be". In her heart she hated Maisie and she hated herself for not having the courage to go and see Bill.

She wondered if he would write to her now; but as she had not heard from him for so long that was asking the impossible. Her days at the beginning of March 1951, were long and bitter and she was filled with remorse and a sense of utter failure: she bore it in silence. In the early days of her marriage to Bill, when they had been happy, she used to go to the Aston Hippodrome with Bill and when it was sing-song time she and Bill would join in, singing with the audience; and one of their favourites was "Keep the home fires burning". She had forgotten. Then suddenly on 6th March, 1951 it all came back: Ivor Novello was dead. That night on the radio there was a tribute and when "Keep the home fires burning" began, she finally broke.

Thursday, 15th March was the day set for the start of the trial; the night before Paget and Fearnley-Whittingstall travelled to Birmingham staying at the Midland Hotel. There is a comradeship within the Bar which is often difficult for others to accept. Meeting in court is very different to meeting for dinner: in the courtroom a lawyer has two causes uppermost in his mind: justice and the client. Over the dinner table those causes are put on one side; and rightly so. On 14th March the four counsel met for dinner. Fearnley-Whittingstall was at his most biting, he was a sensitive man, highly strung and when a man's life lay in his hands he could not forget. Over the dinner table he turned on Ralph Kilner Brown and with his devastating powers of comment brought the conversation round to the church and unlike Jim Crump's 1939 wish "that personalities be kept out of things" joked about

Brown's father. Both were sons of clergymen and Fearnley-Whitting-stall who had served in India and knowing that the Reverend Arthur Brown was a much loved and respected figure in the educational world of Bengal India, said "When I took my gunners across India to join the Burma War the bazaars still rang with the reputation of 'beastly Brown the basher of Bengal'." There was a silence; Bill Fearnley-Whittingstall pushed his glasses back to their normal position and glowered. Paget quickly changed the subject and passed the port. That conversation over, they turned their thoughts and words to other things. In reminiscing now about that night Mr. Justice Kilner Brown said, "as a piece of phraseology it had a wonderful alliteration about it".

In the prison Bill Watkins talked a great deal to the Chaplain, the Reverend F. Thompson, and willingly attended the services joining in whole-heartedly. He prayed regularly, something he had not done for many years. The reality of what was happening to him was lost, he seemed content with life and oblivious of what might happen.

I was in court on 15th March, 1951 as Bill Watkins walked up the steps leading to the dock in Court No. 5 at the Victoria Law Courts. In case, because of my interest in the trial, it should be thought that my eyes did not see what other eyes saw, that my ears did not hear what other ears heard, I give a description of that first day from a reply to an article that appeared in the *Sunday Mercury* saying that a book was being written about the trial and requesting information from anyone who could help, and written to me by a former City of Birmingham ambulance driver who to fill time between shifts would, in 1951, take himself regularly to the public gallery.

"I remember that day, it was a mockery; if I had thought it would have done any good I would have leapt from the public gallery and defended him myself; he looked and was so helpless. He sat in the dock, the most pathetic figure it has ever been my misfortune to see. When he stood he appeared like a slight statue with a drooping chin; he had no collar or tie, his grey suit looked dirty and around his neck was a white knotted scarf. To the amusement of many people in the gallery he was almost as deaf as a door-post. It was obvious that he could not hear what was going on most of the time, he was continuously cupping his hand over his ear to form some sort of trumpet. By his side was a large kindly Warder who from time to time, repeated what was going on. I am only an ordinary man but that day I was ashamed of being there and it has haunted me ever since. It was obvious that Watkins misunderstood so many of the questions for time and again he gave the wrong answer: people laughed at him. . . ." *the letter then continues with a factual account of what happened and then the writer goes on to say* "What a farce of a trial, what a miscarriage of justice. Watkins was said to be of low intelligence, an intelligent man may have acted as he did being in a state of panic. I think the baby came too early and they were not ready for it, I think the baby did slip and was dead when Watkins went back to it after going to see what the shouting was about. I think he then put it in the pillow case. I remember a lot of argument about a second statement. Why no appeal? Why no reprieve?"

After the writer has signed his name he has added the words:

"P.S. the above statement is true to the best of my memory".

Parts of the letter I have not reproduced because they are repetitive and the writer gives very strong views against certain of those involved, with which I personally would not wish to be associated.

Pugh, although the prosecuting solicitor, was certain that if found guilty there would be a reprieve and this thought he imparted to those close to him, but when something worried him he would not tell his wife; on the evening of the first day she could sense that he had something on his mind and that all was not well. Her husband was unduly quiet: she remembers, not because of the case, but because it was her birthday.

After the adjournment a police van took Watkins and the prison officers, who had been with him in the dock, back to the prison; there were no other occupants, except the driver. Watkins sat in the back between two of them and one cannot be certain but he thinks that between the silent sobs he caught the words "Our Father . . ."

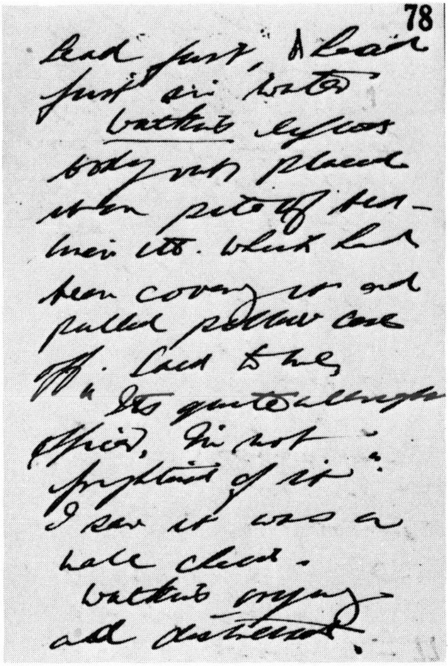

78

head first, & hair
just in water
Watkins lifted
body into place
when piece of lino-
leum etc. which had
been covering it and
pulled pillow case
off. Said to me,
"It's quite all right
officer, I'm not
frightened of it".
I saw it was a
half clock.
Watkins crying
and distressed.

—: *West Midlands Police*

PAGE 78 OF JOCK BLACK'S NOTEBOOK WHICH WAS PRESERVED

—: *Roy Brown: C. S. Bailey (Bromsgrove) Ltd.*

A PHOTOGRAPH OF CLIFTON ROAD TAKEN IN 1978 FROM THE VERY SPOT WHERE ONCE STOOD NUMBER 6/79

—: *Roy Brown: C. S. Bailey (Bromsgrove) Ltd.*

EDWARD ROAD POLICE STATION TO WHICH BILL WAS FIRST TAKEN

—: *Roy Brown: C. S. Bailey (Bromsgrove) Ltd.*

A SECTION OF THE CHILDREN'S COMMON GRAVE AT WITTON CEMETERY

MR. JUSTICE FINNEMORE
"WHEN HIS WARMTH LEFT HIM
HE COULD BECOME ICILY COLD"

W. A. FEARNLEY-WHITTINGSTALL K.C.
"ON HIS DAY HE WAS BRILLIANT"

—: Universal Pictorial Press

R. T. PAGET K.C., M.P.
(NOW LORD PAGET OF NORTHAMPTON)
"HE WAS BOTH ELOQUENT AND LEARNED"

THE TRIAL

COUNTY OF WARWICK – WINTER ASSIZES
BIRMINGHAM DIVISION

> *Victoria Courts, Birmingham.*
> *Thursday, 15th March, 1951.*
> *Friday, 16th March, 1951.*
> *Before: Mr. Justice Finnemore.*

R E X
v.
WILLIAM ARTHUR WATKINS

(Transcript of the Shorthand Notes of Marten, Meredith & Co., 11, New Court, Lincoln's Inn, London, W.C.2, and Walsh & Sons, 4, New Court, Lincoln's Inn, London, W.C.2, Official Shorthand Writers to the Birmingham Assizes.)

MR. R. T. PAGET, K.C. and MR. R. K. BROWN (instructed by the Director of Public Prosecutions) appeared for the Prosecution.

MR. W. A. FEARNLEY-WHITTINGSTALL, K.C. and MR. A. W. M. DAVIES (instructed by Messrs. Hatwell, Pritchett & Co. of Birmingham) appeared for the Defence.

Throughout this transcript the true names of the mother and her son have been transposed by the pseudonyms; Maisie ———— and Michael. The transcript in all other respects is the official record of the trial with the exception of words in italics which are the author's comments.

CLERK OF ASSIZE: William Arthur Watkins, is that your name?
THE PRISONER: Yes.

CLERK OF ASSIZE: You stand charged on this Indictment with the murder of the newly-born male child of Maisie ———— on the 21st January last. Are you guilty or not guilty?

[*The prisoner being very deaf, the charge was repeated to him by a Prison Officer.*]

[*On arrival in the dock, Watkins did not know what to do: he looked around, half smiling and cupped his right hand around his ear and strained forward attempting to hear what was being said.*]

THE PRISONER: Not guilty.

CLERK OF ASSIZE: Prisoner at the bar, the names I am about to call are the names of the Jurors who will try you; if you object to them or to any of them, the time to do so is as they raise the Book to be sworn, and before they are sworn, and your objection shall be heard.

[*The Jury were sworn*]

[*As they were sworn in, Watkins looked blankly at them; there were no challenges.*]

CLERK OF ASSIZE: Members of the Jury, the accused prisoner at the bar, William Arthur Watkins, stands charged upon this Indictment with the murder of the newly-born child of Maisie ———— on the 21st January last. To this Indictment he has pleaded not guilty and puts himself upon his country, which country you are; it is your duty to hearken to the evidence and to determine whether he be guilty or not guilty.

MR. PAGET: My Lord, my learned friend, Mr. Fearnley-Whittingstall, tells me that he has certain legal submissions to make with regard to Exhibit 10, and they are submissions of a nature which are usually made in the absence of the Jury.

MR. JUSTICE FINNEMORE: Is that correct, Mr. Fearnley-Whittingstall?

MR. FEARNLEY-WHITTINGSTALL: Yes, my Lord.

MR. JUSTICE FINNEMORE: Are you going to make it straightaway?

MR. FEARNLEY-WHITTINGSTALL: I do not think this is the time to make it.

MR. PAGET: I am sorry, my Lord, this is a misunderstanding, I am afraid.

MR. JUSTICE FINNEMORE: Very well, it is as well that I know.

MR. PAGET: May it please your Lordship, Members of the Jury, the accused man, William Arthur Watkins, is charged with the murder of the newly-born child whose mother was a Miss —— and whose father the accused Watkins himself was.

Watkins had been living with Miss —— for some five years, and during most of that time they had been living in a small terrace house in Clifton Road, Balsall Heath. They had one child who is three years old and they were regarded by their neighbours as a married couple, and they were living together as man and wife.

In July last Miss ——, who is known as Mrs. Watkins, became aware that she was pregnant. She made no preparations at all, nor did the accused, for the arrival of a baby. No baby's clothes were prepared, Miss —— did not attend or ask any advice at any pre-natal clinic, she did not communicate with her doctor, Dr. Salmon, nor did she make any arrangements with any midwife. Neighbours observed that she was pregnant and that her time was coming. They enquired whether arrangements had been made, and Miss —— in the presence of Mr. Watkins told them that she had booked Dr. Salmon and that a midwife was coming. That was quite untrue. Neither Dr. Salmon nor a midwife had ever been informed.

On the 20th January last Miss —— first felt labour pains commencing, and at 11 o'clock in the morning a neighbour, a Mrs. Revell, came into the house where Miss —— was on a sofa in pain. Mr. Watkins was also in the room, and Mrs. Revell again asked Miss —— whether she was sure that she had booked with a doctor. Miss —— said: "Yes, Dr. Salmon." Mrs. Revell said words to the effect that she did not think it would be long now.

Now, that was 11 o'clock in the morning. At 8 o'clock in the evening the pains had definitely set in. Again Mrs. Revell called round to see if there was anything she could do. Again Mr. Watkins was present, and he on this occasion, when Mrs. Revell mentioned the doctor, said: Yes, he would be going up and was going to fetch the doctor.

MR. FEARNLEY-WHITTINGSTALL: My Lord, this is new, I have had no notice of additional evidence.

MR. PAGET: I am unaware that I have opened anything that is not in the Depositions.

MR. FEARNLEY-WHITTINGSTALL: There is only one interview in the Depositions, and that is 11 o'clock on the 20th January.

MR. PAGET: I am extremely sorry, my Lord, that does appear to be so. There is a statement, of which I will have a copy served on my friend, from this witness. I am afraid I did not observe that this was not done.

MR. JUSTICE FINNEMORE: Had we better not keep to the one that is in the Depositions?

MR. PAGET: I am sorry, my Lord, the second interview was not mentioned before the Magistrates, so that will be dealt with later.

At 3.30 a.m. this baby was born, that is, on the 21st January, which was a Sunday. Now, Members of the Jury, there was nobody present at the birth of this infant save the mother and the accused, Watkins. No doctor or midwife had been sent for and Watkins himself delivered Miss ——— of this baby. He cut the umbilical cord with a pair of scissors, and the baby was then alive. Miss ——— heard it whimper.

The accused then picked up the baby and put it head downwards into a pillow case. In that state, head downwards in the pillow case, he put the baby into a galvanized tub of water, and there the baby drowned and died. Later he returned to Miss ———, removed the after-birth and buried that in the garden. The lid was then put on the tub. It was a galvanized tub with the baby still in that tub dead, and the water was still in the tub, and a pile of clothes was put on the tub, and the door of the room, in which this baby's body in the tub had been left, was wired up with copper wire.

[*Had the defence known of Watkins' phobia of seeing a dead child this would have been submitted as an explanation of his apparent callous behaviour.*]

The next morning between 11 and 12 Watkins saw Mrs. Revell, the neighbour about whom I have told you. He told Mrs. Revell that Miss ——— had had a miscarriage, and he had fetched a doctor and a midwife, but they had gone and that they would not be coming back. All of that was, of course, quite untrue.

Mrs. Revell saw Dr. Salmon and in consequence of what occurred the Police later arrived. When they arrived, which was about 3 o'clock on the 22nd, that is the Monday, they went upstairs; they were taken upstairs by Watkins. Various statements were made, which will be read to you in evidence. They went into that back room and there Watkins showed them the body of this dead baby.

That is the story which will be brought before you in the evidence which my learned friend and I will call, and our submissions upon that evidence are that this is a case of deliberate and premeditated murder, that it was never intended that this child should live, and that is why no arrangements were made for its birth, or for its life, and that arrangements were only pretended. We shall say that this child was deliberately killed and that there does not seem to be any great possibility of an accident when the child is put head first into a pillow case and in that state put into a tub of water.

In my submission it is difficult to imagine any conceivable reason connected with washing a new-born baby that would involve putting it head first into a pillow case. Finally, we shall say that this crime was concealed.

I will now ask my learned friend to call the evidence before you.

MR. BROWN: My Lord, I understand my learned friend who leads, subject to your Lordship's approval, agrees that it is not necessary to call the first two witnesses who speak as to photographs and plans, and that I should proceed straightaway with the third witness.

[*These were Police Sergeant Pountney the Photographer and Police Constable Stanley Miller who drew the plans.*]

MR. JUSTICE FINNEMORE: Mr. Fearnley-Whittingstall, do you want the first two witnesses?

MR. FEARNLEY-WHITTINGSTALL: No, my Lord.

MR. JUSTICE FINNEMORE: Does any difficulty arise about your client's defence, ought the evidence to be called?

MR. FEARNLEY-WHITTINGSTALL: No, my Lord, unless your Lordship thinks so. I am content.

MR. JUSTICE FINNEMORE: There is no provision that it shall be called and so long as he is properly represented it cannot do any harm.

MR. FEARNLEY-WHITTINGSTALL: I agree, my Lord.

MR. JUSTICE FINNEMORE: So long as you are satisfied, that is all right. If at any time you think there is the need to call it, let me know.

MISS MAISIE ———, *Sworn: Examined by Mr. Brown*

Q   Is your name Maisie ———?

A   Yes.

Q   Did you live at 6 back of 79, Clifton Road, Balsall Heath?

A   Yes.

Q   Have you been living there since the 26th January, 1946?

A   No. I have not been there, I have been there just over a year.

Q   You have been living at that address just over a year?

A   Yes.

Q   Have you been living with anybody at that address?

A   Yes, William Arthur Watkins.

Q   William Arthur Watkins, do you see him now?

A   Yes. He is in the dock.

MR. JUSTICE FINNEMORE: The man there, is it?

A   Yes.

[*He pointed his fingers towards Watkins.*]

MR. BROWN: Have you been living with him since January 1946?

A   Yes.

Q   I think you know that he was a married man?

A   Yes.

Q   How has he treated you, Miss ———?

A   Very well.

[*This is corroboration of his gentle way of life.*]

Q   Have the two of you a son, Michael?

A   Yes.

Q   Is that little boy three years old?

A   Three and a half he is.

Q   Is the prisoner Watkins the father?

A   Yes.

Q   Did something happen to you that you noticed in the summer of last year?

A   Yes.

Q   What did you notice about yourself?

A   I missed my periods at the end of July.

Q   Did you not want any more children?

A   Under the circumstances, no.

Q   When you noticed that you had missed your periods did you say anything to Watkins?

A   Yes.

Q   Did you speak about that matter and did he or did he not say anything to you about it?

A   Well, he was worried about it.

Q Did he not say anything about it, can you remember, Miss ——?

A Well, he did not say nothing much at the time.

MR. JUSTICE FINNEMORE: You have told the Jury you did not want any more children under the circumstances. Did he say anything about that, did you tell him that, or what did you tell him? Do you remember, did you tell him you did not want any more children?

A Well, the way things were we did not want any more.

[*The Judge had before him a copy of the depositions and knew what each witness had said in the Magistrates Court : which evidence was written down and signed by each witness.*]

Q How did you know he did not? I mean, did he say so, or did you talk it over together? Do you remember, did you tell him you did not want any more children? (*The witness did not answer*).

Q You know what I mean?

A With me not being married we did not feel as though we could afford to have children.

MR. BROWN: Miss ———, once you realized that you had missed your periods did you make any arrangements about it?

A No.

Q Did you not go to a doctor? You shook your head, does that mean no?

A Yes.

[*Maisie throughout her evidence was very timid and appeared to be awe-inspired by the whole proceedings.*]

Q Did you ever go to a clinic?

A No.

Q After a bit, Miss ———, was it obvious that you were going to have a baby?

A Yes.

Q Did you make any attempt to hide it from your neighbours? You shook your head again, that means no, does it not?

A Yes.

[*Nor did Watkins: as her time came nearer everyone around 6 back of 79 Clifton Road knew that Maisie ——— was pregnant.*]

Q When did you begin your labour pains?

A   On Saturday the 20th.

Q   Was that January of this year?

A   Yes, I think it was the 20th.

Q   About what time was the baby born?

A   Sunday morning about half-past three.

Q   When the baby was born was anybody with you?

A   William Watkins.

[*It seems strange that her answer was not "Bill".*]

Q   Did he help you with the delivery of the baby?

A   Yes.

Q   After the baby was born did you see it?

A   No.

Q   When the baby was born how were you feeling?

A   Very ill.

Q   At the time of this delivery, that is when the baby was born, did you not hear anything from the child?

A   I thought I heard a little cry; I am not sure.

Q   After the baby was born and you heard it cry did anyone else say anything about it?

A   What do you mean—anyone else?

[*The question had to be put in this way because of the rules of evidence.*]

Q   You told my Lord and the Jury that the baby was born about half-past three and you have told my Lord and the Jury that you did not see it again; after it had gone from you did someone say something to you? Do you know how the baby left you, how did it get from you?

A   Well, I suppose the ordinary way.

Q   That is when it came from you, but how did it get away from your bed?

A   Mr. Watkins was there.

[*Again no use of the name Bill.*]

MR. JUSTICE FINNEMORE: Did he take it? (*A pause.*) Mr. Watkins took it, is what she said in effect.

MR. BROWN: I only want to ask you one more question. After Mr. Watkins took it did anyone say anything to you?

MR. JUSTICE FINNEMORE: Did he tell you anything about it afterwards?

A   He just said he had dropped it in the bath.

CROSS-EXAMINED BY
MR. FEARNLEY-WHITTINGSTALL

Q   You told my Lord and the Jury you made no attempt to hide the baby; that is correct, is it not?

MR. JUSTICE FINNEMORE: Hide her pregnancy is what she said.

MR. FEARNLEY-WHITTINGSTALL: I meant that, my Lord. Did all the neighbours know that you were pregnant?

A   I expect so.

Q   You went about as usual. Did Watkins say to you fairly early on that you ought to go to the Welfare Clinic?

A   Yes, he told me to go.

Q   Did you say you would wait?

A   I said I would wait a while.

Q   Can you remember how soon after you told him of your pregnancy that he suggested you should go to the Welfare Clinic?

A   Pardon?

Q   Can you remember how soon after you told him you were pregnant that he said to you you had better go to the Welfare Clinic?

A   He told me to go when I could.

Q   Did you tell him in December that you thought it was dead because you felt no movement? (*No answer.*)

Q   You must give an answer to that.

A   Yes.

Q   Was it true?

A   I could not feel it, no.

Q   You could not feel it move at all. Did he say he had better get the doctor?

A   Yes.

Q   What did you say to that?

A   Well, I would not let him, because I was so bad. He was going to go early in the morning. I was so ill he was afraid to leave me.

MR. JUSTICE FINNEMORE: I think she is on another time now. I think she has come to the actual day.

MR. FEARNLEY-WHITTINGSTALL: Yes, my Lord. Do you mean that

happened on the Sunday, or do you mean that happened in December when you thought the baby was dead?

A   On the Sunday.

Q   I am not asking what happened on the Sunday yet, but what happened in December when you told him that you felt nothing, when you thought the baby was dead. Did he then say you had better go to a doctor?

A   I do not remember him saying that.

Q   Did he ask you before the baby was born once or twice to get the doctor, or to go to see a doctor?

A   Before it was born?

Q   Yes.

A   He wanted to go, and then he was afraid to leave me because I was so ill. He said he wanted to go.

MR. FEARNLEY-WHITTINGSTALL: My Lord, I think again she must be wrong about the day.

MR. JUSTICE FINNEMORE: She is, yes.

MR. FEARNLEY-WHITTINGSTALL: Miss ———, I mean some weeks before then. Did he talk about a doctor, or your going to see one?

A   Yes. Well, I did not expect it was so soon.

Q   That is so, because it was born on the 21st January?

A   Yes.

Q   You did not miss your periods until the end of July?

A   The end of July was the last time I saw them.

Q   You did not expect it, I imagine, for about another six weeks?

A   No.

Q   On the 13th January, that is the week before, did you feel some pains?

A   Well, I was not feeling too grand in myself.

Q   Did Watkins then say he had better get a doctor for you?

A   No. Well, I did not expect it. I thought it was just pains.

Q   Did you have pain about a week before?

A   Yes. I did not take a lot of notice of them.

Q   Did you tell Watkins you had had these pains?

A   Yes. I told him I was not too well, that is all.

Q   I want to find out whether you told him you had pains, not that you were not feeling at all well. You did have some pains, is that right?

A Yes.

Q But you did not think they were labour pains?

A No.

Q Did you still think your baby was not alive?

A Well, I could not feel anything.

Q Then on the 20th, as you have already told us, you felt some pains, did you not?

A On the 21st, I think.

Q You told us you felt some pains on the 20th?

A I think it was on the 21st, on the Saturday.

MR. JUSTICE FINNEMORE: Well, Saturday, anyhow?

A I am not sure, 20th or 21st.

Q It does not matter, it was a Saturday?

A Yes.

MR. FEARNLEY-WHITTINGSTALL: Tell me what happened between you and Watkins. When you felt the pains on the Saturday what did Watkins say?

A Well, he was worried about them, but I did not think it was— at first I did not think it was labour pains, because I thought it was too early.

Q Did Watkins say anything about it?

A Well, he was on nights and he was in bed and said: "If you feel any worse get me up."

[*Watkins was working nights as a labourer at the Hercules Cycle and Motor Co. Ltd.*]

Q You told us when I was asking you about a conversation earlier that a doctor was mentioned on the 20th, the Saturday or the Sunday, is that correct?

A Yes.

Q What was said by Watkins about that?

A He said: "If you feel any worse I will fetch the doctor in", but I would not let him.

Q Was this before the baby was born?

A Yes, because I did not think it was.

Q Did you both go to bed that night?

A Yes.

Q Was the baby born very quickly?

A   Yes, I should think in about half-an-hour.

Q   Did you wake him up and say: "It is here"?

A   I woke him up and said I felt bad.

Q   What did he do?

A   He got out of bed and went downstairs for a drink for me.

Q   Was the baby born then?

A   Then when he come up I was in labour.

Q   Did you suddenly say to him: "It is here"?

A   Yes.

Q   Were you lying in bed?

A   Yes.

Q   Were you in great pain?

A   Yes.

Q   Were you in great pain afterwards?

A   Yes.

Q   Did your pains last for a long time?

A   Yes.

Q   After the baby was born were you still in pain for a long time?

A   Yes.

Q   Was the boy, Michael, sleeping in the same room?

A   Yes.

Q   Was he awake?

A   No.

Q   Can you remember if he woke up and shouted?

A   No. I think he was very good. I do not remember.

Q   Were you crying out, Miss ———? Did you cry out?

A   Yes. I was in pain. I suppose I would.

Q   That is why you cried out, and cried out very bitterly, is that right?

A   Yes.

Q   Do you know what "vague" means?

A   Yes.

Q   Have you got a very vague memory of what happened that morning after the baby was born? (*No answer.*)

Q   Can you remember if you cried out, and Watkins came to you and then started attending to you and cleaning up the bed?

A   Yes.

Q   Where used you to keep dirty washing, in the back room?

A   Yes.

MR. FEARNLEY-WHITTINGSTALL: My Lord, can I have, somewhat prematurely, exhibit 5 shown to me, that is the pillow case?

(*Exhibit 5 was handed to the witness.*) (*To the witness*): That is the dirty pillow case, is that right?

A   Yes.

Q   Would that be kept in the back room until it was washed by you?

A   Yes.

(*The witness withdrew*)

MRS. LILIAN MAY REVELL, Sworn: Examined by Mr. Paget

Q   Is your name Lilian May Revell?

A   Yes.

Q   Do you live at 1 back of 79, Clifton Road?

A   Yes.

Q   And you are a married woman?

A   Yes.

Q   Have you known the prisoner and Miss ———— for some time?

A   Yes, approximately two years.

Q   Were they neighbours of yours?

A   Yes.

Q   Did you know that Miss ———— was going to have a baby?

A   Yes.

Q   About when was that?

A   I noticed when she started to show pregnancy.

Q   About when was that?

A   Roughly about six months.

Q   You knew her as Mrs. Watkins, did you not?

A   Yes.

Q   Do you remember Saturday, the 20th January?

A   Yes.

Q   Do you remember going to see Miss ———— that day?

A   Yes.

Q   About what time was that?

A   In the evening, about a quarter past eight in the evening.

Q   Did you go before the evening?

A No, I think it was the evening.

MR. JUSTICE FINNEMORE: On the Saturday?

A Yes, the Saturday.

MR. PAGET: Cast your mind back to the Saturday, do you remember what you did on the Saturday morning?

A I think my little boy was up there and I fetched him.

Q When you went to fetch your little boy did you see anybody?

A Only Mrs. Watkins and Mr. Watkins.

Q You saw Mrs. Watkins and Mr. Watkins?

A Yes.

Q Did you say anything to Mrs. Watkins, or Miss ———— shall we call her?

A Mrs. Watkins said she did not feel very well and she had got pains in the back.

Q Did you ask her anything?

A I asked her if she thought she was going to have the baby, if she was in labour.

Q Did she reply?

A She thought she had started.

Q This was in the morning?

A Yes.

Q Was anything said about a doctor?

A In the evening.

Q Do you remember anything in the morning?

A No. Not in the morning.

Q Did you then take your little boy and then go home?

A Yes.

Q Did you go and see Mrs. Watkins again in the evening?

A Yes.

Q What happened then?

A I think roughly it was around quarter past eight and she said she felt worse and the pains had gone from her back and gone on her stomach. I said: "In strong labour?", and she said she was going to send for the doctor.

MR. JUSTICE FINNEMORE: Did she mention the doctor's name, or not?

A Dr. Salmon.

MR. PAGET: Was Mr. Watkins present?

A Yes.

Q Did he say anything?

A Just said he would go.

Q Was that for a doctor?

A Yes.

Q Do you remember anything else happening that evening?

A No. I went home.

Q Did you see anybody the next morning, that is the Sunday morning?

A When I was standing on my step talking to my next door neighbour Mr. Watkins came outside.

MR. JUSTICE FINNEMORE: This is Sunday morning?

A Yes. He sent his little boy up, but I could not understand what his little boy was trying to say and I then went up by his door.

MR. PAGET: What happened then?

A He then told me that Mrs. Watkins had had a "miss".

Q Did he say anything else?

A Yes. They had had Dr. Salmon and a midwife.

Q Did he say anything about Mrs. Watkins or Miss ———?

A No. He just said she had had a "miss", that was all.

Q Did you enquire how she was, or anything of that sort?

A No.

Q Did you see Mr. Watkins again that day?

A Yes. I was cleaning my kitchen floor and he came to my door and asked me if I would pop up and see Mrs. Watkins. I said I would in a few minutes.

MR. JUSTICE FINNEMORE: About what time?

A Between 11 and 12 when Mr. Watkins came to my door.

Q This is the second time?

A Yes, that is the second time, between 11 and 12.

MR. PAGET: What did he say?

A Would I pop up and see Mrs. Watkins?

Q Did you go up and see Mrs. Watkins?

A Yes, about five minutes after.

Q Did Mr. Watkins come up with you?

A No. He stayed downstairs.

[*One wonders what Maisie told Mrs. Revell?*]

Q Did you see him again when you left the house?

A   Yes. He was in the kitchen when I left the house when I come out of the kitchen door.

[*One wonders why Watkins did not talk further to her.*]

Q   When you saw Mrs. Watkins did you see any sign of a baby?
A   No.
Q   I think later you saw Dr. Salmon?
A   Yes.

CROSS-EXAMINED BY
MR. FEARNLEY-WHITTINGSTALL

Q   You gave evidence in the Police Court?
A   Yes. A month today.
Q   A month ago?
A   Yes. That is right.
Q   Maybe a month ago your memory as to what was said was a little better than it is now; do you think that is possible?
A   Yes.
Q   Because at the Police Court you told the Magistrate a story a little different from what you have told us today. That is quite likely, that your memory is not quite so good? I want to remind you of what you said at the Police Court: "The next day between 11 and 12 noon"—this is the day before the baby was born—"the prisoner said she had had a 'miss',", is that correct?
A   Yes.

[*In 1951 a Magistrates' Court was frequently referred to as "a police court".*]

Q   That is what you told us today?
A   Yes.
Q   You did not say that the doctor and the midwife had been, but he said that he had sent for the doctor and the midwife. That is not quite the same as saying they had sent for them and they had been?
A   He said they had had the doctor and the midwife.
Q   Let us get this first of all: did you say that the prisoner said they had sent for the doctor and the midwife—did you say that?
A   Yes.
Q   Then you added this: "He said there was no need for the doctor

and the midwife, but that if they wanted them they would send for them".

A   They could get in touch with them, yes.

Q   This is what you said, Mrs. Revell, so far as I can tell from the Depositions, tell me if this is correct: "He said there was no need for the doctor and the midwife but that if they wanted them they would send for them"—is that right?

A   Yes.

MR. JUSTICE FINNEMORE: When was that?

A   On the Saturday morning.

Q   What was he referring to then?

A   Well, he just said if they needed them they would send for them again.

Q   Was that said after he said they had had them?

A   After he told me she had had a "miss".

Q   I want to get it quite clear. He told you she had had a "miss" and had had the doctor and the midwife?

A   That is right.

Q   What did he go on to say after that?

A   He said that she had had the "miss" and they had had the doctor and the midwife when I stepped in the door the first time. He said if they needed them they could get in touch with them.

Q   If they wanted them again?

A   Yes.

Q   He did not use the word "again", of course?

A   No.

MR. FEARNLEY-WHITTINGSTALL: You also said there was no need for the doctor and the midwife, is that correct?

A   I beg your pardon?

Q   You told the Magistrate that Watkins had told you there was no need for the doctor and the midwife?

A   He said they had had the doctor and the midwife.

Q   Just answer the question. Did you tell the Magistrate that Watkins said there was no need for the doctor and the midwife? It is written down as your evidence?

A   I know.

MR. JUSTICE FINNEMORE: Let her see it. Whether she can read this writing I do not know, Mr. Fearnley-Whittingstall, but let her see a

7

typewritten copy. I have put in two red marks, Mrs. Revell. Perhaps the simplest thing would be to read that aloud.

A   "The next day between 11 and 12 noon the prisoner said that she had had a 'miss' and that they had sent for the doctor and the midwife. He said she was not too bad. He said that there was no need for the doctor and the midwife but that if they wanted them they would send for them."

MR. FEARNLEY-WHITTINGSTALL: Stopping there, that is what you said at the Police Court?

A   Yes.

Q   And you signed that, did you not?

A   Yes.

Q   Was it true?

A   Yes.

Q   That is what the prisoner did say to you?

A   Yes.

Q   "There was no need for the doctor and the midwife but if they wanted them they would send for them"?

A   That is right.

Q   At that point you went off, did you not?

A   Yes.

Q   Watkins himself fetched you back to go and talk to his wife?

A   Yes.

Q   Did he stay there while you talked to her?

A   No.

Q   So he left you and his wife alone?

A   That is right.

RE-EXAMINED BY MR. PAGET

Q   Mrs. Revell, when you gave evidence before the Magistrate were you unwell?

A   I beg your pardon?

Q   In fact did you collapse and did you have to be taken from the witness-box?

A   No. I did not collapse, but I did not feel too well in myself.

[*There was a time when she withdrew from the witness-box to drink a glass of water: she did not collapse as such.*]

Q   Did you have to leave the witness-box during your evidence?
A   Yes.

MR. JUSTICE FINNEMORE: I am not sure that this statement is in the least ambiguous; it is for the Jury to decide. There is nothing incoherent about what she said.

MR. PAGET: My Lord, I respectfully agree with you.

(*The witness withdrew*)

DR. ALBERT SALMON, *Sworn: Examined by Mr. Brown*

Q   Is your name Albert Salmon?
A   Yes.
Q   Are you a registered medical practitioner?
A   Yes.
Q   Do you practise at 430, Moseley Road, Birmingham?
A   That is correct.
Q   Will Miss ———— come forward? (*Miss ———— stepped to the front of the Court.*) Do you recognize that lady there, Maisie ————?
A   Yes.
Q   I think she has been a patient of yours?
A   She has never consulted me professionally.
Q   Was she on your list of registered patients?
A   Yes.
Q   Did she ever consult you regarding her pregnancy?
A   Never.
Q   Do you see that man there, the prisoner? Has he ever consulted you?
A   He has never consulted me regarding the woman's pregnancy.

(*The witness withdrew*)

DR. IAN McCRAE SANDILANDS, *Sworn: Examined by Mr. Paget*

Q   Is your name Ian McCrae Sandilands?
A   Yes.
Q   Are you a registered medical practitioner?
A   Yes, I am.
Q   Do you live at 7, Wake Green Road, Moseley?
A   Yes.

Q   At 5.30 p.m. on the 22nd January, that would be a Monday, did you go to 6, Clifton Road?

A   6 back of 79, Clifton Road.

Q   Did you there see the body of a newly-born male child?

A   I did.

Q   Was the child dead?

A   The child was dead.

Q   Did you see Maisie ———?

A   Yes.

Q   Where was she?

A   She was in bed.

Q   Did you examine her?

A   I did.

Q   What did you find?

A   I found she was suffering from the effects of a recent birth, and I arranged for her admission to hospital.

Q   At 11 p.m. on that day did you do anything?

A   I attended a *post-mortem* on the dead child.

Q   Who with?

A   With Professor Webster.

Q   What did that *post-mortem* reveal?

A   It showed that the child had died from asphyxiation due to drowning.

Q   Could you see from that *post-mortem* whether the child had been alive in the sense that it had a separate existence from its mother?

A   It had had a separate existence.

(*The witness withdrew*)

JAMES MATHEWSON WEBSTER, Sworn: Examined by Mr. Brown

Q   Is your name James Mathewson Webster?

A   Yes.

Q   A registered medical practitioner and the Director of the West Midlands Forensic Science Laboratory of the Home Office at Newton Street, Birmingham?

A   Yes.

Q   On the 22nd January, 1951, at 11 p.m. at the public mortuary, did you carry out an autopsy on the body of a newly-born male child?

A   Yes.

Q   Was that child identified to you by Detective Sergeant Black?

A   Yes.

Q   Was the last witness, Dr. Sandilands, also present?

A   Yes.

Q   Did he also identify that child to you?

A   Yes.

Q   What did you find?

A   My Lord, this was a male child, it was obviously newly born. It was 6¾ lbs. in weight, 20½ inches in length, and the condition of the baby was such that it had been born, at least at the end, by a precipitated labour, that is to say, a quick labour at the end. The child had no marks of violence upon it, beyond a pressure mark on the point of the nose. I found that the child had been born alive, that it had had a separate existence, that it had died from asphyxia by drowning, and that the baby was premature.

Q   About how much premature?

A   I should think about the thirty-sixth week instead of the fortieth.

MR. JUSTICE FINNEMORE: Subject to that other things were normal?

A   Yes.

Q   Quite normal apart from that?

A   Yes, quite normal apart from that.

MR. PAGET: Could you also tell my Lord and the Jury how long the child had lived after birth?

A   That is purely speculative. This child had lived sufficiently long to completely fill its lungs. That is a gradual process, it cannot be done in one breath.

MR. JUSTICE FINNEMORE: Was the body perfectly healthy?

A   Perfectly healthy.

Q   Inside as well as out?

A   The child was perfectly capable of continuing to live. It had obviously not received any attention at birth, because the cord, although cut, had not been tied.

MR. PAGET: I think you were handed certain articles of clothing and other articles?

A   Yes.

Q I think in your opinion there is nothing indicative of the death on those exhibits?

A I could not see anything, my Lord, which would be likely to assist your Lordship on this matter.

Q The blood stains were such as you would normally expect in labour?

A Yes.

CROSS-EXAMINED BY
MR. FEARNLEY-WHITTINGSTALL

Q I suppose that the estimate of prematurity is but an estimate, it might be five weeks?

A I could not bind myself to seven days. I would not go as far as six weeks, but it might be five weeks.

Q Just help me on the inflation of the lungs; clearly that would be a gradual process, but about how long would it take?

A That depends upon whether the baby cries, or just breathes, or howls lustily. It may be a matter of 10 to 15 minutes.

Q Which means in the absence of lusty howling the baby would have been placed in a position after birth so that it could breathe easily?

A How do you say the baby had been placed?

Q I am assuming there had been no lusty howling in order to inflate its lungs completely?

A There was no obstruction.

Q So it could breathe easily?

A Yes.

Q It is the easiest thing in the world to take a newly-born baby and turn it over on its face, I should think?

A You are perfectly correct.

Q On examination you found that its lungs were inflated?

A I am quite sure there was no inflation at all.

(*This must be an error in the transcript, inflation of the lungs indicated life.*)

Q Death had clearly not taken place until it had come in contact with the water and that was clearly caused by drowning?

A Definitely.

(*The witness withdrew*)

DETECTIVE SERGEANT JAMES BLACK, *Sworn:*
Examined by Mr. Paget

Q   What is your full name?

A   James Black, Detective Sergeant in the Birmingham City Police.

Q   At about 3 p.m. on Monday, the 22nd January, did you go to the house of the accused?

A   I did.

Q   Were you accompanied by anybody?

A   Inspector Miss Beattie of the Women's Police and Police Woman Coutts.

Q   You and two women policemen?

A   Yes.

Q   Who did you see there?

A   The prisoner Watkins.

Q   What happened when you saw him?

A   I spoke to him. I said to him: "Who lives here?", and Watkins replied: "Me and the woman I live with and the boy."

Q   Did you ask anything?

A   I asked him how old was the boy and he said: "He's three." I said: "Is everything all right?" Watkins said: "No." I said: "What is the matter? Where's your wife?" He replied: "She's ill. She had a baby on Saturday night." I said to him: "What happened?", and he replied: "I was helping her. I got a bowl with water and was bathing the baby. It slipped and I let it fall in the water. The wife was screaming and shouting." I said to Watkins: "Is the baby dead?", and he replied: "Yes." I said: "Where is it now?" He said: "Upstairs. I put it in the back room." I then cautioned Watkins and he made a statement which I took down in writing. I read it over to him and he signed it in my presence.

Q   That is exhibit 9. Look at that statement. (*The statement was handed to the witness.*)

A   Yes, that is the statement.

Q   Will you follow me while I read it?

A   Yes.

Q   This is the statement: "I have been told by Sergeant Black that I am not obliged to say anything unless I wish to do so, also that what I do say will be written down and may be given in evidence. I understand what this means and I wish to make this statement." Did he then sign that caution?

A   Yes.

Q   Then did he proceed: ["I live with Maisie here, she had a baby on Saturday night (20/1/51) we hadn't made any arrangements like. She said she couldn't feel anything you know, and she thought she would be all right. Well I went to bathe it in a bowl of water, to get the blood off it, and it fell in the bowl. The wife was shouting and I didn't know what to do. I put it in the other room away from the baby so as the baby wouldn't see it. I cleaned all the mess and buried it in the garden last night. All the paper and stuff you know. She hasn't had a doctor yet. She said she was all right."] Did he sign that?

A   Yes.

Q   What happened then?

A   I went with Inspector Beattie and Miss Coutts and the prisoner upstairs into the front bedroom, where we saw Miss ———, who was in bed. A small boy, about 3 years of age, was beside her asleep. Watkins, the prisoner, said to Miss ———: "It's the police about the baby. Don't worry, I have told them everything about it." I then told Miss ——— who we were and I left the Women Police with her in the front bedroom.

Q   Then did you go to the back bedroom?

A   I did, yes.

MR. JUSTICE FINNEMORE: With the prisoner?

A   With the prisoner.

MR. PAGET: What was the state of the door?

A   The door was closed and the handle of the door was secured to the door jamb with a piece of copper wire and a piece of string wrapped round the door handle and wrapped around a cup hook on the door jamb.

Q   Did the prisoner do anything about that?

A   Yes. He undid the string and the copper wire.

Q   What happened then?

A   He said: "It's in there." We went into the back room and just behind the door on the right-hand side I saw a pile of clothing and bedding.

Q   Look at exhibit 7.

A   That is the pile of clothing and bedding.

Q   Were some of these articles stained with blood?

A   They were.

Q   What did the prisoner do with that pile of bedding?

A   He lifted it away and underneath I saw a small zinc tub.

Q   Look at exhibit 4, is that the zinc tub?

A   Yes, it is.

Q   That was under the bedding?

A   All this bedding was on top, the lid was in place with the bedding on top of it.

Q   What did he do then?

A   He lifted all the bedding from the top of the zinc tub and laid them over on the floor. He lifted the lid from the top of it, I could see the tub was about half full of water and inside the zinc tub there was the body of a male child, which was head first inside a pillow case, and head first in the water.

Q   What did Watkins then do?

A   He lifted the baby out of the water and laid it on to the pile of clothing on the floor and pulled the pillow case from it.

Q   Look at exhibit 5, is that the pillow case?

A   Yes.

Q   Will you just hold out the pillow case so that we can see its size? (*The witness held out the pillow case.*)

Q   Did he say anything as he pulled the pillow case from the child?

A   Yes. He said: "It's quite all right, Officer, I am not frightened of it." He was crying and he was very distressed.

Q   Did you ask him anything about the umbilical cord?

A   Yes. I asked him who cut the cord and he said: "I did with a pair of scissors."

Q   Did he add anything else?

A   He said: "We hadn't made any arrangements for it. I didn't know what to do. The wife was shouting out. I must have panicked."

Q   What happened then?

A   I then took him from this back bedroom down into the front downstairs room of the house and remained there with him.

Q   What did he say?

A   In this front room he said to me: "I've buried the afterbirth in the garden—up by the hutch. I did it after dark."

Q   Did Miss Beattie and Miss Coutts join you later?

A   They did, yes.

Q   About 5 p.m. did anything happen?

A   Yes, about 5 p.m. when Miss Beattie was present with me I cautioned the prisoner.

Q   What did you say to him?

A   I said to him: "You say you were bathing the baby and it slipped and fell into the water. Did you pick the baby out of the water at any time after it fell in?"

Q   What did he say?

A   He said: "I couldn't have done."

Q   Did you then ask him anything else?

A   Yes. I said to him: "How do you account for it being inside the pillow slip?"

Q   What did he say?

A   He did not reply for a moment, then he said to me: "I got the pillow slip and put the baby into it and then I was washing it over the top of the pillow slip—like." Then he cried and said no more.

Q   Did you ask him anything else?

A   Yes. I said to him: "You say you cut the cord with the scissors, can you find the scissors for me?" He made no reply but took me upstairs to the front bedroom where Miss ———— was in bed and from the adjoining bed he handed me the pair of scissors.

Q   Look at exhibit 8; are those the scissors?

A   Yes.

Q   Then what happened?

A   I then left the room in front of Watkins and went two or three steps down the stairs. Watkins turned back, he put his head round the corner of the door and looked in the direction of Miss ———— and he said to her: "What have you said?"

Q   Did Miss ———— reply?

A   Miss ———— replied: "It's all right. I have told them the same as you have."

[*This is an ambiguous remark. There can be no suggestion that Watkins and Maisie had put their heads together otherwise Maisie would have been charged.*]

Q   What happened then?

A   Watkins looked round and saw I had also stopped and was

listening and he then left the room and came downstairs with me.

Q Did Dr. Sandilands then arrive and examine the child?

A He did.

Q Did you later dig in the garden by the rabbit hutches?

A Yes.

Q Did you find the afterbirth?

A What appeared to be afterbirth was buried there, yes.

Q Did you take the body of the child and the various exhibits?

A Yes. I took them to the mortuary in Newton Street.

Q Who did you give them to?

A Professor Webster saw them there.

Q Were you present at the post-mortem examination?

A Yes, I was.

Q Were you also present at 11.55 p.m. that night when Inspector Quinton charged the prisoner with the murder of the child?

A Yes.

Q Was the prisoner then cautioned?

A Yes.

Q Did he make no reply?

A That is quite correct.

MR. JUSTICE FINNEMORE: The caution of course says he can reply or not as he likes?

A Yes.

CROSS-EXAMINED BY
MR. FEARNLEY-WHITTINGSTALL

Q Of course he had already made a statement to you?

A He made the statement that I have produced as an exhibit at the house.

Q There is no doubt, as you have told us very fairly, he was extremely distressed and distraught?

A He was.

Q When he made the statement to you was it in the room where his wife was, or in another room?

A No. It was in the front downstairs room.

Q I only want to get the order of things about this matter. Miss

——— said: "It's all right. I have told them the same as you", but the prisoner had said first of all to the wife: "It's the police about the baby. I have told them everything"?

A   Yes.

Q   He had in fact told you a great deal?

A   He had, yes.

Q   He then makes the statement, which does not vary, but amplifies what he had said?

A   He had already made the statement.

Q   So far as his wife was concerned all she would know was that everything had been told?

A   Yes.

Q   When she makes the statement to the prisoner: "I have told them the same as you have"—it may be argument, but perhaps you can help us—it may be she knew he had told everything; he had said so?

A   Yes, he had.

Q   You realize that before that the prisoner had told Mrs. Revell there had been a miscarriage?

A   I understand so.

Q   He was perfectly frank when the Police came and said it was the baby?

A   Yes.

Q   And he has told everything?

A   Yes.

(The witness withdrew)

MR. JUSTICE FINNEMORE: Members of the Jury, there is some point of law which has got to be argued and with which you will not be concerned at the moment. I think it might be a convenient time for you to be released now. There will be lunch provided for you on the premises, because, of course, you must be kept.

[*This was about 12.30 p.m.*]

(The Jury retired)

MR. FEARNLEY-WHITTINGSTALL: My Lord, in dealing with exhibit 10, that is the second statement, my instructions are that it was obtained in circumstances which, if they are correct, render the statement inadmissible, in my submission. It will be a matter of evidence and my friend and I were wondering whether your Lordship would prefer to have the Defendant to give evidence.

MR. JUSTICE FINNEMORE: As you like, Mr. Fearnley-Whittingstall.

MR. FEARNLEY-WHITTINGSTALL: I would like him to give his evidence first so that the story can come unaffected by a recent cross-examination.

[*This was the correct procedure.*]

WILLIAM ARTHUR WATKINS, *Sworn:*
Examined by Mr. Fearnley-Whittingstall

Q   What is your name?
A   William Arthur Watkins.
Q   When you went to the Police Station were you interviewed there by the Police?
A   Yes.
Q   How many statements did you sign at the Police Station?
A   One at home and two at the Station.

[*This is where the confusion began.*]

Q   Tell my Lord about the first statement that you signed at the Station?
A   They asked me to make a statement out, and I told them what had happened as far as I could remember as to where the baby was born, I signed that statement, then the Police made me a copy of it.
Q   Did you say whether you could remember any more after you signed that statement, or, just before you signed it, did you tell them whether you could remember any more?
A   I told them that was all I could remember.
Q   Then what happened?
A   Then they told me I had got to make another statement out.
Q   Do you know who it was?
A   The Police.
Q   Do you know which one?
A   The Inspector, I believe it was.

[*This would indicate Mitchell, but there is no evidence to show whether or not Watkins had any knowledge of Police Rank.*]

Q   What happened, what did he say?

A   I got up to the point where I finished off the first statement and the Detective slapped my face both sides and he said he was not going to stop there all night, but get on with it.

Q   How many times did he slap your face?

A   Once each side.

Q   Did he say anything else except that he was not going to stay up there all night?

A   No.

Q   Did he say anything about the girl?

A   The Inspector said that the girl had done it and I was trying to hide her.

Q   Can you remember the words he used?

A   "You know the girl has done it, she is trying to blame you for it."

[*I find it impossible to understand Watkins' answers.*]

Q   How were you trying to hide her? How did he say you were trying to hide it?

A   He said: "I know the girl has done it and she is trying to blame you for it."

Q   Anything else?

A   No.

MR. JUSTICE FINNEMORE: I think, Mr. Whittingstall, that the Officer who he suggests hit him ought to be here. I do not know whether he means the Officer or not.

[*Here the Judge omitted the Fearnley in F.-W.'s name, a happening which normally annoyed him but on this day he let it pass.*]

MR. FEARNLEY-WHITTINGSTALL: As your Lordship pleases. May Chief Inspector Quinton, Inspector Mitchell and Detective Sergeant Black be called into the Court?

(*The three Detective Officers came into Court.*)

Q   Which one of those was it?

A   That one in the middle—no, he is not there, the Detective, I cannot see him there.

MR. JUSTICE FINNEMORE: Is that Inspector Quinton?

A   Yes.

MR. FEARNLEY-WHITTINGSTALL: Is that the Inspector you mean?

A Yes, the one this side.

Q Do you mean he is the one that hit you?

A No.

[*Again Watkins is hopelessly confused.*]

Q Can the Inspector instruct Counsel for the Prosecution as to who else was at the Police Station?

(*Mr. Brown spoke to Chief Inspector Quinton.*)

MR. BROWN: Only these three Officers, Mr. Mitchell, Mr. Quinton and Sergeant Black.

MR. FEARNLEY-WHITTINGSTALL: Did you see those three Officers?

A Yes.

MR. JUSTICE FINNEMORE: Was it one of those who slapped your face?

A No.

MR. FEARNLEY-WHITTINGSTALL: Could you remember what happened after you had begun bathing the baby very clearly?

A At the time I could not, no.

Q When you made the second statement could you remember?

A No. They kept on to me about "What did you do, what did you do then?" I did not remember what I did do.

[*The "They" are completely unidentifiable as Watkins exonerated Quinton, Mitchell and Black.*]

CROSS-EXAMINED BY MR. PAGET

Q Mr. Watkins, you remember making this statement at the Police Station?

A I made two at the Police Station.

Q You made two at the Police Station; will you look at your statement, exhibit 10?

MR. JUSTICE FINNEMORE: The Police Officers should go out of the Court again.

(*The three Police Officers left the Court.*)

MR. PAGET: You are looking at exhibit 10, which is a statement you made: is there any statement which you made other than that?

A That is the third statement.

MR. JUSTICE FINNEMORE: Did he say he signed what is called the second statement?

MR. FEARNLEY-WHITTINGSTALL: Yes, my Lord.

MR. JUSTICE FINNEMORE: Has that been produced at all?

MR. FEARNLEY-WHITTINGSTALL: No, my Lord.

MR. PAGET: You say that at your house you signed one statement?

A   Yes.

Q   Then you say there was a second statement at the Police Station which has not been produced?

A   One at the house, two at the Police Station.

Q   That you say is the third statement?

A   Counting the one at home.

Q   That is the second statement you made at the Police Station?

A   Yes.

[*Again he is confused. His first answer to Mr. Paget after the police officers left the court above indicates this.*]

Q   I put to you that that is the only statement which you made at the Police Station?

A   No.

Q   You say that there is another one?

A   I made two at the Police Station and signed both of them.

Q   Will you look at the statement there, did you sign each page?

A   Yes.

Q   Is that what you mean by signing two statements?

A   No.

Q   You say that there is another statement which we have not seen?

A   Yes. Another one besides this.

Q   I put it to you that you made no such other statement?

A   I made two.

Q   Well, now, as to this statement which you have got in your hand, will you read the beginning—does it say: "I have been told by Chief Inspector Quinton that I am not obliged to say anything unless I wish to": do you see those words?

A   Yes.

Q   Are they true?

A   Yes.

Q   Those words having been said to you did you then proceed to make the statement that follows?

A   Yes.

Q   And Inspector Quinton wrote it down to your dictation?

A   Yes.

Q   Is the statement that you in fact there wrote down true?

A   Up to a point.

Q   Is that statement which Inspector Quinton wrote down to your dictation true?

A   Yes.

Q   Just before you said "up to a point", is it true or true up to a point?

A   The previous statement was up to a point in here.

Q   So that is the "two statements" you made at the Police Station?

A   No, because I said something there that I did not say in the other statement.

Q   I first want to get this clear; you made a statement at the Police Station?

A   Yes.

Q   That is what you refer to as the first statement at the Police Station?

A   *This* one, no.

MR. JUSTICE FINNEMORE: No. That is the second one.

[*Earlier Watkins had said it was the third.*]

MR. PAGET: Is not that what he meant by "up to a point"? Well, I can only put it to you, Mr. Watkins, that your statement that somebody struck you at the Police Station is quite untrue?

A   I made two statements at the Police Station.

[*This answer indicates that he did not hear the question.*]

MR. JUSTICE FINNEMORE: Put that to him again, he did not hear.

A   It is true.

MR. PAGET: How many people were present when you made that statement which is in your hand?

A   The Police Officer who struck me, and the Police Inspector Quinton.

Q   That is two were present?

A   Yes.

Q   And only two?

A   Yes.

8

Q   You saw the Police Officers who came in?

A   Yes.

Q   One was Inspector Quinton?

A   Yes.

Q   You agree that he was present, and Inspector Quinton wrote that statement?

A   Yes.

Q   The other man that was present, was he the other Police Officer you saw there?

A   No.

Q   That is what you say. I put it to you that the other man present was Inspector Mitchell, who was here?

A   No. Another one besides him.

Q   I also want to put one further point to you. When you made that statement which is in your hand Inspector Quinton read it over to you?

A   Yes.

Q   After he had read it over to you you said you wanted to add something else, did you not?

A   When he read it all through up to the finish?

Q   He read what you said and then you said you wanted to add something else?

A   No.

Q   Are you quite sure about that? You then continued your statement?

A   No.

RE-EXAMINED BY MR. FEARNLEY-WHITTINGSTALL

Q   At the Police Station were both the Officers in civilian clothes?

A   Yes.

Q   No one was in uniform?

A   No.

(*The witness withdrew*)
(*The Court adjourned for a short time.*)

DETECTIVE CHIEF INSPECTOR OLIVER QUINTON,

Sworn: Examined by Mr. Brown

The Jury were still out of Court.

Q   What is your full name?

A   Oliver Quinton, Detective Chief Inspector of the Birmingham City Police.

Q   About 6 p.m. on the 22nd January, 1951, did you first see the prisoner at the house and then take him to the Police Station?

A   I did.

Q   How many Officers were present at the Police Station when you saw this man?

A   At the Police Station there would be the Office Constable, there was myself, Inspector Mitchell and Sergeant Black.

[*No name was given to the Office Constable.*]

Q   Will you just look at exhibit 10. You see that exhibit, is that in your handwriting?

A   It is.

Q   Was that written down by you after caution had been administered to the accused?

A   It was.

Q   Was there any other statement given by this man and written by you apart from this one?

A   No.

Q   When that statement was taken down by you, or before it, was any threat or any violence used in your presence to the accused?

A   No.

Q   To any Officer?

A   No.

Q   Or by any Officer?

A   No.

MR. JUSTICE FINNEMORE: What room were you in when the statement was made?

A   In the Inspector's office.

Q   Is that the same room where the Police Officer on duty would be, or not?

A   No.

Q   Who was in the room at the time?

A   Inspector Mitchell, myself, and Sergeant Black, I think, came in twice.

Q   Was there any other Officer there at all at any time?

A   Only Superintendent Blackborow looked in at one stage.

[*George Blackborow would never use violence.*]

MR. BROWN: When the Chief Superintendent looked in did he use any violence to the accused?

A   He did not speak to the accused.

Q   Or use any violence?

A   No.

Q   How long did it take to take the statement?

A   The statement finished at 9.30 p.m. on Monday, the 22nd, and it started at about a quarter to nine.

Q   You have answered my Lord that at the time you and Inspector Mitchell were the two Officers present?

A   Yes.

Q   Other Officers may have looked in during the course of taking the statement?

A   Only Sergeant Black and the Superintendent.

Q   During the taking of the statement at any time was there any pause or interruption in the taking of the final form of the statement?

A   There were probably pauses.

Q   Hold the statement in your hand; you see that it continues to read on until it is finally signed by the prisoner Watkins?

A   Yes.

Q   Was it or was it not read over to him before he signed it?

A   It was.

Q   Before he finally signed was it read over to him?

A   Yes.

Q   How far had you got when it was read over to him?

A   It was when it was finished that it was read over entirely, but there were two occasions on which I thought he had finished and I read the statement over to him, and then he continued.

Q   Can you tell my Lord at what stage it was that you thought he had finished the first time, and also the second time?

A   I could not say that, not to be accurate.

Q   Was any inducement in any form held out to this man to make the statement?

A   None whatever.

Q   Was anything said about the woman, Maisie ———, in regard to her situation so far as any charge in her case was concerned?

A   That was never discussed in his presence at all.

CROSS-EXAMINED BY
MR. FEARNLEY-WHITTINGSTALL

Q   He must have been a very irritating man to take a statement from, with his deafness?

A   Not particularly so.

Q   Was he also distressed, crying at some portion of the time?

A   Not crying, he was distressed, but he looks that way naturally.

Q   We have had from Sergeant Black he was crying in front of him?

A   Not when I was present was he crying.

Q   Did he show any signs of hysteria?

A   No, not at all.

Q   It is a well-known way of treating a hysterical person to slap his face?

A   Yes. It would depend upon the type of person who treated him.

Q   It is a well-known way, I did not say the only way, to slap his face?

A   Yes.

Q   Are you quite sure his mood and behaviour did not tempt anybody to jerk him into coherence with a slap on the face?

A   No, not at all.

Q   I do not quite understand how this statement began in view of your evidence at the Police Court. You went to Clifton Road?

A   I did.

Q   At 6 o'clock?

A   Yes.

Q   You had a very short conversation with him there?

A   Yes, very brief.

Q   You merely told him who you were?

A   That is so.

Q   You told him of what you were going to do with him, take him to Edward Road Police Station?

A   Yes.

Q   What is the distance?

A   Quite short.

Q   Ten minutes?

A   No, more.

[*In a car the journey would take considerably less than 10 minutes.*]

Q   I assume that he was at the Police Station by about 20 past 6?

A   No, that is not so.

Q   Tell me when?

A   He would not get to the Station until probably half-past 7 or a quarter to 8: when I saw him at the house I did not leave straight-away, I had other things to do there.

Q   What happened to him?

A   He just sat there in the presence of someone else.

Q   This is what you said in the Police Court: "At 6 p.m. 22nd January, 1951, I saw the prisoner at 6 back of 79 Clifton Road. I said to him: 'I am a Detective Chief Inspector. I'm going to take you to Edward Road Police Station'." Did you get there at 6, or get there earlier and see him at 6?

A   I got there at 6.

Q   Have you got your notebook here?

A   Yes.

Q   Does it show what time you got there?

A   6 o'clock.

Q   Can I see it? (*The notebook was handed to Counsel.*) You have here: "2 shillings in cash"?

A   That is referring to another case; it is at the bottom of that page.

Q   "6 p.m. Monday I joined Inspector Mitchell at Clifton Road". What did Mitchell show you?

A   He showed me the body of the child.

Q   There was not much to have detained you there, the body of the child, the zinc tub, the clothes and the pillow case. Did you interview that woman there?

A   Yes.

Q   Did you take a statement from her?

A   I did not take the statement, Inspector Miss Beattie took the statement.

Q   In your presence?

A   I was present when the second statement was taken from her.

Q   Do you mean that was taken in between 6 and 9.30 p.m.?

A   In between 6 and 9.30, yes, it was. I came back from the Station to the house after we had taken the prisoner to the Station, it was after that.

Q   He was left at the Station?

A   He was there.

Q   So he was at the Station some time while you were in there?

A   That is so.

Q   That may account for it?

A   I took him to the Station and then I returned to the house.

Q   You did not get back until what time?

A   About half-past 8 or a quarter to 9.

Q   Then you took the statement to which he referred, the second statement at the Police Station?

A   That is so.

Q   What happened between 7 o'clock and a quarter to 9 you know nothing of?

A   No.

(The witness withdrew)

DETECTIVE INSPECTOR JAMES MITCHELL, *Sworn:*
Examined by Mr. Paget

Q   Is your name James Mitchell?

A   Yes.

Q   Are you a Detective Inspector in the Birmingham City Police?

A   Yes.

Q   I think that about 5.30 p.m. you assisted to dig in the garden for the afterbirth?

A   Yes.

Q   When did you come back to the Police Station?

A   Just after 6 o'clock.

Q   Do you remember what time the accused arrived at the Police Station?

A   At the same time, just after 6 o'clock.

Q   Did you remain at the Police Station from then till 9?

A   I did.

Q You were at the Police Station all that time?

A Yes.

Q Did the accused make any statement while he was at the Police Station?

A He made a statement which was taken down in writing by Chief Inspector Quinton.

Q Look at exhibit 10, is that it?

A Yes.

Q Did he make any statement other than that?

A No.

Q Did anybody at the Police Station offer him any violence?

A No.

Q Or any threats?

A No.

Q Was anything said to him about the position of Miss ————?

A No. I did not.

CROSS-EXAMINED BY
MR. FEARNLEY-WHITTINGSTALL

Q What time was that statement taken?

A Half-past 9.

Q That is when it was finished, what time was it begun?

A About quarter to 9.

Q What happened to him between 20 minutes past 6 and a quarter to 9?

A He sat in the office with me.

Q Why so long a wait?

A Well, there were enquiries to be made by Chief Inspector Quinton at the house.

Q Was he asked any question between half-past 6 and a quarter to 9?

A Not in connection with this.

Q Would 20 minutes past 6 be a fair estimate of the time he got to the Police Station?

A Yes.

Q I find some difficulty in reconciling your evidence with what Inspector Quinton has told us. I think he said 7 to half-past—he said he did not get into the Station until about half-past 7, you put it at an hour and 10 minutes earlier, do you?

A   It was after 6.

Q   We all understand that?

A   It was after 6, well, it may have been half-past 6.

Q   I know. That puts it an hour earlier than he said. He said half-past 7. Did Inspector Quinton leave when he had taken the prisoner to the Police Station?

A   He did.

Q   You remained there with him?

A   I did.

Q   Was he hysterical at all?

A   Well, he was upset.

Q   Was he crying?

A   He did cry.

Q   Did he cry during the statement?

A   No.

Q   Did he cry before the statement was taken, by which I mean immediately before?

A   Well, he sort of cried before the statement was taken. He was upset.

Q   Was Inspector Quinton there?

A   No.

Q   What do you mean "upset": how did he manifest it?

A   Well, he started sobbing.

Q   I said crying, I meant sobbing. Was he sobbing?

A   Yes.

Q   Sobbing while he was being taken through the statement?

A   No. Not during the statement. He was quite composed then.

Q   You know, of course, that it is one way to treat a person who is overcome with emotion to smack his face to pull him together, do you not?

A   I would not do it in the case of the prisoner.

Q   You know it is one way of treating a person who is hysterical.

A   Yes; if he is hysterical, yes.

Q   Did his deafness interfere with the taking of the statement?

A   Well, he hesitated during the time that Mr. Quinton was taking the statement down.

Q   This statement I am going to suggest to you (I am not complaining) was obviously question and answer?

A   No.

Q   Just look at it. Do you mean to say this man whom we have
seen in the witness-box begins in this way: "It is true I have lived
with Maisie ———— for five years as man and wife"?

A   That is what he said.

Q   Are you seriously saying he began the statement: "It is true I
have lived with Maisie ———— for five years as man and wife"?

A   That is what he said.

Q   Without any question?

A   Without any question.

Q   You see, without complaint, an Officer sometimes put it into
better language than an ill-educated prisoner uses?

A   Yes, that is so.

Q   Did he go on: "I met her when she came to lodge at my home
in Aston"?

A   He did say that.

Q   "I have a son by her, aged 3 years"?

A   Yes.

Q   You are serious, are you?

A   I am quite serious.

Q   Was there any other Officer there besides yourself at any time
along with this man?

A   No.

Q   Did you or anybody else leave in order to get some tea?

A   No.

Q   Did you have no tea?

A   I did, it was fetched.

Q   Did he have tea?

A   Yes, he had a cup of tea.

Q   So you had tea brought you?

A   Yes.

Q   He begins the final sentence of the statement in these words,
which bear, as far as I can see, no connection with the rest of the
narrative: "The house is a small terrace one and we have people at
either side. We have lived there two years"?

A   Yes.

Q This man really had the brains to start talking about the size of the house and the nature of its architecture?

A Well, he said it was a small house.

Q And the proximity of the neighbours?

A He said it was a small house with people on either side of him.

Q Look at the sentence before: "I never heard it cry out. The only person in the house besides the wife and I was my son aged 3 years"; it bears an inconceivable relation, does it not, the length of time they have been there, to the events of the 21st January?

A No, but that is what he said.

Q I am sure he said it, but was he not asked if it was a terrace house?

A No.

Q And how long he had been there?

A No.

Q I am not suggesting it was wrong to ask him questions?

A He was asked no questions.

Q Had you made up your mind to charge him?

A No.

Q Why had you not made up your mind?

A We had made up our minds to charge him, but what it was to be remained to be seen.

Q Why did you say you had not made up your minds to charge him?

A For one thing there had been no post-mortem made on the dead body of the child.

Q There had not been when he was charged?

A Yes, there had.

MR. JUSTICE FINNEMORE: Mr. Fearnley-Whittingstall, the post-mortem was at 11 o'clock that night. Had you not made up your minds to charge him at quarter to 9?

A We had a good idea he would be charged.

Q Had you made up your mind to charge?

A I must have done.

MR. FEARNLEY-WHITTINGSTALL: Why did you say "No" a little while ago?

A Well, it depended to some extent on the post-mortem of the child.

Q   Why did you say "No" a little while ago when I asked you?

A   We had not made up our minds on the specific charge.

Q   Not until I reminded you you were entitled to ask questions, you had not made up your minds. I am suggesting you went to the boundary line in asking him questions?

A   He was not asked questions.

Q   I am suggesting it is quite inconsistent with your duty not to ask him questions, if you had not made up your minds to charge him?

A   Well, it was fairly obvious to us he would probably be charged.

MR. JUSTICE FINNEMORE: Since you found out the child had been alive, I suppose?

A   Yes.

RE-EXAMINED BY MR. PAGET

Q   You agree that the "house is a small terrace one and we have people on either side", is of no consequence and has got nothing to do with the statement?

A   I agree.

Q   Can you suggest any reason at all why he should be asked a question which is quite inconsequent?

A   No. I do not see any reason why he should have been asked that.

Q   Just one thing, you saw Watkins in the witness-box this morning. He was asked to identify you?

A   Yes.

Q   It may be you observed he was having great difficulty in hearing what was said to him?

A   Yes.

Q   Was he as deaf as that in the Police Station?

A   He did not seem so to me.

(*The witness withdrew*)

MR. FEARNLEY-WHITTINGSTALL: This is a matter for your Lordship. Your Lordship has heard the evidence. It seems quite inconceivable that this man would have invented this story if it had not been true. I do submit also that nobody could have made this statement, even if it had been made by a man with higher intelligence than this man has, without being asked questions. That he should have started in this way, unless he was answering questions which were put by those persons who were interrogating him (I do not complain that they were interrogating) seems inconceivable. I do say nobody could say he was not being asked any question at all and then allege this is the result of a person's spontaneous attempt to tell a story. That is really something which cannot possibly be accepted.

[*Undoubtedly the answer given by Watkins could have given the impression that he was not telling the truth.*]

MR. JUSTICE FINNEMORE: It does not make it inadmissible.

MR. FEARNLEY-WHITTINGSTALL: No, my Lord, but it throws some doubt on the word of the Officer who was there with him between 20 minutes past 6 and a quarter to 9. It would certainly not make it inadmissible, but on the question of credibility. You have had the story of this man in the witness-box and it was told in a way, I submit, which carries conviction. In a charge of this nature it is for your Lordship to have some feeling that the story might be true. I submit it is quite dangerous to let in this document. It is in a sense a precedent which creates danger.

We have also got an objection of inconsistency, and it is a substantial one, as to the time this man went to the Police Station, namely, whether it was half-past 6 or half-past 7. These two Officers went together and there is some doubt about that part of their evidence, some doubt about evidence which says this is a spontaneous outburst by this man, and not the result of question and answer (again I say there is no complaint about that). Bearing in mind all the evidence and the nature of the matter it must stand in strong relief to that portion of the evidence and must give a little doubt when given on behalf of the Police, in denial of what he says.

MR. JUSTICE FINNEMORE: I do not think I can exclude it, Mr. Fearnley-Whittingstall.

[*As an onlooker sitting in Court, it was at this point that I felt the case was lost.*]

MR. FEARNLEY-WHITTINGSTALL: As your Lordship pleases.
(*The Jury returned into Court.*)

HELEN ANNE BEATTIE, Sworn: Examined by Mr. Brown

Q. What is your name?

A   Helen Anne Beattie Inspector of Birmingham City Police.

Q   On the 22nd January this year at about 3 o'clock did you go to 6 back of 79, Clifton Road, Birmingham?

A   Yes.

Q   Did you go with Detective Sergeant Black and Police Woman Coutts?

A   I did.

Q   When you got to that address did you see anyone?

A   I saw the prisoner.

Q   Did Detective Sergeant Black introduce you to him?

A   He did.

Q   Did you hear Sergeant Black say something to Watkins?

A   Yes.

Q   What did he say?

A   He said: "Who lives here?"

Q   What did the prisoner reply?

A   He said: "Me and the woman I live with and the boy."

Q   Did Sergeant Black say something else?

A   Yes, he said: "How old is he?"

Q   Did the prisoner reply to that?

A   Yes; he said: "Three".

Q   What did Sergeant Black say then?

A   "Is everything all right?"

Q   What was the prisoner's reply to that?

A   The prisoner said: "No".

Q   Did Sergeant Black say something else?

A   Yes, he said: "What's the matter?"

Q   Did the prisoner reply to that?

A   Yes, he said: "She had a baby on Saturday night."

Q   Then what did Sergeant Black say in answer to that?

A   "What happened?"

Q   What did the prisoner say?

A   "I was helping her, I got a bowl and some water and was bathing the baby and I let it drop into the water. The wife was screaming and shouting."

Q   Did Sergeant Black then say something?

A   He said: "Is the baby dead?"

Q   Did Watkins reply to that question?

A He replied: "Yes."

Q Did Sergeant Black then say something?

A He said: "Where is the baby now?"

Q What was the reply?

A "Upstairs."

Q Then was the prisoner cautioned by Sergeant Black?

A He was.

Q Did he then make a statement?

A He did.

Q Will you just look at exhibit 9? That statement has been read, Miss Beattie. It starts: "I live with Maisie here, she had a baby on Saturday", and it ends: "She has not had a doctor yet. She said she was all right." Is that the statement that was made by the prisoner and taken down by Sergeant Black?

A Yes.

Q Then together with Miss Coutts and Sergeant Black and the prisoner did you go to the front bedroom?

A Yes.

Q Was anybody there?

A Mrs. Watkins, Maisie ———, was in bed and a little boy was in bed with her.

Q Did you hear anything said?

A The prisoner said to ———: "It's all right—it's the police about the baby. Don't worry, I've told them all about it."

Q Did the prisoner Watkins and Sergeant Black then leave the room and did you and Miss Coutts remain with Miss ———?

A Yes.

Q Later on, did you join the prisoner and Sergeant Black in the front downstairs room?

A Yes.

Q Did you hear Sergeant Black caution him?

A I did.

Q After the caution did Sergeant Black ask a question?

A He did, he said: "Did you take the baby out of the water after it fell in?"

Q What did he reply?

A The reply was: "I couldn't have done."

Q Did Sergeant Black ask another question?

A Yes.

Q What was that?

A He said: "How do you account for it being in a pillow slip?"

Q What was the reply to that question?

A "I got the pillow slip and put the baby in it and then I was sort of washing it over."

Q When he was asked those questions and made those replies in what condition was he?

A He was very distressed and he was crying.

(*The witness withdrew*)

DETECTIVE CHIEF INSPECTOR OLIVER QUINTON,
Recalled: Examined by Mr. Paget

Q Your name is Oliver Quinton and you are Detective Chief Inspector in the Birmingham City Police Force?

A I am.

Q Did you go to the prisoner's house on the 22nd January?

A I did.

Q About what time did you get there?

A 6 p.m.

Q Who did you see when you got there?

A Inspector Mitchell and Sergeant Black, the prisoner and the woman Miss ———.

Q Did you say anything?

A To the prisoner?

Q Yes.

A I did. I said: "I am a Detective Chief Inspector. I am going to take you to Edward Road Police Station where you will be detained whilst further enquiries are made into the matter."

Q What happened then?

A Soon afterwards we took him to Edward Road Police Station where he was detained.

Q When you say "Soon afterwards", about how long afterwards?

A It would be, I should say, about 7 o'clock the time when we got to the Station.

Q Between 6 when you arrived and 7 o'clock, did you do anything else?

A   I was having a look round the house and saw the body of the child and saw the woman, Watkins, yes.

Q   While you were doing that where was the prisoner?

A   He was in charge of one of the other Officers, I believe Sergeant Black, or Inspector Mitchell.

Q   You took him back to the Police Station; what happened there when you got there?

A   At the Police Station I said to him: "I am not satisfied that the child's death was an accident—being found head first in a pillow case in the bath of water."

Q   What did he say?

A   He said: "I suppose I panicked and we didn't want the child."

Q   What happened then?

A   He went on to make a statement, which I took down in writing.

Q   What time was that?

A   That was as near as I can say a quarter to 9.

Q   Had you been at the Police Station from about 7, when you say you arrived, to quarter to 9?

A   No. I had been back to the house on other enquiries.

Q   So, was it when you got to the Police Station the second time that he said about having panicked and not wanting the child?

A   It was.

Q   It was the second time?

A   Yes.

Q   Can you describe how the statement came to be taken at a quarter to 9?

A   Well, he finished that remark that he did not want the child and then was saying: "I will tell you", and I cautioned him. Then I told him I should take it down in writing.

Q   What room at the Police Station was this in?

A   In the Inspector's office.

Q   Who was present?

A   Inspector Mitchell was present.

Q   Yourself and the accused?

A   Yes, that is so.

Q   Three of you. Did he then make the statement?

A   He did.

9

Q   Did you write that statement down to his dictation?

A   I did.

Q   Was it read over to him?

A   It was.

Q   Did he sign it?

A   He did.

Q   Was it read over to him once or more than once?

A   Actually, the first part of the statement would have been read on more than one occasion, because part way through the statement I thought he had finished and I then read the statement back to him, and he initialled certain alterations. Then he continued on with the statement, which I continued to write. That occurred on two occasions, but when he finally finished I read it all over to him. The alterations I had made were all initialled and he signed it.

[*This could well be why Watkins thought that there were three statements.*]

Q   Will you just follow the statement as I read it?

A   Yes.

MR. FEARNLEY-WHITTINGSTALL: May one have the alterations as they come?

MR. JUSTICE FINNEMORE: Yes.

MR. PAGET: If there are any alterations to which I do not refer please point them out. The statement begins: "I live at 6 back of 79 Clifton Road, Balsall Heath. I shall be 49 years old tomorrow."

A   There is an alteration there. I wrote "29" in the first instance and it was altered to "49" and he initialled the alteration.

Q   "I have been told by Chief Inspector Quinton that I am not obliged to say anything unless I wish to, but that whatever I do say will be taken down in writing and may be given in evidence. I understand that caution, I want to tell what happened." Did he sign that?

A   He did.

Q   Then he goes on: "It is true I have lived with Maisie ———— for 5 years as man and wife. I met her when she came to lodge at my home in Aston. I have a son by her aged 3 years. In August or September last year my wife told me she had 'missed'. When we knew she was pregnant I told her to go to the Welfare but she said she would wait a bit. My wife told me she did not want another baby. I did not mind if we had had another baby. Two or three times I asked her to go to the Doctor or the Welfare but she did not go. I made no arrangements myself for the baby, and we had nothing prepared. This Saturday, 20th January, 1951, Maisie was not well, she had pains in her back. I offered to fetch the doctor but she said 'No' "?

    A   There is an alteration there initialled.

    Q   What is the alteration?

    A   The next word "and".

    MR. JUSTICE FINNEMORE: That was deleted?

    A   No. I wrote "but" in the first instance.

    MR. PAGET: "but" should be "and"?

    MR. JUSTICE FINNEMORE: "but" altered to "and"?

    A   Yes. "and she did not ask me again."

    MR. PAGET: "she did not ask me again. During the night she was much worse. I got into bed with her. I went off to sleep. At about a quarter to four on Sunday morning (21st January, 1951) she woke me up and said, 'It's here.' I got up and could see the baby was born. I got my things on. I went downstairs and got a pair of scissors, came back and cut the cord. I did not try to get any help. I went downstairs again and brought up a bowl of water. It was a zinc bowl. I got the water out of the kettle, it was still warm and added some cold to it. I brought the water upstairs. I picked the baby, pulled a pillow case off one of the pillows on the bed. I wiped some blood off the baby with a shirt. I was holding the baby over the bowl of water, when my 'wife' shouted and I slipped the baby into the pillow case and dropped it into the bowl of water. I went to the wife and cleaned up the bed a bit. I took the bowl containing the baby into the other bedroom. I thought it was dead. I put the lid on the bowl and some dirty clothes on top of it. When I went back into the front bedroom I told my 'wife' the baby was dead. My wife asked me what I was going to do with it and I told her I didn't know. I have never looked at it until the Police came today"?

    A   There is an alteration there, the word "Police".

    Q   What should it be?

    A   I had written something else before it and over-written it with "Police".

    MR. FEARNLEY-WHITTINGSTALL: Something quite trivial?

    A   Yes.

MR. PAGET: "It was dead as far as I knew. I buried the afterbirth in the front garden. I never told anyone."?

A   Alteration in the word "never". I had got "I told".

MR. JUSTICE FINNEMORE: You put in the word "never"?

A   Yes.

MR. PAGET: "I buried it Sunday night at dark. Today I went with the Police to where the baby was still in the water. It was still head first in the pillow case, as I had put it. I cannot say whether the baby was alive or not. I did not bother to find out; once I had dropped it in the water I did not bother. I was afraid afterwards to have a look at it. It is true we didn't want this baby. I lost my head and did not know altogether what I was doing. I was afraid to get assistance after the baby was in the water. *My wife was very worried when she knew what I had done and I have had no sleep since.* (Author's emphasis.) My wife had nothing to do with this. She was in bed all the time and I had my back to her when the baby went into the water. She did not know the baby was dead until I told her. She said she was sorry it all happened. She did not know whether it was a boy or girl until I told her it was a boy. She never actually saw the baby, but must have seen its head because she said it had black hair. She never saw it in the water, because the lid was on the bowl when I carried it out."

A   There is an alteration to the word "when", I think apparently I had missed the "w" off in the first instance.

MR. JUSTICE FINNEMORE: A spelling correction?

A   Yes.

MR. PAGET: "The zinc bowl was used chiefly for dirty clothes. When I dropped the baby in the water, I dropped it about 2 feet from the bowl. I did not touch the baby otherwise. I never heard it cry out. The only person in the house besides the wife and I was my son aged 3 years. The house is a small terrace one and we have people at either side. We have lived there two years. If I drown the baby I did it in a panic." Did he sign that "W. A. Watkins"?

A   He did.

Q   Subsequently that night did you charge him with the murder of this child?

A   I did.

Q   When you did that had the post-mortem taken place?

A   Yes.

Q   Did you caution him on charging him?
A   Yes.
Q   Did he make any reply?
A   He did not reply.

CROSS-EXAMINED BY
MR. FEARNLEY-WHITTINGSTALL

Q   What is the lighting in the bedroom?
A   Quite good. There was an electric light.
Q   How many?
A   The one bulb.
Q   Where is it, in the centre of the room?
A   I am nearly sure it is on the wall. It is on the wall in the second bedroom, at any rate.
Q   I am not concerned with the second bedroom.
A   I am not sure. It had been put in I should think by an amateur, probably the prisoner.
Q   On the wall?
A   I am not sure about it.
Q   Was there a lamp shade?
A   I do not think so. I am not sure.
Q   You do not know either way?
A   No. I do not think there was. I am not sure.
Q   Do you know whether it was just a bracket sticking out from the wall—you would not know which wall either?
A   I think it was a holder screwed dead on to the wall. It was in the second bedroom; I am nearly sure it was in this room, too.
Q   It is a small room?
A   That is so.
Q   There are two beds in it?
A   Yes.
Q   One occupied by the baby, Michael?
A   Yes.
Q   The other a double bed?
A   That is so.
Q   This man has a perfectly good character?
A   Yes.

Q   He is separated from his wife?
A   Yes, that is so.
Q   He has been completely regular in his weekly payments to her?
A   That is correct, since she summoned him.

[*There had in fact been some arrears but whenever a summons was issued he always paid up in full.*]

Q   Well, yes. There has been an Order made and he has been completely regular in his payments?
A   Yes, that is so.

(*The witness withdrew*)

DETECTIVE INSPECTOR JAMES MITCHELL, *Recalled:*
Examined by Mr. Brown

Q   Is your name James Mitchell?
A   Yes.
Q   You are a Detective Inspector in the Birmingham City Police?
A   Yes.
Q   On the 22nd January, 1951, did you go with Detective Sergeant Black to the garden of 6 back of 79, Clifton Road?
A   I did.
Q   About what time would it be?
A   At half-past 5 in the evening.
Q   Did you help Sergeant Black to dig in the garden?
A   Yes.
Q   Is there a small rabbit hutch in the garden?
A   There is.
Q   Near that small rabbit hutch about 18 inches below the surface did you find something?
A   Yes.
Q   I think that was what appeared to be a small afterbirth? *(pause)* —Wrapped in paper, was it?
A   Yes.
Q   Did you some time later at Edward Road Police Station see the prisoner?
A   I did.

Q   About what time would it be that you got to Edward Road Police Station?

A   At half-past 6.

Q   Did you see the prisoner there at that time, or later?

A   At that time.

Q   Was any other Officer present when you were there?

A   Chief Inspector Quinton was there at the same time.

Q   Did he say anything to the prisoner?

A   Well, he left then, it was later on he spoke to the prisoner.

Q   About what time would it be that Mr. Quinton said something?

A   About a quarter past 9.

Q   What did Chief Inspector Quinton say to the prisoner then?

A   He said to the prisoner: "I am not satisfied that the child's death was an accident being found head first in the pillow case in the bath of water."

Q   Did the accused say anything in answer to that statement?

A   Yes. He said: "I suppose I panicked. We did not want the child."

Q   Then was he cautioned by Mr. Quinton?

A   Yes.

Q   That he need not make a statement unless he wished?

A   Yes.

Q   Did he make a statement?

A   Yes.

Q   Did Mr. Quinton take it down?

A   He did.

Q   Was that at the prisoner's dictation?

A   Yes.

Q   Look at exhibit 10. Is that the statement?

A   Yes.

Q   Does it begin, after setting out the caution: "It is true I have lived with Maisie ———— for five years as man and wife", and goes on and finally ends in the last paragraph: "The house is a small terrace one. We have lived there two years. If I drown the baby I did it in a panic."?

A   Yes.

Q   Is that the statement which Mr. Quinton wrote down from the dictation of the prisoner?

A   Yes.

Q   Were certain corrections made in that statement?

A   There were.

Q   At any time before the final reading over was it read, or was part of it read over?

A   Part of it was read over, I think on two occasions.

Q   Were the corrections initialled by the accused, as well as the signature at the beginning and at the end?

A   Yes.

CROSS-EXAMINED BY
MR. FEARNLEY-WHITTINGSTALL

Q   He is not a man of very high intellect?

A   I should say he was below average intelligence.

Q   Was he very distressed at the Police Station?

A   He was upset.

Q   And sobbing?

A   Yes.

Q   Did you see anybody smack his face?

A   No.

Q   Or hear anybody say "We don't want to be here all night"?

A   No.

Q   He had already made one statement?

A   He had made a statement previously, yes.

Q   At the Police Station he made another?

A   He made another at the Police Station.

Q   Were there any questions asked of him?

A   No.

Q   It seems a little odd it should begin in this way: "I live at 6 back of 79 Clifton Road, Balsall Heath. I shall be 49 years old tomorrow", if nobody asked him how old he was?

A   Well, he mentioned his age.

Q   I am sure he did when he was asked?

A   No. He was not asked.

Q   Then this admission from a man below average: "It is true I have lived with Maisie ———— for five years as man and wife". Are you really saying he starts off, when the object of his detention at the

Police Station is the death of a baby, by going back five years and saying: "It is true", unless someone had said: "Is it true?"?

A   It is true. When he made the statement he was composed.

Q   That is not the question. Are you telling my Lord and the Jury that this man starts off his statement: "It is true I have lived with Maisie ———— for five years as man and wife" without someone having said to him: "Is it true you have lived with this woman for five years as man and wife?"?

A   No, that is what he said.

Q   Did he say it in answer to a question?

A   No. He was not questioned.

Q   Does it not strike you now as a little odd?

MR. PAGET: With respect, my Lord, if this statement is being challenged, surely these questions should have been put to Inspector Quinton who is the man who took it?

[*At this point Fearnley-Whittingstall turned on Paget and said: "That was ridiculous nonsense. I suppose you were out hunting on Saturday and took a toss and landed on your head!"*]

MR. JUSTICE FINNEMORE: That is a matter of comment, of course.

[*I do not know whether or not the Judge heard Fearnley-Whittingstall's remarks, but if he did this observation was both twofold and an example of his brilliant wit.*]

MR. FEARNLEY-WHITTINGSTALL: This Officer was there. I am not putting these questions to someone who was not there at the time. (*To the witness*): No questions at all?

A   No questions at all.

Q   He then goes back to the time he met her: "I met her when she came to lodge at my home in Aston"?

A   Yes.

Q   Without any question being asked about that?

A   No. He was willing to tell us.

Q   I am sure he was willing. I am not complaining of question and answer. I am merely saying it is surprising that there was no question and answer, in accordance with your duty, and above all that this man of low intelligence should produce this statement straight off the reel without any question from you or anybody else?

A   He was not questioned.

Q   And then he goes back: "In August or September last my wife told me she had missed"?

A   Yes.

Q   Then at the conclusion again this man with his low intelligence says: "I never heard it cry out.", then suddenly says: "The only person in the house besides the wife and I was my son aged 3 years. The house is a small terrace one. We have people on either side. We have lived there two years."—says that again without any question?

A   Yes.

Q   Really. Another point: "At about a quarter to 4 on Sunday morning", in brackets "21st January, 1951". Are you seriously telling anybody that those were the original words that he used: "About quarter to 4 on Sunday morning", then "21st January, 1951"; that this man in the dock (there is no complaint) said that without being questioned?

A   He was not asked a question.

Q   That again you are swearing to the Jury this man says: "I went off to sleep"—full stop—"At about a quarter to 4 on Sunday morning (21st January, 1951) she woke me up and said 'It's here'," and nobody said: "I had better put the date in"?

A   The date is put in in brackets.

Q   By whom?

A   Mr. Quinton.

Q   I put it to you again, it was not his language but Quinton's?

A   It was his language, except the date. That was obviously the 21st January, 1951.

(The witness withdrew)

MR. JUSTICE FINNEMORE: If you want to ask Inspector Quinton anything you are entitled to, if you think it is worth while.

MR. PAGET: I would like to, my Lord.

DETECTIVE CHIEF INSPECTOR OLIVER QUINTON,

Recalled: Further Examined by Mr. Paget

Q   You have heard the question which was put to Inspector Mitchell?

A   I have.

Q   In the course of taking this statement, was that the statement as given by Watkins, or were questions put to him from time to time?

A   There were no questions put to him at all.

Q   With regard to the matter of the date, where you have got down: "At about a quarter to 4 on Sunday morning", and then in brackets: "21st January, 1951", what did Watkins say?

A   He did not give the date there. He just said "Sunday morning" and I put the date in in brackets.

MR. JUSTICE FINNEMORE: Do you want to ask him anything, Mr. Fearnley-Whittingstall?

FURTHER CROSS-EXAMINED BY
MR. FEARNLEY-WHITTINGSTALL

Q   I gather you said: "I am not satisfied the child's death was due to an accident"?

A   That is correct.

Q   "being found head first in the pillow case in the bath of water"?

A   That is correct.

Q   Then he answered: "I suppose I panicked. We did not want the child"?

A   That is so.

Q   So you cautioned him?

A   Yes.

Q   Asked him whether he would like to say anything?

A   I gave him the caution as written down.

Q   The ordinary caution then?

A   Yes.

Q   Then you tell us he immediately starts off with the words: "It is true I have lived with Maisie ——— for five years as man and wife"?

A   That is how he started.

Q   Without anybody saying: "Is it true?"?

A   Nothing was said to him at all. That is exactly how he started.

Q   I assume you had made enquiries as to how long they had been staying there?

A   At that stage, no, I had no idea.

Q   Had you asked Miss ———— how long she had been living with this man?

A   No. I had not.

Q   Had you been asking her questions?

A   Yes.

Q   And that was not one of them?

A   No. I had not.

Q   When did you learn they were not married?

A   When I spoke to the woman I knew they were not married.

Q   That is after he had been taken to the Police Station?

A   No. I was told by one of the Officers they were not married. Before that I got it off the woman.

Q   I thought you said after you had spoken to the woman?

A   Yes.

Q   You did not speak to the woman until he had been taken to the Police Station?

A   I spoke to the woman before we took him to the Police Station.

Q   And learnt then they were not married?

A   Yes.

Q   Did she tell you anything about not being married?

A   She told me they were not married.

Q   Did she tell you she had lived with him for five years?

A   No.

Q   Did you not ask?

A   Not at that stage.

Q   Were you not interested to know?

A   Oh, I should have got to know, and I did get to know later.

Q   You got to know by a piece of enormous fortune without ever asking that question, because this man blurts it out at the beginning of his statement?

A   That is what he told me.

Q   As far as you know it is true?

A   I believe it is true.

Q   Here is something you wanted to know and you never asked the woman, you never asked the man, but you get the information when you question this man on the occasion of the death of his baby?

A   That was not material.

Q   Is that the narrative, is that the fact?

A   That is what he said, but that was not important to my enquiry at the time.

Q   It conveys something; for instance, if he had been living with her for only three months and it was another man's baby?

A   To a certain extent, yes.

Q   So the incident of relationship would be of some interest, would it not?

A   Yes.

(The witness withdrew)

MR. PAGET: That is the case for the Prosecution. Before the Magistrates the accused said: "I plead not guilty and reserve my defence. I do not desire to call any witnesses here."

MR. FEARNLEY-WHITTINGSTALL: I call the accused. Your Lordship will appreciate that I am in some difficulty because he is very deaf.

WILLIAM ARTHUR WATKINS, Sworn:

Examined by Mr. Fearnley-Whittingstall

Q   Is your name William Arthur Watkins?

A   Yes.

Q   Are you aged 49?

A   Yes.

Q   And you live at 6 back of 79, Clifton Road?

A   Yes.

Q   Are you a labourer?

A   Yes.

Q   Your earnings are £9 a week?

A   Yes.

Q   Are you a married man?

A   Yes.

Q   Have you four grown-up children?

A   Yes.

[*This answer is nonsense.*]

Q   All grown up?

A   Yes.

[*This answer is also nonsense.*]

Q Have you been making your wife a regular allowance in accordance with the Order?

A Yes.

Q For the last five years have you been living with Maisie ———?

A Yes.

Q Is Michael, the 3-year-old boy, your son?

A Yes.

Q Have you lived at this address for two years?

A Yes.

Q At the beginning of August did Miss ——— tell you she had missed her July period?

A Yes.

Q What did you say?

A I asked her to go to the Welfare, or get a doctor.

Q What did she say?

A She said she would leave it a bit until later.

Q Did you carry on, both of you, quite normally after that?

A Yes.

Q In December did she say anything to you?

A She said that she could not feel anything moving inside.

Q Was anything else said after that?

A Well, she fell in the snow just before Christmas in the yard.

Q Did you say anything to her when she told you she could not feel anything?

A No.

Q What happened in January? Can you remember, before the baby was born?

A Yes. She said her back felt bad and she had to lay down for about half a day, and after she said she felt better.

Q When was that, do you know?

A The second week in January.

Q Do you remember the Saturday before the baby was born?

A Yes.

Q Did she have pains then?

A Yes.

Q Do you remember Mrs. Revell coming?

A Yes.

Q   Can you remember what was said, or what you heard being said in front of Mrs. Revell?

A   Maisie said she was going to get a doctor and I said "Yes". After Mrs. Revell went out she said she did not feel so bad, so she would leave it a bit longer.

Q   Why did you not get the doctor?

A   Well, she said she did not want one, she would leave it.

Q   Did you think the baby was going to be born then?

A   No.

Q   If the baby was still alive about when did you expect it to come?

A   We thought about March.

Q   About another five weeks?

A   Yes.

Q   What happened early Sunday morning?

A   On the Friday night I had worked all night, I am working nights, and I came home the Saturday morning. She said she did not feel very well. I lit the fire and helped with the housework and the shopping. We went to bed on the Saturday night and some time that night she woke me up and said the baby was born. I think it was about half-past 2. Well, I ran downstairs and put the kettle on the gas, got the scissors, went back upstairs, helped with the baby. Then I went down and fetched the bowl with water to wash the baby.

Q   How did you carry the water up?

A   With my two hands.

Q   Where was that zinc bowl?

A   It was downstairs.

Q   Was there a kitchen downstairs?

A   Yes. The back kitchen.

Q   You carried the water up in that?

A   Yes. I went to wash the baby. Michael woke up and he cried, and Maisie was crying about the mess on the bed, and I turned round sharp and dropped the baby in the bowl in the water.

Q   How loud was Maisie crying?

A   Well, loud enough for me to hear her.

Q   Where was the pillow slip then?

A   In the back bedroom.

Q   Was it dirty?

A   Yes. It had been put there for washing.

Q   Did you always put the dirty washing in the back bedroom?

A   The upstairs washing, yes.

Q   You dropped the baby in the water?

A   Yes.

Q   What light was on?

A   The electric light.

Q   Is that on the wall?

A   In the middle of the room.

Q   Does it hang down without a shade?

A   It hangs down over the bed.

Q   What did you do after you dropped the baby?

A   I took all the bedclothes and I put some clean clothes on the bed.

Q   Why did you not pick the baby out of the water?

A   No, I left him in there. Well, I was worrying about Michael being awake, and Maisie crying.

Q   That bowl was about half full of water?

A   Yes.

Q   Was the baby head first in, or sitting in?

A   Head first in when I got it out.

Q   Did you see it go in?

A   No. It slipped out of my hand as I turned round sharp.

Q   Slipped out of your hands?

A   Yes.

Q   Did you try to kill it?

A   No.

Q   How long were you tidying up?

A   I think about a quarter of an hour.

Q   What happened when you came back?

A   Well, I saw the baby's head in the water and I carried it in the back bedroom, and I went to get this pillow slip to put it in, and I could not and it dropped in the water, and I left it there.

Q   Why could you not?

A   Well, my nerves.

Q   Did you put it inside the pillow slip?

A   Yes. I went and put it inside.

Q   And put it back in the water?

A   Put it back in the water, yes.

Q Had you got anything that you wiped the baby with while you were bathing it?

A Yes, the towel.

Q Where had you got the towel from?

A From downstairs, and the flannel when I fetched the water up.

Q Was the flannel there in the zinc bowl, or where was the flannel?

A Downstairs.

Q Did you bring it up, or not?

A Yes.

Q When you carried the baby in, you put the lid on top and some clothes on top of that?

A Yes.

Q What did you do to the door?

A I fastened the door with some string to keep Michael from going in there, because all the dirty clothes were on the floor and everything.

Q What did you do when you got back to the bedroom?

A Went back to bed.

Q Did you sleep?

A No.

Q What happened to Maisie?

A She said she felt all right, and she dozed off to sleep.

Q The next day what happened, that is Sunday?

A Well, I just took Michael out for a walk and fetched the paper, came back and cooked the dinner.

Q Did you see Mrs. Revell?

A Yes.

Q Did you tell her you had sent for the midwife and the doctor?

A Yes.

Q It was not true, was it?

A No.

Q Why did you tell her that?

A Well, I do not know.

Q Can you think why you told her that?

A No.

Q Did you tell her that she had had a "miss", that is that Maisie had had a "miss"?

10

A Yes.

Q That was not true?

A No.

Q What were you going to do with the baby's body?

A I do not know.

Q Had you got any idea about it?

A None at all.

Q That night did you bury the afterbirth?

A Yes.

Q Next day the Police came?

A Yes.

Q Did you tell them perfectly truthfully that the wife had had a baby?

A Yes. The Police asked me where it was and I took them up in the bedroom and showed them.

Q Did you say to Maisie: "It's the Police about the baby. I have told them everything"?

A Yes.

Q Later on did you make a statement?

A Yes.

Q She said to you: "I have told them the same as you have"?

A Yes.

Q You had told them everything?

A Yes, everything.

Q That evening were you taken to the Police Station?

A Yes.

Q What happened there?

A We went about 7 o'clock. I took Michael with me, left him where the Police were. We went and wrote that statement out, I signed it and stayed there. They said: "Do you want a cup of tea?" I said: "Yes, please." They gave me a cup of tea and I started to drink it. The Detective stood by me and said: "Take it off him", and put it on a shelf and said: "Come on, we are not going to stop here all night. Make out another statement." I told him I could not remember what happened, and then they made this other statement out. You have got it here.

Q In that statement you say that you put the baby in the pillow slip before it was in the bath?

A Yes.

Q Is that right?

A When it was in the back room when it was dead.

Q Did you put the baby in the pillow slip when it was alive at all?

A No.

Q Why did you not get help after the baby was in the water?

A Well, I was that flustered I did not know what I was doing.

Q Can you read?

A Yes.

Q Just take that statement. Just find the place where it says: "I went downstairs and I got a pair of scissors": do you see that?

A Yes.

Q "came back and cut the cord." Did you know anybody who you could have got help from at that hour of the morning?

A No.

Q "brought up a bowl of water. It was a zinc bowl. I got the water out of the kettle, it was still warm and added some cold to it. I brought the water upstairs. I picked the baby, pulled a pillow case off one of the pillows on the bed". Was that true or not?

A No. The pillow was off the bed the previous week ready for washing. That was in the back bedroom.

Q How many pillows are there on the bed?

A Two on the bed.

Q "I wiped some blood off the baby with a shirt. I was holding the baby over the bowl of water, when my 'wife' shouted and I slipped the baby into the pillow case and dropped it into the bowl of water". Was that true?

A No.

Q "I went to the wife and cleaned up the bed a bit."

MR. JUSTICE FINNEMORE: You had better ask him if he did say it, or not.

MR. FEARNLEY-WHITTINGSTALL: Did you say these things to the Police?

A Yes. But I did not know what I was saying part of the time because they had me there so long making the statement out, and this one as well. I did not know what I was saying.

Q We have heard you were sobbing for some time; what sort of state were you in when you made the statement?

A   I could not remember what had happened; I told the Police I could not remember.

Q   Before you were arrested had you got any idea what you were going to do about the baby?

A   No.

Q   Or its body?

A   No.

Q   Is it true that you never looked at it until the Police came?

A   No, I had not touched it after.

Q   At the end of that statement you say: "If I drown the baby I did it in a panic": did you mean drown on purpose, or let it drown, or if the baby drowned through anything you did?

A   I could not say. I was in such a panic. It slipped out of my hands and I forgot all about it. That is what I meant to say.

Q   Can you remember if it was 2 feet from the bowl when you were beginning to wash it? How were you holding it?

A   My two hands like *that*. [*Watkins held his two hands out*] Reaching down for the flannel washing it.

Q   Can you remember what you did with the flannel?

A   Yes. I brought it for Maisie to have a wash with the same flannel. Afterwards I took it downstairs again in the kitchen.

Q   Is that where it was kept?

A   Yes.

CROSS-EXAMINED BY MR. PAGET

Q   Mr. Watkins, you say that your wife told you in December that she thought the baby was dead?

A   Yes.

Q   Was that a reason for going to the doctor or not going to the doctor?

A   No.

Q   In January did you still think the baby was dead?

A   Yes. As far as we knew.

Q   Was that not an urgent reason for going to the doctor?

A   Yes. I wanted to fetch the doctor and she said leave it a bit.

Q   If you thought your wife was carrying a dead child was it not urgent that she should go to the doctor?

A   Well, I suppose, yes.

Q   Why did you not?

A   Well, she kept saying she was all right, leave it.

Q   Did you tell your Counsel that you expected this baby to arrive in March?

A   In March, yes.

Q   The dead baby or the live baby?

A   I do not know.

Q   You knew perfectly well that the baby your wife was carrying was alive, did you not?

A   I did not know.

Q   Do you remember on the Saturday Mrs. Revell coming to see you?

A   Yes.

Q   Do you remember her coming about 11 o'clock in the morning?

A   Yes.

Q   Did she ask your wife how she was?

A   Yes.

Q   Did your wife say that she had got the pain in her back?

A   Yes.

Q   Did Mrs. Revell ask her: "Are you booked up for the doctor?"?

A   Yes.

Q   Did your wife reply: "Yes, Dr. Salmon"?

A   Yes.

Q   Did Mrs. Revell say: "You will not have long now as it looks as if your labour has started"?

A   I could not say about that. I did not hear her say that.

Q   Did Mrs. Revell say something about your wife's labour having started?

A   I do not know. I did not hear her say that.

Q   In fact your wife's labour had started in the morning? At any rate you knew she was in labour in the morning?

A   Well, she had been like that about a week before nearly all day.

Q   That went on all day. Did Mrs. Revell come and see you again in the evening?

A   I do not remember.

Q   I am putting it to you that Mrs. Revell came about 8 o'clock in the evening and your wife said the pains had moved round to the front; do you remember her saying that?

A   No.

Q   Do you remember Mrs. Revell saying anything to you about fetching the doctor?

A   On the morning and I said "Yes".

Q   What about in the evening?

A   She did not say anything about it in the evening.

Q   Did you tell her you would be fetching the doctor?

A   I told her on the morning I would fetch the doctor.

Q   Why did you not?

A   The wife said leave it, she did not feel so bad, wait a bit longer.

Q   Was your wife booked with Dr. Salmon?

A   Yes, her panel doctor.

Q   Had she consulted Dr. Salmon, or arranged for him to attend her confinement?

A   No.

Q   Why did she tell Mrs. Revell so?

A   The wife said she was going to send for the doctor, and I said: "Yes, we will."

Q   Had she prepared any clothes or not, or anything for this baby?

A   Not that I am aware of, no.

Q   Why not?

A   I do not know.

Q   It was not intended that this baby should live, was it? That is the reason, is it not?

A   What?

Q   The reason why no preparations were made was because it was not your intention that the baby should live?

A   No.

Q   What do you mean by that answer, that it was not your intention that the baby should live?

MR. JUSTICE FINNEMORE: (*To the Prison Officer who was standing beside the prisoner in the witness-box*): Ask him this, Officer: whether they wanted another baby or not.

THE PRISON OFFICER (*to the witness*): Did you want another baby, or not?

A   Yes. I was not particular about it.

MR. JUSTICE FINNEMORE: Tell him that his wife has said that she did not want another child. Ask him if that is right.

THE PRISON OFFICER: That is what your wife said, that she did not want another child, is that right?

A   Yes. We said the same about the first one.

MR. PAGET: Did you want another child?

A   I did not mind.

Q   Do you remember saying anything to the Inspector, did you say anything about not wanting the child to Inspector Quinton?

A   No.

Q   Did you say to the Inspector: "I suppose I panicked. We did not want the child"? Do you remember saying that to Inspector Quinton?

A   No.

Q   When you went to the Police Station before you made the statement do you remember the Inspector saying to you: "I am not satisfied that the child's death was an accident being found head first in a pillow case in the bath of water"; do you remember Inspector Quinton saying that to you?

A   Yes.

Q   What did you answer?

A   I do not remember.

Q   Inspector Quinton says that you answered: "I suppose I panicked. We did not want the child."?

A   I did not say about not wanting the child.

MR. JUSTICE FINNEMORE (*To the Prison Officer*): Ask him what he did say.

THE PRISON OFFICER: Do you remember what you did say?

A   I said: "I suppose I have dropped it in the water in a panic." I did not say about not wanting the child.

MR. PAGET: Will you look at the statement which you made and signed on the first page of exhibit 10? Did you say there: "I did not mind if we had had another baby"?

A   Yes.

Q   Is that true?

A Yes.

Q That is what you are saying today, is it not, that you did not mind if you did have another child?

A Yes.

Q On the bottom line of page 2 and the top line of page 3, you went on to say: "It is true we did not want this baby." Do you see that passage: "I cannot say whether the baby was alive or not. I did not bother to find out; once I had dropped it in the water I did not bother. I was afraid afterwards to have a look at it. It is true we didn't want this baby." It is true you did not want this baby?

A No. What made me say that, I was so long in the Police Station and made the other statement out. I did not know what I was saying.

Q I know, we have heard you say that, but it is true you did not want this baby?

A It is not, no.

Q Very well. I will not take that any further. Now we come to the night when this baby was born. Do you agree that if somebody put a live baby head first into a pillow case and then put that pillow case and the baby into a bath of water head first, they could do it with no intention save to kill it?

[*Fearnley-Whittingstall was on his feet before Paget had completed the question.*]

MR. FEARNLEY-WHITTINGSTALL: That is hardly a question this witness can answer. I should have thought it was an astonishing question. It is hardly a question which a deaf labourer below average intelligence can answer. I am merely doing what I am allowed to do, which is object.

MR. JUSTICE FINNEMORE: It is obvious, is it not? If anybody puts a child like that into a bath of water you would think it was not for any other purpose but to destroy its life. But it is for the Jury to say, of course.

MR. PAGET: You now say that you did not put that child into the pillow case while it was alive?

A That is right, I did not.

Q Until this afternoon have you said to anybody that you put it in the pillow case if it was dead?

A Yes. I told the doctor at the prison.

Q Do you remember when Sergeant Black came to see you on the Monday at your house?

A Yes.

Q Do you remember you there took him up to see this child?

A Yes.

Q And the child was then in the tub, was it not?

A Yes.

Q And the lid was on the tub?

A Yes, on the tub.

Q And the tub was concealed under a pile of old clothes?

A The washing was on top of it, yes.

Q You took the child out of the tub, did you not?

A Yes.

Q And the child was then head first in the pillow case?

A Yes.

Q You took the child's body out of the pillow case?

A Yes.

Q Did you say to Sergeant Black: "It's all right, Officer, I am not frightened of it"?

A Yes.

Q Did Sergeant Black ask you who cut the cord?

A Yes.

Q You said that you did?

A Yes.

Q You produced the pair of scissors?

A Yes.

Q Then you said to him you had not made any arrangements for the baby's arrival?

A Yes.

Q But you did not know what to do?

A Yes.

Q And that your wife was shouting out and that you must have panicked?

A Yes.

Q All that is true, is it not?

A Yes.

Q Then he took you downstairs into the front room?

A Yes.

Q   Then you told him that you had buried the afterbirth in the garden?

A   Yes.

Q   That was true?

A   Yes.

Q   Then he cautioned you; do you remember his giving you a caution?

A   Yes.

Q   Then Sergeant Black said to you: "You say you were bathing the baby and it slipped and fell into the water": did you pick the baby out of the water again at any time after it fell in?

A   Yes.

Q   You replied: "I couldn't have done"?

A   Yes.

Q   Then did he ask you: "How do you account for it being inside the pillow slip"?

A   Yes.

Q   Was that not the time to tell Sergeant Black that it was inside the pillow slip because you put it there after it was dead?

A   Yes.

Q   Is that what you said to Sergeant Black?

A   No.

Q   What you said to Sergeant Black was: "I got the pillow slip and put the baby into it and then I was washing it over the top of the pillow slip like": is that what you said to Sergeant Black?

A   Yes.

Q   You said that to Sergeant Black?

A   Yes.

Q   Was it true?

A   I told him at the Police Station.

Q   We are dealing with what you told him at your house?

A   I did not say that in the house.

Q   Did you not?

A   No.

Q   Do you remember that the lady Inspector Beattie was present in your house?

A   Yes.

Q   She was not at the Police Station, was she?

Q   All that is a correct account, according to you, of what happened?

A   Yes.

Q   Did you understand what you were saying when you said all that?

A   No, because I had already made one statement out before this.

Q   Well, so far is this all correct?

A   More or less, yes.

Q   Did you understand what you were saying when you said all this was correct? (*No answer.*)

Q   Then you go on to say: "I picked the baby": do you mean by that you picked up the baby?

A   Yes.

Q   "pulled a pillow case off one of the pillows on the bed": is that correct?

A   Yes.

Q   That is correct?

A   That is what is down *here*, yes (*pointing to the statement*).

Q   Yes. Is that what happened?

A   No.

Q   Why did you say so?

A   I do not remember saying so.

Q   You signed each page of this statement, did you not?

A   Yes.

Q   It was read over to you?

A   Yes.

Q   If it is not correct that you pulled the pillow case off one of the beds, why did you say so?

A   I was that upset I was not taking no notice what he did read back to me.

Q   How do you think he got it that you pulled this pillow slip off one of the pillows on the bed?

A   I do not know.

Q   Then you go on: "I wiped some blood off the baby with a shirt": is that right?

A   I told him I wiped some blood off the baby with something, and he said: "Was it a shirt?" I did not know what it was.

Q   At any rate, you wiped some blood off the baby with something and it may have been a shirt?

A   Yes.

Q   "I was holding the baby over the bowl of water, when my 'wife' shouted": is that right?

A   I said she cried out.

Q   Whether she shouted or cried out you were holding the baby over the bowl of water?

A   Yes.

Q   That is quite right, is it not?

A   Yes.

Q   Then you go on: "and I slipped the baby into the pillow case and dropped it into the bowl of water": is that not what happened?

A   That is what I did after, when it was in the back room.

Q   It is not what you said here, is it?

A   I said it there, but that was after it was in the other room.

Q   "I went to the wife and cleaned up the bed a bit": that is correct, is it not?

A   Yes.

Q   "I took the bowl containing the baby into the other room."?

A   Yes.

Q   That is right, is it not? "I thought it was dead"?

A   Yes.

Q   "I put the lid on the bowl and some dirty clothes on top of it."?

A   Yes.

Q   Why did you not mention that that was when you put the baby into the pillow case?

A   I was that mixed I did not know what I was saying.

Q   At any rate, your nerves were sufficient to enable you to carry that into the back bedroom with the dead baby in it, to put the lid on, and to put the clothes over it. You did that, did you not?

A   I did it, yes.

Q   Then you wired up the door of that room?

A   Yes.

Q   You then in the night buried the afterbirth?

A   That was on the Sunday night.

Q   And the next day you told Mrs. Revell that your wife had had a miscarriage?

A   Yes.

Q   It was not true?

A   No.

Q   That you had sent for the doctor and the midwife?

A   Yes.

Q   That was not true, either?

A   No.

Q   What was the point of that, save that you had killed this baby?

MR. JUSTICE FINNEMORE: Why did you tell Mrs. Revell that, unless it was that you had killed the baby?

A   I do not know.

RE-EXAMINED BY MR. FEARNLEY-WHITTINGSTALL

Q   In your first statement did you say this: "Well, I went to bathe it in a bowl of water, to get the blood off it, and it fell in the bowl. The wife was shouting, and I did not know what to do"?

A   Yes.

Q   Was that true?

A   Yes.

Q   At any time did you intend to murder this baby?

A   No.

(The witness withdrew)

(The Court adjourned for a short time.)

MR. FEARNLEY-WHITTINGSTALL: That is my case, my Lord.

MR. PAGET: May it please your Lordship, Members of the Jury, I now have to address you on behalf of the Prosecution and to deal with the defence that Mr. Watkins has put up. Now this case falls into three parts: what happened before this fatal night; what happened during the night; what happened afterwards.

As to what happened before, the total failure to make any preparations for this birth, or that this child should live, the failure to prepare any cot or any clothing, the failure to attend at any clinic or welfare centre, the failure to notify any doctor or midwife, in the submission of the Prosecution took place because there never was any intention that this baby should live, because this man had decided that the baby should die.

Now, what is the alternative suggestion put forward. Firstly, it is said that in December Miss ——— thought that the baby within her was dead. If that was so, was it not an additional and greater reason for going to the doctor immediately? If she thought it was still dead in January was not that a greater reason? If that were so, why was it that they were expecting it to be born in March which is wholly inconsistent with the first story?

The second thing which is said is: Oh, but this baby was premature. It was not to be expected that it would be born for a month or perhaps five weeks. That is true enough. But the preparations for a baby that is expected and intended to live are not left to the last four or five weeks. And here look at the last day. She had begun labour at 11 o'clock, when Mrs. Revell was around her. She said then that she had booked a doctor, and that that doctor would be fetched. He was not.

At that late stage the preparations, or the lack of preparations are, in my submission, consistent with only one interpretation. It was not intended that this child should live.

Now, let us just consider what happened on this night. That really has come down to a very small issue indeed. Nobody now suggests that if this child was first put into a pillow slip, and then, in a pillow slip in which he was head first, put into that tub of water, that that could have been done with any intention other than the intention of killing or murdering that baby. Nobody now suggests otherwise.

The question is: was he put into that pillow slip whilst he was still alive? He was certainly in it. He was certainly in it head first. He was certainly head first in the water, because that is how the body of this baby was found. Well, this prisoner was asked, when this was fresh in his mind and new in his mind, to account for how the baby got into the pillow slip. As to what he said you have two versions. You have what Sergeant Black said was the answer he gave on being asked to account for the baby being in the pillow slip. What he said to Sergeant Black was: "I got the pillow slip and put the baby into it, and then I was washing it over the top of the pillow slip like".

Miss Beattie, the lady Police Inspector, has a slightly different

MR. JUSTICE KILNER BROWN
PHOTOGRAPHED WHEN HE BECAME A Q.C.
"AS A JUNIOR COUNSEL HE WOULD GIVE AS MUCH ATTENTION TO THE
CASE AS WOULD THE SILK HIMSELF"

—: Universal Pictorial Press

MR. JUSTICE MICHAEL DAVIES
"IN 1951 AN UP AND COMING YOUNG MAN FOR WHOM MANY COULD
FORESEE A GREAT LEGAL CAREER"

A NUMBER 5 TRAM DEPICTED IN VICTORIA ROAD IN 1951 FROM A
PAINTING BY R. K. CALVERT; NOW IN THE COLLECTION OF BRIAN JARVIS
"IT WAS TO W. M. TAYLOR'S THAT BILL
RUSHED TO BUY THE 'FOUR AWAY CHAIRS'"

—: *Roy Brown: C. S. Bailey (Bromsgrove) Ltd.*
NUMBER 136 VICTORIA ROAD ASTON AS IT STOOD IN 1978

In replying to this letter, please write on the envelope:—

Number 7122 ... Name WATKINS W.A.

BIRMINGHAM Prison 31/3

Dear Doss,

I am writing this letter to you as perhaps it may be the last but please God I am hoping for something to turn up at the last minute I am still keeping my chin up I went to Church this morning (Sunday) and I prayed hard I know you are all doing your best for me. I have arranged visit on Monday. Well Doss it is a funny life please try and don't worry too much, we have both made mistakes but we had a long time together so try and think of the past when we were happy together. I was very pleased you came up to see me remember me to all my friends in Victoria Rd.

Well in case Doss good bye and God Bless you all I am sorry things have turned out like this for the childrens sake one thing as they say I was always a good father XX to them XX Good Bye Doss X

Don't worry too much

No. 243 (21442—3-11-42)

—: Roy Brown: C. S. Bailey (Bromsgrove) Ltd.

THE LAST LETTER FROM BILL TO DOSS

ALBERT PIERREPOINT

"SUDDENLY I FELT SORRY SEEING A MAN LOOKING SO SAD AND JUST
WAITING TO DIE"

THE SCENE OUTSIDE WINSON GREEN PRISON IMMEDIATELY AFTER THE
NOTICE OF EXECUTION HAD BEEN DISPLAYED

recollection of his reply, and I would submit to you that that is significant, because sometimes it is said that Police Officers always seem to remember the same thing. This is what Miss Beattie said he said: "I got the pillow slip to put the baby in, and then I was sort of washing it over". When he is asked, when it is fresh in his mind, how the child got into the pillow slip, he does not suggest for one moment that the child was put in later and after it was dead.

Then we come to the detailed statement which he made at the Police Station. Now it says he was upset at the Police Station; doubtless he was. But none the less that statement tells a coherent story. As to all the facts in it, save as to this pillow slip, he says it is correct. In that statement he says he took the pillow slip off a pillow on the bed. How on earth did that statement get into the document which he signed, unless he said it? Who would invent that, and why, unless it was true?

Of course, it does not fit the present story, that the child was only put into that pillow slip after it was dead and in the bath. He makes it perfectly plain in that statement, as he had previously made it plain to the Police Sergeant and to the lady Police Inspector, Miss Beattie, that he put the baby into the pillow slip before it was dead. The story that it was put in downwards is, in my submission to you, Members of the Jury, an afterthought, which we hear of today.

Really, what is the alternative story? He says that this baby slipped into the water while he was washing it, and his wife was crying out because there was some mess in the bed. When it slipped into the water he did not look to see whether it was head first, or otherwise, and he did not think of picking it out. Members of the Jury, is that even a remotely credible story? It is said that he had panicked and lost his nerve. But had he? He had got nerve enough to put that bath into the back room and to cover it up with clothes, to wire up the door, to take the afterbirth and to bury it, and to go and see Mrs. Revell and to tell her his wife had had a miscarriage, and, also untruthfully, that the doctor and the midwife had been there. Does this sound so very panicky?

Members of the Jury, I must put this to you as a case of a planned murder; a murder which was intended in advance, that it was never intended that this child should live, that the murder was carried out, that the body was concealed, and an untrue story told to account for

11

what had happened that night, that when the Police came there was a different story to that which had been told to Mrs. Revell. Now, when the difficulties involved by the pillow case are recognized, there is yet a different story for you.

In my submission, Members of the Jury, if you have any doubt, then the accused is entitled to the benefit of that doubt, but it should be a reasonable and substantial doubt. If you have no real doubt then, however unpleasant that duty may be, it is your duty to find this man guilty.

MR. FEARNLEY-WHITTINGSTALL: May it please your Lordship, Members of the Jury, it is now for me, in accordance with the rules of procedure, to address you finally on behalf of this man, and may I remind you of something that I am sure you have got in the forefront of your minds, that in dealing with this man and a woman like that you are dealing with two people living in fairly low circumstances of civilization. You are dealing with two people—there is only evidence about the man, but you saw the woman—who undoubtedly both of them have comparatively low mental abilities.

When one hears Prosecuting Counsel talking about the absence of preparations for the coming child, and cross-examining the man, and addressing the Jury about preparations for the birth and the reception of the baby being left to the last five weeks, one wonders whether it is appreciated on all sides that you are dealing with persons who are not of the type who necessarily obtain a cot and layette and buy pretty things for the coming child, even within two or three days of its birth.

But there is no doubt, is there, as to one thing, and that is that this child was not conceived until the end of July, and by the ordinary process of nature its birth would be expected somewhere in the region of the first week in March, maybe the last week in February. A great deal has been made of the frank admission that this baby was not particularly welcome in advance—in their words: "We did not want another baby".

I do not suppose it is the first woman, or the first man, who having had one child, then finding another one conceived, has said: "Well, we don't want it". But it is a very different thing, of course, from not wanting a baby, to conceive a wicked scheme to do away with that child's life when it is born. Mr. Paget said on behalf of the Prosecution, and I suppose, therefore, it is part of their case, upon which they rely in order to extract from you a verdict of guilty, that this was a planned murder.

Let me say that whether it be planned murder or not, nothing looks like being less planned. At what stage is this planning for murder supposed to have begun? Let me deal with the first part of this case, which is the evidence of the Prosecution, and the evidence of the woman, who so far as I know has not seen this man, and she certainly has not seen him so that she could conceive with him a plan for the defence. What was this evidence? That when she commenced her pregnancy he at any rate said to her, whether he wanted the baby or not: "You had better go to the clinic".

She is the one who, more than he, did not want the child. That would be natural, because she would have the household task of looking after it. She had already got the little boy, Michael, I suppose something of a handful, and it was not a particularly rich place, and the burden of looking after the baby was something which at her age, (and one assumes she was slightly stupid), she did not want. Maybe she deferred going to the clinic, as she has told you she did,—and this is evidence called on behalf of the Prosecution,—and said: "Oh, no, I will wait a bit". Maybe she thought it was a false alarm, or maybe she thought she would have an early miscarriage and there would be no need for her to go into the clinic to take medical advice.

There is no doubt that this is evidence brought by the Prosecution, and that he did not suggest any operative procedure to her. His first reaction was: "Well, you had better go to the clinic". If she had taken his advice then there is no doubt that officially the pregnancy of this woman would have been known.

A planned murder, Members of the Jury? This woman going round amongst her neighbours with her growing pregnancy so that the neighbours would know. I said that he was not in a particularly intelligent class of Society, and not particularly intelligent. But does one really imagine he would be so stupid, if from the first or from any stage up to the last month or so, it was planned and determined that this child when born should be destroyed, because there would be all the gossip of the neighbours then asking, "Where is the baby. She obviously has had it, what has happened to it?" All that would in the end be bound to have aroused enquiries from official sources.

She has an accident, falling in the snow. You heard this man give his evidence about that. Was that a brilliant lie? She confirms it, that she felt no move in December, and told him she thought the baby was dead. Mr. Paget said that of course that was a leading reason for going to the doctor; carrying a dead baby about would be dangerous. Well, you and I and he know that is correct. But people in this walk of life many a time must have heard of a still born child. Unless they had some medical knowledge, unless they had some culture and imagination, particularly imagination, would they think that the mother of a still born child had gone through some considerable danger in carrying a dead child? It was simply the way she said it, she could feel no movement, and thought the baby was dead.

Again, the evidence of the Prosecution is that on the 13th January, or that weekend, a week before the real events occurred, she had been in some pain. She had lain down, and she recovered. That plays some small but important part in the understanding of this sort of thing, because, when a week later she also had some pain, it might well be in the back of both their minds that this was but a repetition of what had happened some seven or eight days before, and did not necessarily mean that these pains were labour pains, indicating with certainty the birth of this child.

And the evidence is there that he wanted her to go to the doctor, or wanted to fetch his doctor to her. She said: "No, it will be all right". That is the evidence in this case. Did planning for this murder begin after she said: "No, it will be all right"? The planning for this murder, —the idea cannot have been in the man's mind if his 'wife' is telling the truth. And he has said the truth is that when her pains began on the Saturday he said something about fetching the doctor, but she said: "No, it is not necessary, it will be all right". Did it mean that she thought it was a repetition of what had happened some seven or eight days before? It was the kind of statement by which she might reassure herself in the hopes that it would be all right, and certainly might reassure him that it was going to be all right.

Do you think that the man went to bed, having planned a murder, expecting the birth? Do you think he would have gone to bed that night with that on his mind? That is the evidence. Has that been invented? Do you think in the imagination of this man that that was part of the story he has told you, and told to the Police from the very first. Members of the Jury, a planned murder, and the man going to bed, when the case for the Prosecution is that they expected the birth of the baby, but when it was born it was going to be destroyed. Would he not stay up and wait for the birth, and destroy it when it was born, in case its cries roused the neighbours next door? But it had occurred before he could awake in time and carry out what he intended to do.

Take the conversation with Mrs. Revell, and take it as she disclosed it in the Police Court. It was then she said she had booked Dr. Salmon, or she was going to Dr. Salmon, one or the other. The uncertainty in Mrs. Revell's mind is as to exactly what was said. There may have been discussions then about labour beginning. This baby was not really expected by this ignorant couple for some four or five weeks. Again, this might have looked like a false alarm.

What was the motive in doing away with this child? This is a man of good character, and this is a woman who is, after all, the mother of the child, living with him as his mistress for five years. There is no evidence to show that the other child, Michael, has not been affectionately looked after. Does the evidence indicate that this man is that kind of a murderer,—it is not too high to put it to say,—that kind of a monster?

This child is born—is not this a matter for your imagination, trying to picture this almost Hogarthian scene—in a little room, 12 ft. × 11 ft. At some time, at 2 o'clock in the morning (this is confirmed by Professor Webster) there was this precipitated birth. This child was born quickly and she tells him: "It's here".

Had the planning of the murder really begun before then? Do you think he would not have carried it out with some elementary skill? What would have been easier when the baby was born than to turn it for a few seconds upside down on the bed, or on a pillow? There would be no sign of injury. Life would hardly have entered into that child just separated from its mother.

Instead of that, this murderer planning his scheme, acting with elementary skill, goes down, puts on the kettle, warms water, adds cold water to it, half fills that bath, and the evidence is that it was half filled when it was found by the Police. He goes back upstairs, carrying that zinc bath, in order to tidy up and to wash that baby. Are you surprised that he was a bit unnerved. It is a fairly unnerving

thing, one would imagine, for anybody who has no medical knowledge, no nursing experience, to see a woman in the process of childbirth or to see a woman immediately after the birth of a child. And
next door, sleeping, Michael, three years old; and this murderer
midwife.

Could they really have called the neighbours at 2.30 in the morning?
I suppose they could. Rousing a neighbour would mean leaving his
wife, the wife who was crying, groaning, or making some other noise,
crying that she was going through terrific, intense pain.

In circumstances like that (I use the expression 'wife' because it has
been used today) I say his whole instinct would be to stay by her for
as long as possible, if he could, maybe going to bring up the water,
the washing of the baby, but he would have coped with those
circumstances, and stayed by her side.

Members of the Jury, is this charge murder? Surely the fact that at
2.0 or 3.0 in the morning he roused no neighbours cannot possibly
be a point which tells in your minds, or in your judgment. Let us just
picture that night. I will take the alternative stories. He was washing
the baby with a flannel in warm water. Michael woke up and shouted.
His wife uttered a cry, and he dropped the child. He says, you know,
in one of his statements, the last statement, the Police took at the
Police Station: "I was holding it about 2 feet above the bath, or
something like that", and he went through a gesture in the witness-
box. That is not the position a man who intends to drown the child
would hold the child if this was a planned murder.

Do you not think that the moment he had got the bath he would
have put it then and there straight into the water, giving it no chance
to utter a cry, or a whimper? Do you not perhaps think that if he
intended to drown this child he would not have done it in the presence
of the child's mother, and not in the presence of his own son? Do you
bring the water to the child you are going to drown? The man,
whatever the state of his mentality, would surely in those circumstances
have taken this child to the water downstairs and drowned it there, if
this were a planned murder?

But whatever you think of a man's mind, and you have seen this
man (and you are the people who are going to judge him to the best
of your ability) through the fairly short time that you were watching
him in the witness-box, do you really think he could, and would,

have committed that murder in the presence of the woman in a small room, and in the presence of his own son?

Is not this much more consistent: The fact that whatever happened happened in that room; and the situation is that of a man whose mind is quite unhinged by the suddenness of events which are thrust upon him, the sudden and unexpected birth of that child; there was the woman with whom he is living in miserable circumstances; all at a time when few people are at their best, namely, half past two or three o'clock in the morning.

When you come to judge this case, picture will you please, in the light of those circumstances, and wonder for yourselves whether this man really knew what he was doing; whether he was acting at all with any kind of deliberation, or with the vague idea: "I must wash the baby, I must tidy up the mess, and I must do this, that, or the other". In my submission to you, the way he acted is entirely consistent with a vague sort of unformed intention, with no sense of order, but in the sense of how to set about the matter, what A, B, C, D, E or F might do I must do that way. Simply, the first thing to do is to warm water.

When you have pictured that scene will you give it what weight you think is right? In my submission, it is fantastic to submit this is a planned murder when he brings the water to the child, and does not take the child to the water.

Members of the Jury, subject to the directions which you will receive from my Lord, I consider, and I may be entirely wrong, that there are three verdicts you can obtain in this case. One, a verdict of guilty. You can find him guilty of murder if you come to the conclusion that he deliberately intended to destroy the life of this child. You can find him guilty of manslaughter if you think that he acted with such gross negligence as amounts in law to manslaughter when he was dealing with the child. You may find him not guilty of both these charges if you think that this was an accident.

Consider the story which he told to the Police at first; that part of the story has never varied. You may think that there is a very sound reason why this part of the story has never varied in any way. While he is necessarily in circumstances of mental uncertainty and distress—he is taken by surprise as to what really happened, and it has unhinged his mind—the memory of this rather stupid man may very well have become at first blank, so infirm that when he tried to adjust events in his own recollection, when he is trying to say: "What did I do next, what really happened after that?", when he really does not know, he sometimes gets the order wrong.

One might say: No, that kind of thing will come after the baby had fallen into the water, or at any rate come after the crying from his wife. Is it unlikely, is it impossible, that he was bathing this child when the wife suddenly let out a cry and he was startled, and he attended her first? If that tub was part full of water that baby could have been left but a few seconds; maybe it fell when his wife cried out in this miserable room, maybe he was startled by the cry, and his son cried out, and perhaps he then and there dropped the baby by sheer accident, and this sheer accident could have killed the child.

Then he went away, but deferred coming back because he did not want to see the baby dead in the bath. It is possible, it is human, is it not? It could happen, could it not? Thereafter, being something of a moral coward, he put the lid on the tub and took it and the baby into the next room.

Members of the Jury, one of the most significant matters, you may think, in the whole of this case, is a statement made in answer to a question when he was being interviewed by Sergeant Black. This is what Sergeant Black said: "Did you take the baby out after it had fallen in the bath?" What is the answer? It is: "I could not have done." I submit to you that that is an answer of the utmost significance in trying to discover the truth in this case. A liar, a planned murderer, would have said: "Yes, I did. Immediately I let it fall I picked it up again." He would not know whether scientific evidence would be called to say how long that baby had been in the water, and indeed there has been no such evidence in this case.

If he had murdered that baby and he was asked: "Did you pick it out when it had fallen?", surely he would have said: "Yes, I did. I found it was dead. I was horrified, and then I put it back." But his answer is: "I could not have done."

Certainly not: "I did not"; certainly not: "I did." The answer of the prisoner was: "I could not have done"; not: "I do not think I could have done, because I should have remembered if I had, or some other sequence would have followed if I had done."

It was a perfectly ordinary answer, and unprepared, in reply to the question: "Did you take the baby out after you had let it fall?". "I could not have done", is in my submission to you, the answer of an innocent person. It cannot be the answer of a person who has conceived a scheme, who has carried out that scheme, and who is preparing a lie to hide the execution of that scheme. It cannot be; it just will not work that way.

Look at the other answers he made. Are they not a vague answering, the answers of a man completely and absolutely haunted by the misery and the dreadful things that have happened, and the futility of that night? I will deal with them later on, but you shall have the worst views and you shall have the best, and you shall make up your minds as to whether they are not the answers of a person who just does not know exactly what happened; who after all is being asked a lot of questions, certainly at the house, by police officers.

We know, Members of the Jury, that that evening, the Sunday evening, he buried the afterbirth, and all the time in that room, inside that tub, covered with a lid, and over-covered with clothes was the body of that baby, and the door is tied. Is that the action of a person who has planned a murder, and who has carried it out? What was he going to do with the corpse? He had buried the afterbirth, why not bury the corpse, if this is a murder which has been planned?

We know he told Mrs. Revell that she had had a miscarriage. So far as Mrs. Revell was concerned, the baby was not really expected for some four or five weeks, and a miscarriage could have taken place. We know also it was a lie. But, you know, someone who has had this kind of experience, someone who has gone through this dreadful scene, acted with clumsiness if you like, certainly in the circumstances of the horror in which this man dealt with this sudden and unexpected birth in this dreadful room, is not likely to tell the neighbours the baby was born and: "I dropped it in the bath." Is that likely, unless of course it was murder? Then he would say: "The baby was born, I was bathing it and it fell." To cover up his tracks he would tell the neighbours immediately. The Police could be sent for, and the story is shipshape. The bath is emptied, the baby is lying in the tub, no water is there, and certainly its body is not enclosed in a pillow slip.

Do you think he really did take the pillow slip first of all and push the baby in and then immerse it in the water with the deliberate intention of drowning it? Then, having carried out his intention, took it into the next room and left everything there for all to see? What happens when the Police came? He was absolutely frank. He may have lied to Mrs. Revell, but I submit that the lie to Mrs. Revell is not in the words of a person who has executed a planned murder. It is not the action of a planned murderer who has carried out his job.

When the Police come and they say to him: "Who lives here?", he answers: "Me and the woman I live with, and the boy." "How old is the boy?"—"He's three." Then the Police officer asks: "Is everything all right?" "No," he replies. "What is the matter? Where is your wife?" He replies: "She is ill. She had a baby on Saturday night." There is no question then of trying to shift his ground; no question then of trying to say there was a miscarriage. Do you think a planned murderer would not have disposed of the body of that child before any police could come and make the enquiries that would be set on foot, and which Mrs. Revell certainly set on foot?

There is another feature of this case; Watkins deliberately gets Mrs. Revell on the Sunday to go and talk to his wife. He says to her: "She wants to see you." He goes and fetches her, takes her to his wife and leaves them alone. Do you think a man would leave a woman with the frailty of mind that a woman like Miss ——— must have been suffering from after having gone through the experience of giving birth to a child without any skilled attendants, being in miserable pain, with another woman?

She was in that condition the whole of Sunday, and the doctor came and found her extremely ill. Do you think he would have left her alone with Mrs. Revell if he had got the body in the back room for which he was responsible as the murderer, and left her alone so that perhaps Miss ——— could blurt it out and give away the fact? In my submission to you, Members of the Jury, if he was a murderer he would never have taken that truly fantastic course of action.

Let me go through the rest of the conversation that took place when Sergeant Black was there. "She had a baby on Saturday night," says Watkins. Black says: "What happened?", and the reply is: "I was helping her. I got a bowl of water and was bathing the baby. It slipped, and I let it fall in the water. The wife was screaming and shouting."

Members of the Jury, does not that part of it ring true? "The wife was screaming and shouting"; does it not make the circumstances of this evening with which this man was dealing quite terrible to imagine, and does it not justify to you my submission that he was an utterly unnerved and at all times a fairly feeble-minded creature, acting in an utterly unnerved and, in those circumstances, an utterly feeble-minded way?

The officer said: "Is the baby dead?", and Watkins replied: "Yes." Then the officer asked: "Where is it now?", and Watkins said: "Upstairs. I put it in the back room." He goes to his wife and says: "It is the Police about the baby. Do not worry. I have told them everything about it." Thereafter he is not with her. You see, up to that time his story has been that told to Mrs. Revell: "It was a miscarriage." Then, suddenly, the baby is born, the baby is dead, it is put into the back room. He says: "I have told them everything about it."

It is quite consistent, is it not, when he says to her: "What have you told them?", and she replies: "The same as you"? In other words, everything about it—everything about it. Members of the Jury, that does not mean that they had put their heads together and concocted a lie, because if they had you might think there would be no discrepancy in the story, if this was a planned murder. Can you imagine for a moment, and please ask yourselves this important question, a man saying, as undoubtedly he did say: "I slipped the body in the pillow case, and then put the body in the tub"? Can you imagine this man telling that story? From whom had they got that story? From whom did Mr. Paget get the opening: "I slipped the body into the pillow case, and then put the body and pillow case straight into the water"? They got it from this man's own statement.

Members of the Jury, can it be said that that was the statement of someone who had schemed a murder and carried it out? Second-rate intelligence he may have, but do you really think that if at any rate he had thought out his job and had got his scheme going he would have told that story? Is it not far more consistent with the fact that the man on that morning when the baby was born had precious little idea of what he was doing? And the next day when he was being interviewed by the Police had precious little idea of what he was saying?

Members of the Jury, if either or both of these submissions by me to you are correct, can you convict this man of murder, of deliberately taking away the life of that child?

Much has been made of the second statement, and it is my duty to go through it, or, at any rate, certain parts of it. May I deal with the first statement he made when he was in the house: "I live with Maisie here, she had a baby on Saturday night, we hadn't made any arrangements like. She said she could not feel anything you know," that is consistent with the other statements and he is telling the truth.

"She thought she would be all right," in other words, it would be born normally. "Well I went to bathe it in a bowl of water to get the blood off it, and it fell in the bowl. The wife was shouting and I did not know what to do." You may think it would be equally true to say: "I did not know what I was doing."

"I put it in the other room away from the baby so as the baby would not see it"—that is Michael—"I cleaned all the mess and buried it in the garden last night. She has not had a doctor yet. She said she was all right."

Members of the Jury, if that is true, is that the account of a murderer? Does that show you that this man deliberately drowned this child? The wife was screaming and shouting, and the time was 3 o'clock, with all the other occupants of the room besides this man and this recently born baby, and screaming and shouting. His wife screaming and shouting, and his own son awake in the next bed and crying too.

Then he is taken to the police station, and whether you think that some part of that statement was obtained by question and answer, or whether you do not, is a matter for your deliberations, and maybe you will think it seems a little odd. I hope you will take both these statements with you when you go into that room to consider the verdict you are going to give in this case. It seems a little odd that this man with this low intelligence was allowed to make this statement without being asked a few questions by the Police to direct his mind to the essential points.

Do you think when they said they were not satisfied with his explanation and would he like to make another he would, unasked and with no questions put to him, begin: "It is true I have lived with Maisie ——— for five years as man and wife"? There would be no complaint by me, it would be a perfectly reasonable thing to do on the part of the Police. Members of the Jury, can you read through this statement, as you will do, and come to the conclusion that it was the uninspired outpourings of this man without his mind being directed along the tramlines of thought by the Police by any single question?

Well, Members of the Jury, it is a matter for you. But, you know, if you come to the conclusion that some questions were asked, then of course the order in which those things are written down is very significant, is it not? He describes the birth, when he went off to sleep, when he was wakened up and told: "It's here." "I got up and could see the baby was born. I got my things on. I went downstairs and got a pair of scissors, came back and cut the cord. I did not try to get help." It would be the most natural thing for the officer to say: "Did you try to get any help?", and he would answer: "No."

"I went downstairs again and brought up a bowl of water. It was a zinc bowl. I got the water out of the kettle, it was still warm, and added some cold to it. I brought the water upstairs. I picked the baby up, pulled a pillow case off one of the pillows on the bed. I wiped some blood off the baby with a shirt." Members of the Jury, "I picked the baby up," and if the question was asked: "Where did the pillow come from?", and he said: "I pulled the pillow case off one of the pillows on the bed", and it was written down, it would not necessarily mean, would it, that he had in fact done things in that order; picked up the baby and then taken off the pillow slip, and that the pillow slip with the baby in it had then gone to the zinc bowl, and the baby had died there?

You will see that pillow slip, it is in a filthy state, and you may think that even in that house it was something which was not in use, and that the story is true that that particular pillow slip was in the back bedroom, where these people used to put their dirty laundry before it was washed. They obviously would keep it in the back bedroom, they obviously would not want it in the kitchen. It is quite consistent with such habits of domesticity, and it follows immediately that that is quite correct, that the pillow slip was amongst that dirty laundry and was kept in that room.

If that was so he would be unlikely to get that pillow slip until the baby was dead, and until he wanted to put the corpse in the zinc bath, also in the back room. I think he would want to do that because it was a dreadful sight, and to give this wretched corpse some kind of a shroud. It would be the instinct of the man when he found the child was dead to put it into the pillow slip and let that pillow slip be some kind of a shroud.

Let me go on with the statement now: "I wiped some blood off the baby with a shirt. I was holding the baby over the bowl of water when my wife shouted"—all the way through, from the very start, this point comes in—"I was holding the baby over the bowl of water when my wife shouted." She screamed, or she shouted, or some violent noise came from her. She was in intense pain and distress. If you can picture that scene, is it unlikely that this man could have dropped the child as he says he dropped it then?

In this statement he says: "I slipped the baby into the pillow case and dropped it into the bowl of water. I went to the wife and cleaned up the bed a bit." Before anything was done by this man there was a cry, a shout, from his wife. So it goes on: "My wife asked me what I was going to do with it, and I told her I did not know." A planned murder! And he says: "I did not know what I was going to do with it." Is it not likely that, with this corpse in the next room, sudden and unexpected in its arrival in this world, and equally sudden and unexpected in its death, and with this man in that state of mind, of course he did not know? Is not that part of the story true? Is it not utterly inconsistent with a murder which is planned?

The statement goes on: "I have never looked at it until the Police came today. It was dead as far as I know." Then: "I cannot say whether the baby was alive or not. I did not bother to find out once I had dropped it into the water I did not bother." Members of the Jury, is not that what I more or less suggested to you—"bother" may not, of course, be a very fair word—but having dropped it into the water, and started up to go to his wife, he did not dare go back because he thought with some certainty that dropping it into the water, a child only a few minutes old, had been fatal to its life? If he had been asked by the Police: "Did you bother to find out?", the answer would be: "No, I never went back and picked it up," but he said: "I could not have done"; the answer will go down: "I did not bother to find out."

"It is true we did not want this baby." Of course it is true they did not want it. Previously he had said, and it is not inconsistent: "I did not mind about having the baby." You know, Members of the Jury, not wanting a baby and not minding about one are quite consistent. To want something is not necessarily to actively desire it, but now it is coming "I do not mind" means "I do not actively resent it." Although they said they did not want this baby, they were expecting it in five weeks time and they were going to make preparations after the end of January. If that is so, is that a murder which is planned?

"I lost my head and did not know altogether what I was doing. I was afraid to get assistance after the baby was in the water. My wife was very worried when she knew what I had done and I have had no sleep since." Members of the Jury, that also would be true, that also would be consistent with the fact that he had started and dropped this living creature, or let it fall—one or the other—into this bath of water, had not gone back, and both parties knew that it was dead. Is that the worry of a woman who knows that a murder has been planned?

You see, the Prosecution cannot have it both ways, can they? They cannot say "This man intended to murder this child, and one of the things we submit to you is, of course, no preparations for its birth were made; and this woman, according to the man, was worried at what he had done, because she was a participant in making no preparations for the birth in January, if that was a guilty thing to do." Is he telling the truth when he says she was very worried when she knew what he had done? Members of the Jury, I submit to you that he is telling the truth. If he was planning a murder she must have known also, must she not, if part and parcel of the plan was to make no preparations whatsoever to welcome the birth of this child? Is he just saying that to protect her, or has it just come out as he tells the story: "She was very worried as to what I had done." If he is telling the story to protect her; why not say this was an accident?

Members of the Jury, I have asked you this question before, may I ask you again: do you really think a murderer would have told this story, whether it was right or wrong, about putting the baby in the pillow slip, and then putting the pillow slip and baby into the water in the tub? Do you really think a murderer who has planned the murder would have told that story, or is it not as I have said to you the uncertain story of an absolutely uncertain man? That is very, very far removed from the mind of a man which has been made up to carry out the job, and has carried it out from start to finish, from completion of the plan to the execution of the plan.

Then the statement goes on: "My wife had nothing to do with this. She was in bed all the time and I had my back to her when the baby went into the water. She did not know the baby was dead until I told her. She said she was sorry it all happened. She did not know whether it was a boy or a girl until I told her it was a boy. She never actually saw the baby, but must have seen its head because she said it had black hair. She never saw it in the water, because the lid was on the bowl when I carried it out. The zinc bowl was used chiefly for dirty clothes. When I dropped the baby in the water I dropped it about 2 ft. from the bowl." I have made my observations to you upon that.

Then: "The house is a small terrace one, and we have people on either side. We have lived there two years. If I drown the baby I did it in a panic." Members of the Jury, that does not mean, does it: "If I murdered the baby by drowning it I did it in a panic"? It means this: "If there was something I did, dropped it, and I drowned it, I was in a panic." Again we get these same circumstances, bathing the baby in this dreadful little scene, and suddenly disturbed by the nerve shattering scream of his wife in pain.

Members of the Jury, those so far as I know are the circumstances of this case. Upon those circumstances and upon that evidence you will judge this man. May I just say this to you, that when a jury sitting in an important case like this, trying a man for murder, has given its verdict, that is the end of their job. It would be quite wrong, whatever your verdict, that you should worry about it afterwards. Once you have done your job, you have done it, and you are entitled to bring a shutter down upon your mind and forget the case. I would never say to a Jury: "You might worry about this afterwards." It would be wrong, whichever way your verdict went, for you to worry about it afterwards.

Once you say Guilty or Not Guilty your job is done, your worries are gone. Your worries will last while you bring your conscientious minds to find out what is the truth.

May I also say this to you: when you give the verdict at which you arrive you will be asked whether it is the verdict of you all. In asking you that question, the learned Clerk of the Court really means, and the question really means, is this the verdict of each of you, because the verdict which the foreman gives in your name must be the one which any one of you would give if you were sitting alone in that jury box, and were the sole judge of this case, and the sole mind to decide it, and the sole voice to announce the decision.

It is no use A and B saying: "Well, the other ten say so-and-so, so

SIR FRANK NEWSAM
"NOT UNIVERSALLY A POPULAR MAN"

J. CHUTER EDE
THE HOME SECRETARY WHO FAILED TO EXERCISE THE PREROGATIVE
OF MERCY

—: *Universal Pictorial Press*

IVOR NOVELLO

"KEEP THE HOME FIRES BURNING" WAS A FAVOURITE SONG OF BILL AND DOSS. NOVELLO DIED ON 6TH MARCH, 1951. WHEN A RADIO TRIBUTE BEGAN DOSS FINALLY BROKE

—: *Universal Pictorial Press*

DONALD PEERS

"A FAMILY FRIEND"

W. E. LOVSEY

AT HALF TIME ON 31ST MARCH, 1951, HE WAS CALLED AWAY FROM VILLA PARK TO GO AND SEE BILL

—: *Roy Brown: C. S. Bailey (Bromsgrove) Ltd.*

DAVE WALSH

ASTON VILLA'S BRILLIANT CENTRE FORWARD WHO SCORED, ON 31ST MARCH, 1951, A FINE GOAL AGAINST SHEFFIELD WEDNESDAY

W. A. FEARNLEY-WHITTINGSTALL K.C.

"HE JUST SAT, ALONE, IN THE VAST EMPTY COURTROOM . . .
IT WAS AS IF THE CURTAIN HAD COME DOWN"

"BILL WATKINS, SECOND RIGHT FOREGROUND, WITH ORLANDO KELLETT AND SUPPORTERS." THIS AND THE FIRST PHOTOGRAPH ARE THE ONLY PHOTOGRAPHS OF BILL WATKINS KNOWN TO BE IN EXISTENCE

perhaps they are right, and I will conform in that view." It has got to be the verdict of each one of you. The responsibility may look to be collectively discharged, and it is collectively discharged. But, notwithstanding the fact that it is a collective discharge, it is an individual responsibility up to a percentage of 100 per cent. Therefore, as I say, when you have come to your verdict you can forget this case.

When you come to consider the verdict with open minds, of course, you take the advantage of other people's ideas. You take advantage of the juryman on your left, or on your right, or behind you. You turn it over in your own minds, but it is no use taking other people's views unless it appeals to you as right.

May I put that responsibility into words other than my own, which I would ask you to bear in mind when you come to consider what your verdict ought to be: "This above all, to thine own self be true, and it must follow, as the night the day, thou canst not then be false to any man."

MR. JUSTICE FINNEMORE: Members of the Jury, I propose to sum up to you tomorrow morning, and you can bring fresh minds to hear it, and I will bring a fresh mind to do it. As you probably know, until recent years, in a trial of this kind the Jury would not be allowed to separate at all until the trial was over, but that has been relaxed now, and you can go to your own homes. As you have been told in another connection, do not worry about this case, do not discuss it with anyone, do not discuss it at all. It can be discussed when you retire at the conclusion of the case.

(*The Court adjourned until tomorrow.*)

All stood and bowed to Mr. Justice Finnemore. Watkins was taken back to Winson Green escorted by the warders who had been his day-long companions. They travelled by police van. That night 15/16 March, 1951, Watkins slept in a single cell in the hospital wing of the prison.

Friday, 16th March, 1951.

SUMMING-UP

The Court resumed at 10.30 a.m.

MR. JUSTICE FINNEMORE: Members of the Jury, as you know, this man, William Arthur Watkins, is charged with the murder of the newly-born child of Maisie ————, in the early morning of Sunday, 21st January of this year. My duty is to tell you what is the law; your duty is to find the facts and to give your verdict on them.

The law on murder for the purposes of this case, at least, can, I think, be stated to you really quite simply. The crime of murder consists in a person unlawfully killing another person with malice aforethought. Nobody suggests that there was any lawful reason for this man killing that child, if he did kill it. If you are satisfied that he killed the child you then have to ask yourselves did he do it with what is called malice aforethought.

That, Members of the Jury, is an old phrase, and it does not mean what perhaps you might think it means at first sight. It is not necessary in the crime of murder to have a long prepared plan, or premeditation. You can murder, to use a homely phrase, on the spur of the moment. What malice aforethought is is that it was a deliberate act, because every voluntary act has to be preceded, even though it may be by what we sometimes call a split second, by intention. It must be a deliberate act, and it must be a deliberate act intended either to kill the person, or at least to cause grievous bodily harm (I do not think you will have to consider the question of grievous bodily harm in this case).

What you have to decide is whether it is proved that this man killed that child by a deliberate act intending to do so. If in fact you come to the conclusion that he did place that child in that tub of water and leave it there, I should not think that any person in possession of his senses could come to any conclusion other than that he intended to do it to destroy the life of the child.

The word "malice", as I told you, means intention. That intention may be quite plain from what a man says. Somebody may say "I am going to shoot that man", and actually goes and shoots him; there is evidence of express malice, of his deliberate intention to do it.

In many murders, perhaps most, men do not speak like that, and you have to gather what is the intention of the person, what was his intention, by what he does, and the rule of our law, and I think you will agree it is common sense, is this, that a man is presumed to intend the natural result of what he does. I should not think that anybody can contend that there can be any natural result of deliberately placing a little child in a tub of water other than to destroy its life.

You will probably find that this case will come down mainly to this point, are you satisfied that this man by a deliberate act placed that little child in that tub of water that morning. If he did, though it is entirely for you, I should not think you would have, or could have, much hesitation in deciding that he did so for the purpose of ending the child's life. If he did it does not matter whether he thought about it for a long time before, or whether he thought about it only at that time. It does not matter if he lost his head; it does not matter if he acted in a panic; if in fact he deliberately placed the child in that tub of water so that it died, that would constitute the crime of murder.

Learned Counsel who appeared for him also said to you, quite properly, that you might have to consider, and indeed must consider, another verdict, which is that whilst he asked you to say you are not satisfied this man did this deliberately with the intention of murdering the child, maybe he acted in such a way that he was guilty of the crime of manslaughter.

Now, the crime of manslaughter is different from murder in this sense, that a person unlawfully kills someone else without ever intending to do it at all. If you do something which is unlawful and somebody dies as a result, although you never intended to kill, though indeed you never intended to do that person serious harm at all, you would then be, or might be, guilty of manslaughter. That would depend upon the same point I have put to you already.

We know in fact what the defence in this case is. The defence in this case is: "I did not put the child in that tub at all. I was quite properly getting ready to bath the child, somebody shouted from the bed and as I turned round, in my horror the child slipped into the water and I went across to the bed to see what was the matter with the woman. I never bothered about the child any more. I never meant to drown it, but when I dropped it in the bath I left it there".

Members of the Jury, this, of course, is again for you, and you have to decide as to whether you think that story is true. Let us assume it is true, or may be true. I think it will be very difficult, if that is the proper view of the facts to take, to escape the view that this man is at least guilty of manslaughter. Now, in this country you have not got to go about rescuing people. If you go by the side of the river and see somebody drowning in the river, one hopes one would always be prepared to help that person, but it is not a crime if you do not.

Of course, in the case of a little child with its own parents it is another matter altogether. I should think you would probably want to consider very carefully whether there could be any answer, if that is a real answer, to a charge of manslaughter, because you might well say: "Well, the child slipped in the bath with the man actually there, and for him to leave his child in it, at the very least it can only be a sample of the grossest carelessness, and is indeed quite astonishing behaviour altogether", so astonishing altogether that the Prosecution say it did not happen, you ought not to believe it. If you do believe it then you will say at the very least this is about as obvious a case of manslaughter as you could possibly have. After all nothing could be easier than to pick the child out, it would take one second, two seconds, possibly three. He did not do it. As he said himself, he did not bother.

The third alternative is one to which you must not shut your minds, —but I confess it seems to me it may be a very difficult one for you to find at all,—that this man is not guilty altogether. Of course if having considered all the evidence, you are not satisfied that either deliberately, or by the grossest negligence and callousness, the child fell into the bath, he is entitled to be acquitted altogether.

Members of the Jury, I think, therefore, I should suggest to you that if you are satisfied he put that child into the bath—that is murder. If you are not satisfied about that, but are satisfied that having dropped the child into the bath accidentally he took not one single step to rescue it—that at least is manslaughter. If, as I said, you are not satisfied of either of those matters, he is not guilty altogether.

You have been told already by Counsel, and I have to set out again, and I daresay you know it already, that nobody in this country may be convicted in this country of any crime until it is proved. We are not entitled in this country to charge a man with a crime and then say: "Now, prove you did not do it". If the Crown says this man has committed a crime, the Crown must prove it, and must prove it to the full satisfaction of the twelve jurymen. If you are left, therefore, in any reasonable doubt on any point in the case you must always resolve that doubt in favour of the prisoner. It is not for him to prove to you that he is innocent; it is for the Prosecution to prove to you that he is guilty. If they fail to do it then you must say: "So much the worse for the Prosecution, but so much the better for the man who is accused."

We sometimes say the onus of proof is on the Prosecution. Every man is presumed to be innocent until he is proved to be guilty. You are the people who have to decide that, and you only. Let me make this quite plain, I am going to review shortly with you, as I must, the evidence. It is not for me to express an opinion about it, at least, if I do you are not bound by it at all. You have got to make up your minds, and you have got to accept the responsibility. It is your responsibility alone. So remember, please, you alone are the judges of fact in this case. Therefore, whether the case is proved beyond reasonable doubt is for you to decide.

If you ask me what reasonable doubt means, I do not know that I can tell you any more than that it is the sort of doubt which would stop you acting in some very important matter in your own lives. It does not mean, of course, some fanciful or imaginary doubt. You were not there, you did not see what happened in that room. You have got to apply your common sense. You have to apply the ordinary standards you would apply to the ordinary things of life. Then when you have done that if you are satisfied you will say so. If you are not satisfied you equally will say so.

Members of the Jury, I did mention to you that apart from the verdict of murder there is the alternative verdict of manslaughter. It is hardly necessary to say to you that if you say "This man did drop this child into the bath and he did intend it, but today he seems a pretty poor type, his intelligence is low, he looks a rather miserable specimen, we think it enough to find him guilty of manslaughter", you cannot of course, do that. It would not be right. What you have to decide is whether the facts, if you find them true, satisfy you that this case is murder, or if it is only manslaughter, or that there is no evidence at all. You do not have to consider the question of what follows, you have to decide on the evidence what crime, if any, has been proved against this man.

Now, the facts are not really very long and they are not complicated. They depend partly on certain indisputable facts, and also to a considerable degree on what this man himself said. Now, Members of the Jury, the indisputable facts are, of course, that early on the Sunday morning this little girl was born [*Mr. Justice Finnemore here made a slip of the tongue; the baby was a male child.*] and that very shortly afterwards it died by drowning. You had evidence from Dr. Sandilands and Professor Webster to satisfy you that this child was a person that had had an actual separate existence of—it is only indeed a little time— some 10 to 15 minutes, or less. The child was healthy, normal, but born a little previously, and, but for the fact that it was drowned, it would have gone on living as any child normally would.

The other thing you know is that its life came to an end because somehow or other—it could not have got there itself—it got into this tub of water, where indeed its body was found on the Monday, the 22nd January last, when the police went round to that house. You know that, and you know that the child must have got into that tub of water through the agency of one or two people, either the woman, Miss ———, or the prisoner. On the evidence that you have heard I should think you would be fully satisfied that it was not the woman, who was in bed ill, weak, in considerable pain, quite apart from the fact that this man says it was his fault.

Whether he did it purposely, or whether it was an accident I am not discussing at the moment. Those are the facts. You know the other facts. You know that you have to decide what this man has himself said about it.

It is an unhappy story, it is a sordid story. In most homes that you know about the arrival of a little child is an event of rejoicing and happiness. But, of course, there is sometimes in the world the tragedy of what is called the unwanted child. The Prosecution put this case to you on that footing. They say that this was a child which the woman did not want, and it was a child which this man did not want, and when it arrived it was very quickly by this man destroyed.

Members of the Jury, I mentioned to you about premeditation, and the Prosecution, as you know, have put this case to you as being a planned murder, planned before the child ever arrived, premeditated in the strict sense of the word. Well, they point out to you a number of facts,—nothing had been arranged for the child, the woman never went to a clinic, no clothes for the child, no preparation of any sort or kind,—as evidence of that.

On the other side it is said that you must bear this in mind, this man himself suggested to the woman more than once that she should go to the clinic, or she should go to the doctor, and they also point to the fact that the child did arrive four, or possibly five, weeks sooner than expected. In effect, they say that there really is no evidence on which you ought to find that this murder was planned before the child was ever born.

Members of the Jury, you may well hesitate on that point, but it does not matter; it is not an essential part of this case. Whenever this man decided to do it, if he did, it is murder, just as much as if he had planned it weeks before. It may be, of course, a far worse kind of murder if the planning for the destruction of this child's life took place before it was ever born. But whether it did or not, if on that early Sunday morning he did destroy this life by a deliberate act, that is murder. Just the same it does not matter whether it was premeditated, or whether it was not, in the sense of being planned before the child arrived.

Now, these two people, Maisie ———— and this man, had been living together for some five years. They had one child of their own, the little boy, Michael, aged 3. We were told this man had four children of his own of the other marriage, who were all grown up to the maturity of life. The only importance of that is this, you are not dealing with inexperienced people, you are not dealing with two young people to whom this sort of thing had never happened before. This was the father of five children, four of whom had grown up, and this little boy. The woman herself had also had this one other child before. It is a matter, you may think, of some importance. I do not know, but there it is.

[*Mr. Justice Finnemore relied on the unchallenged evidence of Watkins that he had four grown up children.*]

We are told that somewhere about the end of July last the lady missed her periods and was suspicious, naturally, that she was pregnant. Later on it became quite obvious that she was. She said to you quite frankly that she did not want any more children. She said she did not want to go to the doctor and she kept putting it off. She did say in this man's favour, and you must not forget it, that he suggested she should go to the clinic. She agrees there were no arrangements made as to clinic or doctor, or about the clothes, or anything of that sort at all.

She said that on the day,—this may be of some importance,—this Saturday she had pain, and she was seen on that day by Mrs. Revell. Of course, it is quite obvious by that time her condition was plain to be seen by any of her neighbours, and was seen by Mrs. Revell. That is another point that the Defence makes to you, that it was no good planning out to kill this child, because the neighbours would know this woman was pregnant, and when they found it had gone they would ask what had happened to the child. That is a point you must determine.

The Prosecution say they were probably going to say what in fact was said. They say that the day after, when this man met Mrs. Revell, he said: "She has had a miscarriage", which, of course, was not true, and that is the explanation of how Mrs. Watkins' (as she was called) condition had come to an end. There it is. Undoubtedly on that Saturday Mrs. Watkins, or Miss ——— (whichever name you like to use, it really does not matter) had reason to suppose something was happening, because, if you believe Mrs. Revell she told Mrs. Revell in the morning that she thought she had started.

Later that day, again if you believe Mrs. Revell, she told Mrs. Revell that the pains were worse, and they had moved from the back to the stomach. Mrs. Revell said to her: "Well, you are already in strong labour". Miss ——— said that she was going to send for her doctor, Dr. Salmon. Mrs. Revell said on that occasion the Prisoner Watkins was there and said he would go for the doctor. But what Miss ——— said about it was that he was ready to go for the doctor, but she said: "Well, do not do it just yet, I am not sure they are labour pains because it is too early". He also said at night: "If it gets any worse get me up, and if you are any worse I will fetch the doctor". She said: "Do not do that yet".

That is the position, that on the Saturday there was, to put it at its least, reason to suppose that something like that was near at hand.

The only other matter you ought to know about what happened before that material day is that in December Miss ———, as she told you, could not feel any movement in her body and that the child was dead. She had a fall in December, and again in January, she still thought she could feel no movement, and thought in fact that the child was dead, and all that would happen would be a miscarriage. Of course, it is said at once, all the greater reason to have gone to the doctor. One would have thought everybody knows that under those circumstances the health, indeed the life, of the mother might very soon become in serious danger. But you must always remember the people you are dealing with in this case. You have seen the prisoner, and you have seen the woman, and it is for you to say whether it helps you at all on this point that both of them may have thought on that Saturday, in spite of these pains, that whatever it was it would not be a live child.

That is, if it is right, what Miss ——— told you that she really thought in December and January, that the child was no longer alive.

Well, however that may be, early on Sunday morning she became involved in much greater pain and she woke up the prisoner and told him what was happening. He went downstairs, I think he said to light the gas and get something for her, and the child was born in about half an hour, she tells us, and you remember what Professor Webster said—that at all events towards the end it would happen rather quickly. There was nobody else there.

This man did not do what you might think the rather obvious thing, even at half-past two or three in the morning, that is going next door to Mrs. Revell, who obviously is a kindly neighbour, to say: "Will you come and help?". He looked after things himself, and he got the scissors and cut the cord, as you have heard, and then undoubtedly very quickly he took the child away from the woman. There is no doubt about that. She says after the birth had taken place she never saw the child again at all.

Then comes the problem of what happened next. Of course nobody else was there, and the only people who can tell you anything about it, and indeed in large measure the only person who can tell you anything about it, is the prisoner himself. A little later we shall have to look rather carefully at what he said at the time, and at what he said to you in the witness-box yesterday.

You know this, that somehow or other the child got into that tub and, of course, as you would expect, very quickly drowned. There is no doubt, as I have told you, this child was born alive. There is no doubt it had a separate existence, and she [*Again Mr. Justice Finnemore makes a slip of the tongue. The baby was a boy.*] was fully under the protection of the law in this country, as any grown-up person would be.

What he says is, he went downstairs and brought up a bowl of water, you saw the zinc bowl, with a view to washing the child in it. Unfortunately, the little boy woke up and called out, and his wife said something about coming to clean up the mess on the bed. As he turned round sharply the child slipped into the bath. He says that he was washing the child about 2 feet above the bowl at the time. It may be, I do not know, but it is something for you to consider, that there was no injury on the child's body at all. Professor Webster said the only mark on the child was a little mark on the end of the nose, which appeared to have no significance, no bruise, no mark of violence or blow of any sort at all. The only thing the matter with the child was that it was asphyxiated by drowning.

What is said by the Prosecution is that story is quite impossible and quite untrue. What they say is: "Here is the child's father and the child is alive, and he puts it in the water". As I say, there was nobody else there except this man and woman, therefore it is important for you to see what accounts he gave of the murder.

The first thing is this: On the Sunday morning he got up, he tells us he went and bought a paper, took the little boy for a walk and cooked the dinner. While he was out in the morning he met Mrs. Revell, his next door neighbour, again. It is for you to consider this matter, but it is of some importance, of course. When he saw Mrs. Revell he said that Mrs. Watkins had had a miscarriage. He said they had had the doctor and a midwife, and I think he said yesterday he did not say how his wife was. Of course, what he said there was quite untrue. He agreed it was untrue when he was in the witness-box. He had not had Dr. Salmon, he had not had a midwife, and, of course, his wife had not had a miscarriage, she had had a live child.

Members of the Jury, remember whom you are dealing with and the type of man. It may be surprising he did not say this: "We had a most terrible time last night. Quite unexpectedly this child arrived. I was bathing it, had a most terrible accident, it dropped in the water and it is dead. What in the world are we to do?". But he does say, by that time he was for some reason trying to hide it. He told Mrs. Revell: "There was a miscarriage. My wife did have the child and a midwife to look after her".

It was quite properly put to Mrs. Revell that that is not quite what she said before the Magistrates in the Court below. Whether it is or not, Members of the Jury, it is for you to decide how far you think this matter is important. This is what Mrs. Revell said, and we know she was very much upset in the Magistrates' Court. As you know, evidence in the Magistrates' Court is all taken down in writing, and this is what she said: "The next day between 11 and 12 noon the prisoner said that she had had a 'miss' (meaning miscarriage) and that they had sent for the doctor and the midwife. He said that she was not too bad. He said there was no need for the doctor and the midwife, but that if they wanted them they would send for them". I do not know whether you find that very difficult to understand. It is for you to decide entirely. Do not take my view, it is not for me, it is for you.

I should think that appeared to mean that the prisoner said they had sent for the doctor and the midwife when the miscarriage took place the night before. He then went on to say: "The wife was not too bad. There was no need for a doctor and a midwife, but if they wanted them they would send for them". You may think that what that meant was he did not need the doctor and midwife any more, but it is for you.

What is important, and there is no dispute about this, is that this man did say there had been a miscarriage, which was wrong, and he did say he had had a doctor and midwife, and had sent for them. That is also untrue. How far it helps you in the general matter is for you to decide, but we have got to face the facts. On the Sunday morning when all the trouble was over and he had had time to settle down he is telling Mrs. Revell something about the night before which was all untrue in the only material and important particulars.

Mrs. Revell later at his request—remember that—went to see the woman and she found the woman ill, and, again, as a kindly neighbour well might, she took it on herself to call the doctor. That, of course, is how this matter came to light, because as soon as the doctor came he saw that she was in need of attention and arranged for her to go to hospital. Then, of course, once matters had started like that, it very quickly got into the hands of the police.

It was 3 o'clock on the Monday when the police came to the house. That was Sergeant Black and he was accompanied by Miss Beattie and another policewoman. He saw the prisoner, told him who he was and he was told that this man and the woman and the boy lived there. He then said: "Everything all right?". Watkins said: "No." "What is the matter, where is your wife?". Watkins said: "She is ill. She had a baby on Saturday night." He is telling that part truthfully. The policeman then said: "What happened?", and Watkins said: "I was helping her. I got a bowl of water and was bathing the baby. It slipped and I let it fall in the water. The wife was screaming and shouting."

It is right to pause to point out to you at that stage he has given the account of an accident. He was bathing the baby and it slipped into the water. Then the officer said: "Is the baby dead?". Watkins said: "Yes." "Where is it now?". Watkins said: "Upstairs."

Watkins was then cautioned. As you know, Members of the Jury, when a man is being asked questions when the police are enquiring into what may be a crime, and it begins to look as though he may be involved himself, he is cautioned, in other words he is told he need not say anything unless he wishes, but if he does it will be taken down and may be given in evidence.

After that had happened at the house the prisoner made a statement to Sergeant Black: "I live with Maisie ———, she had a baby on Saturday night. We had not made any arrangements like. She said she could not feel anything, you know, she thought she would be all right. Well I went to bathe it in a bowl of water, to get the blood off it, and it fell in the bowl. The wife was shouting and I didn't know what to do. I put it in the other room away from the baby so as the baby wouldn't see it. I cleaned all the mess and buried it in the garden last night. All the paper and stuff you know. She hasn't had a doctor yet. She said she was all right."

In other words, all he says is this was an accident, the baby falling into the water while he was quite properly bathing it. Well, then the officer went upstairs with Watkins, and Watkins said to the woman: "It is the police about the baby. Do not worry, I have told them everything about it". Then Miss Beattie was left with the woman, and the prisoner and Sergeant Black went to the back room.

You know what the state of the room was, the door was tied up with string and a piece of copper wire—quite a sensible thing to do, of course, because there was a little boy of three years in the house. Well, when they got inside there was a pile of clothing, which you have seen identified, and you need not trouble about it, some stained with blood. When those articles were pulled away, underneath was the zinc bath, which you saw.

An astonishing part of this story is that the tub was still half full of water, with the lid still on, and in the water was the baby. This may be the crucial part of this case. The baby was then in a pillow case head first, with one of its little legs protruding out of one end, and it was head first in the water. Watkins lifted out the body in the pillow case and then said this: "It's all right, officer, I am not frightened of it". He told the officer he had cut the cord with the scissors. He was very distressed and crying at that time.

He then said: "We had not made any arrangements for it. I did not know what to do. The wife was shouting out and I must have panicked." Members of the Jury, that may mean one of two things. It might mean, and I think he does mean there plainly, that he panicked after the child had fallen into the water, and that is his explanation of why he did nothing, presumably, to take it out again, which you may think was as simple and obvious a thing to do as there could have been in the world. That is the story.

He said: "I buried the afterbirth in the garden—up by the hedge. I did it after dark." Quite plainly, whatever else he had in mind, at that time he meant, you may think, but it is for you, to conceal this altogether, and took the afterbirth away and buried it. He had not apparently decided what to do with the body then. When you add that to what he told Mrs. Revell the previous morning you will see there was a very strong case that he was trying to hide altogether what had happened.

At 5 o'clock he was cautioned again. Of course, you see, the Officer was not quite satisfied with that explanation. He said to the prisoner: "You say you were bathing the baby and it slipped and fell into the water". Then he asked the obvious question, and I expect you thought of it straightaway: "Did you pick the baby out of the water again at any time after it fell in?". Watkins replied: "I could not have done". That is another matter for you to think about later on.

Later on he said he did. He told you in the witness-box he did take it out, because he put it in the pillow case after it had gone in the water. That is what he told you later. Then at the interview with Sergeant Black he goes on to say something of great importance. The Sergeant said: "How do you account for it being inside the pillow slip?". This is probably the core of this case, which I am sure occurred to you long ago, that if a man was washing a baby and it fell into the bath, how in the world could it happen that it was in fact head first in the pillow case, and the officer says he did not reply to the question for a moment. Then Watkins said: "I got the pillow [*sic*] and put the baby into it and then I was washing it over the top of the pillow slip like". That is for you, whether it makes any sense to you, I do not know.

If it is true that he put that baby into the pillow slip just before it went into the water, well, of course, it is bound to throw a very grave doubt on the story that he was washing the child properly at the time that the accident—as he says it was—occurred.

He was then very distressed, cried again, and he produced the scissors. Then he went to the room where the woman, Miss ——— was with the two lady police officers, and he spoke to her: "What have you said?". Miss ——— said: "It is all right, I have told them the same as you have". I do not think you need think there is anything unduly sinister in that. It is, of course, possible that they agreed what they had to say, and she said: "I have told the story". It is, of course, for you to decide. It is open to the interpretation: "I have told them the truth, the same as you have". It is open to you to consider, but do not worry about that.

The officer did find the afterbirth where Watkins said he had buried it by the rabbit hutch. Later this man, as you know, was taken to the police station and then other officers dealt with what happened there. In as much as some of that is in dispute, you have to make up your minds where the truth lies. I would just remind you that Miss Beattie was with Sergeant Black at the main part of this conversation, which was at the opening part, which was when the prisoner said: "She had a baby on Saturday night. I was helping her. I got a bowl and some water and was bathing the baby and I let it drop into the water. The wife was screaming and shouting". Sergeant Black asked: "Is the baby dead?" and Watkins said: "Yes". They then went upstairs and Miss Beattie did not hear what happened when they went into the back bedroom and got the pillow with the baby's body in it. But she was there when he was cautioned and when Sergeant Black said: "Did you take the baby out of the water after it fell in?" and the prisoner said: "I could not have done". Then Sergeant Black said: "How do you account for it being inside the pillow slip?" and the prisoner replied: "I got the pillow slip and put the baby in it and then I was sort of washing it over".

As you know, Members of the Jury, what he says now is that he put the baby into the pillow slip after it was drowned. I do not know whether he ever said that, or that he ever said why, having done that, he put it back in the water again. That you may have to consider when you come to deal with the whole matter.

The accused was taken to the police station, and he was told there by Inspector Quinton that he was going to be detained there while inquiries were made about this matter. Then he said to him, again this is of great importance if you are satisfied it is true: "I am not satisfied that the child's death was due to an accident"—being found head first in the pillow case in the bowl of water. I daresay you are not surprised to know he said that. Then the prisoner said, according to Inspector Quinton: "I suppose I panicked and we did not want the child". It is entirely for you, Members of the Jury, and nobody else, to decide what that meant, and what importance you ought to attach to it.

What the Prosecution say is that in effect that is as near as does not matter a confession. When he is faced with the question to which it is difficult to think what the answer could be: "How do you account for the child being found head first in the pillow case in the bowl of water?", the Prosecution say he could not think of any answer to that. He says: "Well, I suppose I panicked and we did not want the child". In other words, he is saying: "We did not want the child and I panicked. When it did come I got rid of it". If you think it means that, of course it is a statement of the greatest possible, and of the gravest possible, importance, but it is for you to consider.

He later made another statement at the police station. Before referring to that you must remember that he said there is a discrepancy. He said that when he got to the police station he made a statement, which he says was signed. The police say he did not and there is no other statement except, of course, this statement, the one I am going to read to you in a moment. It is signed in two or three places, it is signed on each page, as indeed is the custom when the statement goes on to more than one page. The officer did say that on two occasions the man stopped his statement, and the Inspector thought he had finished and therefore read over to him what he had said, this man went on again to add something else, and that that happened twice. Whether that is the explanation of his saying he made more than one statement at the Police Court or not I do not know.

He does say: "Well, they took this statement off me and having given me a cup of tea took that off me, and said: 'We are not going to stop here all night. Give us another statement'." The Police completely deny that. If they did say that, or anything like it, it was most improper, and if the man made the statement after an incident of this sort, you ought not to pay much attention to it. Of course, the Chief Inspector says no such thing happened. Inspector Mitchell says no such thing ever happened—"we took down the statement as he gave it. When he stopped the statement was read over to him and he then said there was something more. Nothing was suggested to him and they did not try to make him make the statement. Indeed, the beginning of the statement, which he signed himself, says he had been cautioned. That means that he need not say anything unless he wanted to, and if he did, it would be taken down in writing and may be given in evidence.

Members of the Jury, he then made a statement. If it is true it certainly does go a very long way, the Prosecution say the whole way, to a confession that he deliberately drowned this child. As I say; that is for you. That is what the Prosecution say. What the Defence say is this, what the man himself says: "I was very upset, I was very distressed, I was very troubled, and I did not really know what I was saying". That is entirely a matter for you to consider. It is for you to decide whether or not you think the man was upset and distressed, only two days after the event happened, going to make a statement in which he confesses, if you think that is what he means, to having committed the grave crime. Please remember this, you are dealing with a man who has been described as below average intelligence. Do not therefore use against him odd phrases or words, which you yourself would use carefully, and which he might not. He is not mental defective or anything like that; he is a man of some years and experience in the world. If in fact he did say certain plain statements of fact about what he did, you are quite entitled to say: "Well, after all who knows better than he what he did that night, and what he said two days after that he had done. It is probably true".

Of course, you will also apply to what he says the evidence given you about surrounding circumstances. If I indicate the sort of thing you might consider while the statement is being read it is merely something for you to think about, I am not trying to suggest for a moment what conclusion you ought to come to. But you may, for example, think this, you may think, I think you must think this, that if this child accidentally fell into that bath of water it is well nigh beyond the bounds of credibility that its own father, with it at the time, would not immediately pick it out, without thinking about anything at all, but rather goes away and spends ten to 15 minutes tidying up the bed, and then goes to the bath, puts the lid on, carried it into the back room, and covers it up with all this clothing.

If his account is right he took the baby out of the bath, then put it into the pillow slip, and then put it back into the water, the dead baby in the pillow slip. Then you may wonder what in the world he was doing that for, and why he was doing it. You may think—I do not know, it is for you—that it is far more credible that the child was put into the pillow slip first. That is what you have got to ask yourselves— why? Can you think of any other reason than that he was then intending to drown, not to bath, the child, to drown it in the tub of water. That is the sort of matter you have to ask yourselves. I am not supplying the answers; you must supply them.

As I say, consider what the man says now; consider what he says in his statement to the Police, then you have to apply your judgment and your reason in deciding where the truth lies.

Anyhow, this is what he says: "It is true I have lived with Maisie ———— for five years as man and wife"—do not think any the worse of him for that, lots of people do that without committing murder. "I met her when she came to lodge at my home in Aston. I have a son by her aged three years. In August or September last year my wife told me she had 'missed' "—it was in fact true, we know now, but that does not matter. "When we knew she was pregnant I told her to go to the Welfare but she said she would wait a bit. My wife told me she did not want another baby. I did not mind if we had had another baby. Two or three times I asked her to go to the Doctor or the Welfare but she did not go"—she agrees with that—"I made no arrangements myself for the baby, and we had nothing prepared"— I suppose you would not expect him to.

"This Saturday, 20th January, 1951, Maisie was not well, she had pains in her back. I offered to fetch the doctor but she said 'No,' and she did not ask me again. During the night she was much worse. I got into bed with her. I went off to sleep. At about a quarter to four on Sunday morning (21st January, 1951) she woke me up and said,

'It's here.' I got up and could see the baby was born. I got my things on. I went downstairs and got a pair of scissors, came back and cut the cord. I did not try to get any help. I went downstairs again and brought up a bowl of water. It was a zinc bowl. I got the water out of the kettle, it was still warm and added some cold to it. I brought the water upstairs"—now follows the important passage—"I picked the baby"—I suppose "picked the baby up"—"pulled a pillow case off one of the pillows on the bed. I wiped some blood off the baby with a shirt. I was holding the baby over the bowl of water, when my wife shouted and I slipped the baby into the pillow case and dropped it into the bowl of water. I went to the wife and cleaned up the bed a bit". He says that is not so, he never pulled the pillow case off a pillow on the bed at all, it was a pillow case he got in the back room when he went there. He says it is not true he slipped the baby into the pillow case and then dropped it into the bowl of water, and he says he made that statement because he really did not know what he was doing at the time.

Then the statement goes on: "I took the bowl containing the baby into the other bedroom. I thought it was dead. I put the lid on the bowl and some dirty clothes on top of it. When I went back into the front bedroom I told my wife the baby was dead. My wife asked me what I was going to do with it and I told her I didn't know. I have never looked at it until the Police came today. It was dead as far as I know. I buried the afterbirth in the front garden. I never told anyone. I buried it Sunday night at dark. Today I went with the Police to where the baby was still in the water. It was still head first in the pillow case, as I had put it. I cannot say whether the baby was alive or not. I did not bother to find out once I had dropped it in the water I did not bother. I was afraid afterwards to have a look at it. It is true we didn't want this baby. I lost my head and did not know altogether what I was doing. I was afraid to get assistance after the baby was in the water. My wife was very worried when she knew what I had done and I have had no sleep since. My wife had nothing to do with this. She was in bed all the time and I had my back to her when the baby went into the water. She did not know the baby was dead until I told her. She said she was sorry it all happened. She did not know whether it was a boy or girl until I told her it was a boy. She never actually saw the baby, but must have seen its head because she said it had black hair. She never saw it in the water, because the lid was on the bowl when I carried it out. The zinc bowl was used chiefly for dirty clothes. When I dropped the baby in the water, I dropped it about 2 feet from the bowl. I did not touch the baby otherwise. I never heard it cry out. The only person in the house besides the wife and I was my son aged 3 years. The house is a small terrace one and we have people at either side. We have lived there two years. If I drown the baby I did it in a panic."

Members of the Jury, I do not propose to comment to you about that statement. You have heard it commented upon by the Prosecution, who say it is a plain confession that he put the baby in the pillow slip first, then dropped it into the water. You have heard the comments of Counsel for the Defence, that that was the statement of a distressed, ill-educated and not very intelligent man, who said a number of things that he did not really mean. You are the judges of how far that statement helps you.

As I say, the two crucial points are whether he put this child in the pillow slip before it went into the water; and, of course, whether he did it deliberately, and whether the explanation suggesting that they did not want the child is the explanation. But why he did what it is alleged he did, and what it is alleged he did is for you to consider, and it is for you to consider whether that statement is going very near indeed to saying he actually did it.

Members of the Jury, those are the facts put forward by the Prosecution. You have only to ask yourselves whether they have satisfied you so far that this man deliberately put the child into that tub of water. He has given evidence, and he is not bound to, but he is entitled to, as every accused man is entitled to in these days, to give evidence on his own account. He told you his wife missed her July periods, he told her to go to the welfare and get the doctor, but she said she would leave it to a bit later on. She told him in December and again in January that she could not feel anything of the child, and the child was probably dead.

He agrees that on the Saturday before she was in pain, and Mrs. Revell came. And he says that they were not expecting the baby for about five weeks, and did not know whether it would be alive or not. But on this particular weekend he worked on nights on the Friday and on the Saturday morning his wife said she was very ill, so he did the house-work. You have heard already the conversation that took place with Mrs. Revell about her being in labour pains. He said he went to bed on the Saturday night, and about half-past two she woke him up and said the baby was born. He ran downstairs, put on the gas, got the scissors, helped with the baby, got the bowl of water, washed the baby over the zinc bowl he brought up from downstairs. He went on washing the baby, Michael woke and cried, Maisie, the wife, cried out about the mess on the bed. He said: "I turned round sharply and dropped the baby into the bowl. The wife shouted loud enough for me to hear. The pillow case was in the back bedroom. The electric light was on"—it is not a case of something happening in a dark room.

"The electric light hangs over the bed"—I do not think it matters whether it was over the bed or on the wall—"I left the baby in the water because Michael was crying and because the woman was crying. The baby was head first in the water. I did not try to kill it."

"I was about fifteen minutes tidying up. I saw the baby's head in the water. I went to the back bedroom. I took the baby out of the water, put it into the pillow slip and put it back." He said: "I got a towel and a flannel and brought it upstairs. That was in order to wash the child."

He then says: "I put the bowl in the back room and put clothes on top of it, and fastened the door because of Michael. I then went back to bed. The woman said she felt all right, and dozed off to sleep. On Sunday I took Michael for a walk, bought the paper, and cooked the dinner. I did tell Mrs. Revell we had sent for the doctor and midwife. That was not true. I did say the wife had had a miscarriage. That was not true. I had no idea what to do with the body."

"It was on Monday, 22nd January, the Police came, I made a statement"—I have read that to you, it is Exhibit No. 9. "I got to the police station about 7 o'clock. I made a statement, then signed that. They gave me a cup of tea; they took it off me and said they were not going to stop all night, I must give them another statement. He said: "I did not put the baby in the pillow slip while alive." With regard to the statement that I have referred you to already, the part of the statement in which he said: "I picked up the baby, pulled a pillow case off one of the pillows on the bed," he says: "I did not know what I was saying." When he said: "I slipped the baby into the pillow case and dropped it into the water"—again he said: "I did not know what I was saying."

If he said: "If I drowned the baby I did it in a panic," he does not remember saying about that; anyhow, he did not mean he deliberately drowned it.

Members of the Jury, that is his account, and that is the account you have to consider, in answer to the charge. You have got to consider how far it appeals to your reason and your judgment. You have got to make up your minds, not whether you are fully satisfied it is true—there is no burden of that sort put on the Defence—but what you have got to think about is: does it raise in your minds any real doubt about the matter. That is what he has got to do. The Prosecution have to prove he murdered that child, that is to say, that he deliberately put the baby into the bowl of water.

If by his evidence, through his Counsel's speech and his Counsel's cross-examination he has raised in your minds any real doubt about the matter, then of course he is entitled to be acquitted.

I think the only other thing I have to tell you is that late that night, about five minutes to twelve, he was formally charged with the murder. That was because the post-mortem had to take place first in order that it could be established that this child was a live child or not. Professor Webster's report and the evidence he gave in the witness-box made it quite plain that this child had had its own separate existence. If anybody ended that existence it is, as you would expect, under the laws of this country, murder, if it is done under the conditions explained to you at the beginning.

He was then charged with the murder of this child, and he was cautioned. He then made no reply. It does not mean, of course, that he has got no reply to make; when a man is cautioned he is told he need not reply unless he wants to. He had already made a statement. It really means he had nothing further to say at that time.

Members of the Jury, that is the whole of this case. It is for you to decide the proper verdict to return. You remember the warning I gave you at the beginning, you must not convict this man unless you are satisfied beyond doubt. On the other hand, if you are satisfied beyond doubt, you must not shrink from returning a verdict according to the decision to which you have come. You hold the scales of justice. You owe a duty to this man; you owe a duty to the public as well.

The life of that little child undoubtedly was lost. If it is proved it was lost because this man deliberately drowned it, it is your duty to find him guilty. If you are not satisfied about that, but you are satisfied it was through the criminal negligence of this man, you will find him guilty of manslaughter. If you are not satisfied about either, then of course he is entitled to be acquitted.

I think you ought to have the statements with you, and if there is any other exhibit, or anything you want, of course you may have it if it will help you in your deliberations. Then I am going to ask you to take these statements, consider them and the evidence, and then tell me how you find. If there is anything else you want you will ask for it.

(The Jury retired at 11.50 a.m.)

(The Jury returned into Court at 2.15 p.m.)

THE CLERK OF ASSIZE: Members of the Jury, are you agreed upon your verdict?

THE FOREMAN OF THE JURY: We are.

THE CLERK OF ASSIZE: Do you find the accused, William Arthur Watkins, guilty or not guilty of murder?

THE FOREMAN OF THE JURY: Guilty.

THE CLERK OF ASSIZE: You find him guilty of murder, and that is the verdict of you all?

THE FOREMAN OF THE JURY: Yes.

THE CLERK OF ASSIZE: Prisoner at the Bar, you stand convicted of murder. Have you anything to say why the sentence of death should not be pronounced upon you according to law?

THE PRISONER: No.

SENTENCE

MR. JUSTICE FINNEMORE: William Arthur Watkins, the Jury have found you guilty of murder, for which the law of this country provides only one sentence, and that is that you be taken from this place to a lawful prison and thence to a place of execution and there suffer death by hanging, and that your body be buried within the precincts of the prison in which you shall have last been confined before your execution, and may the Lord have mercy on your soul.

The Chaplain added "Amen". The shorthand writer missed this (understandably) and also did not report that the same prison warder, who earlier had to shout into Watkins' ear, now had the unenviable task of repeating the death sentence word by word. Watkins turned to him and smiled.

EPILOGUE

The Jury returned on the afternoon of Friday, 16th March, and after they had given a finding of guilty, the Chaplain passed to Mr. Justice Finnemore a small square piece of black material which he placed on top of his wig. As he started to speak, the dreaded, yet only possible sentence, it was obvious to all in court that Watkins had a vague air about him; so the Judge paused and asked the warder, who earlier had repeated questions to Watkins, to repeat the sentence of the Court. It was a macabre setting—a young lady who had prepared all the prosecution's evidence burst into tears; yet there seemed little other emotion within the Court. Nearly everyone present believed that the sentence would never be carried out. As the warder repeated the long sentence, word by word, Watkins turned to him nodding his head and smiling. When it was over he turned away from Mr. Justice Finnemore and still with a smile on his face, slowly followed the leading warder down the stairs.

In the court room Fearnley-Whittingstall, his body drained with pent-up emotion, bowed with the other counsel to the Judge: he departed and Fearnley-Whittingstall was lost for words. Paget sensing the emotion and knowing his opponent so well, turned to Kilner Brown and indicated, without saying a word, that it was time to go. Alderson touched Michael Davies on the shoulder and the two went into the dock and down the stairs. Pugh and his Clerk, Norman Brown, sitting in the well of the Court quietly bundled up their papers; and as they left, Pugh was heard to say "he won't swing". Others in the court room quietly left leaving the great orator alone. Fearnley-Whittingstall had done his best and his best had not been good enough. He just sat, alone, in the vast empty court room which over the past two days had been his stage. It was as if the curtain had come down.

Earlier in the day, before he had made his speech to the Jury, he was observed writing in the gentleman's lavatory. The Superintendent in charge of the courts had put up a notice above the urinal which read "Please do not throw cigarettes into this urinal". Fearnley-Whittingstall was seen to take out his pen and write underneath "it makes them soggy and difficult to light". At one point in the trial, the previous day, he had rounded on Paget (who was a very keen hunting man and later Master of the Pytchey Hunt) and said "that was ridiculous nonsense. I suppose you were out hunting on Saturday and took a toss and landed on your head." His wit could be sardonic and biting; his remarks to his colleagues were often outrageous, but the little smile lurking on his lips took away all offence and this led to the realization that it was all a legpull, and with it there was no malice.

His quotations were brilliant and Mr. Justice Finnemore to his dying day never forgot his opening in a case in the very same court room some two years later. Coincidentally on that day his junior was Mr. R. K. Brown. His brief then was in a civil case in which heavy damages were sought for a youth of 17 who had suffered the most terrible injuries. He looked at the Judge and began thus: "When one considers the appalling injuries sustained by this once happy, carefree youth, the icy fingers of the Snow Queen clutch at one's heart."

As he sat alone in the court room, this man who earlier in the trial had been so witty, who later in his career was to make an opening so brilliant as the one quoted, could only repeat to himself the quotation he had earlier spoken with all the strength and feeling of a great advocate "This above all, to thine own self be true, and it must follow, as the night the day, thou canst not then be false to any man."

Some twenty minutes later the Superintendent in charge of the courts, thinking the court room empty, came to lock up. He coughed when he saw the back of a barrister wearing his wig: he had no idea who it was. "Sorry, sir," he said, and the figure did not turn. The Superintendent left and moments later saw the great advocate move with enormous speed towards the robing room.

Meanwhile in the cells Alderson and Davies gave comfort to Watkins; as did the warders. On the journey back to the prison for the last time Watkins questioned the warders as to what was going to happen to him. All the time that he had been in Winson Green prior to the trial he had been anxious to do everything that was asked of him. He was always apprehensive of unwittingly doing anything that was wrong. The warders on this journey assured him that all would be well; and they were sincere. Generally when a person was found guilty of murder there was nothing but coolness mounting to unshown anger from the officers. They had a job to do but in the case of Watkins they felt differently. They had come to know him over the past weeks as a gentle soul. One officer told me that generally a prisoner in similar circumstances would not be told that the officers thought there would be a reprieve. "We have," he told me "a remarkably high record of successfully forecasting whether or not there would be a reprieve: no officer at Winson Green thought that this sentence would be carried out and I felt confident in telling Watkins so at the earliest opportunity: I meant what I said." He went on to tell me that after it was all over a number of officers were quietly angry that there had been no reprieve for Watkins. Many comparisons were made with other capital cases where there had been a reprieve. The general consensus throughout Winson Green was that if ever there was a case for a reprieve: this was it.

This, it must be remembered was in 1951. Three cases in 1978 have caught my eye and I think it proper, now, that for the case of Watkins to be seen in true perspective, other cases of this era must be compared with the trial of 1951. My comparison is simply to show how things have changed over the last twenty-seven years. I could find no similar case in 1951 to compare with this trial; this does not mean that there were no such cases, simply that my research did not reveal them.

Firstly from *The Birmingham Post*, 25th April, 1978, under the heading "Teenage Mother jailed for killing seven-week-old son" there appeared the following report:

> A teenage mother and her husband took their unwanted baby in a shopping bag on a motor-cycle, a court heard yesterday.
>
> The boy died when he was seven weeks old and his body showed 30 different marks of violence.
>
> Mr. Desmond Fennell, Q.C., prosecuting at Nottingham Crown Court said the injuries included: broken ribs, human bites, burns, and "a massive anvil-type blow to the head", which fractured his skull.
>
> Mr. Justice Mais, who said the baby was subjected to "the most indescribable acts of cruelty," jailed the mother for five years and the father for two years.
>
> He said he hoped never again to have to listen to such details of injuries inflicted on a small boy.
>
> X—— and Y—— of Mansfield, Notts., admitted manslaughter, and a joint charge of cruelty with her husband, Y—— (24).
>
> The mother's plea of not guilty to murder was accepted by the prosecution.

Mr. Brian Appleby, Q.C., defending the mother, said she married in Holland when she was only 16.

"She regarded her father as old-fashioned and dictatorial. She would literally have married anyone to get away from home."

He said this was a tragic but classic case of baby battering. The girl was emotionally unprepared for childbirth, and saw the baby as a liability.

Mr. Fennell said that after marrying, the couple moved into a small caravan in Mansfield. On the day before his death—on October 10 last year—a neighbour heard the baby screaming.

Secondly from *The Birmingham Post*, Tuesday, 22nd May, 1978, under the headline "Man killed crying baby son" there appeared the following report:

A Birmingham man who killed his 11-month-old son because he would not stop crying, could not tell his wife what he had done.

Birmingham Crown Court heard yesterday that after killing the baby he collected his wife from work as usual. They sat watching television, it was not until the following morning that the mother found her son dead in his cot.

X—— Y——, (23), of Z——, Birmingham, pleaded guilty to the manslaughter of his son J——. He was sentenced to three years' imprisonment.

Mr. Justice Gibson told X—— Y—— that it was a "grave and dreadful act, carried out in anger and resentment at the demands of a child."

X—— Y——'s plea of not guilty to murdering the child was accepted by the prosecution.

Mr. John Gorman, Q.C., prosecuting, said X—— Y——, a builder's labourer, looked after J—— in the evenings while his wife had a part-time job. J—— was found dead in his cot on the morning of October 28 last year. Medical evidence showed that he was dead when Mrs. X—— Y—— returned from work the previous evening. He had died from injuries to the head and abdomen, consistent with heavy blows from a fist.

X—— Y—— told police later that he had a headache, and J—— kept crying. He said: "I just went mad and kept hitting him. It seems like a nightmare. I tried to tell my wife, but I couldn't."

Mr. John Field Evans, Q.C., defending, said X—— Y—— was not normally violent, and he was very fond of the baby. He was an immature young man faced with a situation which he could not control and he was "shattered" by what he had done.

Thirdly from the *Evening Post* (published in Reading), 20th June, 1978, under a massive headline saying "MONSTER KILLER" and a sub-heading of ". . . tortured and shook toddler to death" there appeared the following report:

A three-year-old boy was tortured and shaken to death by a "monster", a court heard yesterday.

Labourer E—— F—— crudely "circumcised" G—— H—— 10 days before he died with a pair of nail clippers, Mr. David McNeil, prosecuting, told Liverpool Crown Court.

E—— F——, 24, who was jailed for a total of 15 years, admitted manslaughter, wounding with intent by circumcision, causing grievous bodily harm with intent by scaldings, and inflicting grievous bodily harm burns. He denied murdering G—— H——.

G—— H——'s mother, Miss J—— K——, 24, who was living at the time with E—— F—— in ——, Liverpool, admitted wilfully neglecting her son.

Mr. Justice Hollings told E—— F——: "It is difficult to know how to punish a person who has no feelings for human pain.

"The culmination came when, weakened from his other injuries through your ill-treatment, you shook that boy to death."

Mr. McNeill said E—— F——, who may or may not have been the child's father had tortured him by scalding his legs, burning his toes and shaking him so vigorously that he died from brain damage.

G—— H—— was taken to hospital when his mother called in a neighbour. She thought he was having a fit. He died from irreversible brain damage by shaking.

J—— K—— had known E—— F—— since she was 16. They had a sexual relationship from time to time and she went to live with him in —— just before Christmas.

After the child's death she was heard to describe E—— F—— as "a monster."

"In the final stages of the little boy's descent to death E—— F—— attempted to force his mouth open with a toothbrush and in doing so broke two of his teeth, ruptured his gum and broke the toothbrush," said Mr. McNeill.

Mr. Justin Price, Q.C., defending E—— F——, said E—— F——'s treatment of the boy was gross brutal ignorance in the desire to get him clean.

But E—— F—— did not intend to kill G—— H——, Mr. Price added.

Mr. Eric Somerset Jones, Q.C., defending J—— K——, said she was infatuated with E—— F——.

The Judge said that J—— K—— was plainly under the influence of E—— F—— but had failed sadly in her duty to her child. The maximum for the offence was two years' imprisonment. J—— K—— would be sentenced to 18 months, he said.

When I read these cases my mind goes back to the afternoon of Friday, 16th March, 1951 when William Fearnley-Whittingstall was addressing the jury and said in commenting on the prosecution's view of his client: "There is no evidence to show that the other child, Michael, has not been affectionately looked after. Does the evidence indicate that this man is that kind of murderer—it is not too high to put it to say" and then he paused and after a break said "that kind of monster". The effect on the jury was almost electric.

On the night of 16th March, 1951, William Arthur Watkins was taken to the condemned cell which had already been prepared in readiness. He was told to take off his own clothes and put on prison clothes—a suit with tie up laces and no buttons; a similar shirt: this he willingly did and as the two officers prepared for their long vigil through the night Watkins ate a hearty supper, smoked a number of cigarettes, read a little and seemingly went happily to sleep.

The Captains and the Kings departed to other cases and other courts and England prepared for the next day to mourn those who were killed in the terrible train crash at Doncaster. The 10.06 a.m. express from King's Cross to Doncaster on Friday, 16th March, had crashed at Balby Bridge Junction: at least fourteen were dead and at that time an unknown number injured.

On that same day Queen Elizabeth and her younger daughter, Princess Margaret, visited Boreham Wood Studios to see the best of England's actors and actresses making the Festival of Britain film, *The Magic Box*. Robert Donat and Maria Schell were on set and Donat, the possessor of a voice of such depth and poignancy, fluffed his lines. "I was so nervous," he said. The Chancellor of the Exchequer, Hugh Gaitskell, announced that there would be a new coin struck— a festival crown. Mr. Attlee the Prime Minister was due to go into hospital the following Wednesday; Jack Buchanan was to take over the lead in *King's Rhapsody* following the death of Ivor Novello; Princess Elizabeth was in Cheltenham fulfilling a programme that had had to be postponed because of her recent chill; George Wigg, Labour M.P. for Dudley, was rebuked by the Deputy Speaker, Major J. Milner, for reading a newspaper in the chamber of the House of Commons; Wigg replied that he did not have a pair of reading glasses with him and he was checking what Mr. L. D. Gammon (the M.P. who was speaking at that moment) was saying against what he had written previously and then went on to slate Mr. Gammon; B.S.A. acquired the share capital of Triumph Engineering Co. Ltd., the makers of Triumph motor cycles; Woodrow Wyatt, the energetic Labour M.P. for Aston, was reported as saying that "the Tories' childish tricks are bringing Parliament into disrepute"; he was referring to Churchill's night after night constant attempt to catch the Government out and suddenly spring a vote, which because there were more Tories in the house late at night, they would win—"What a hope," declared Wyatt. "They will get tired long before we do"; 9,440 London dockers staged a token strike as a result of proceedings taken against seven dockers charged with conspiring to incite an illegal strike. The Chief Metropolitan Magistrate, Sir Laurence Dunne was listening to the seventh day of the case and on this day, 16th March, 1951, one of the advocates before him appearing for some of the defendants was Mr. Sidney Silverman, M.P.—oh yes! a lot happened on that day and in between all the other news *The Birmingham Mail* found space to include under the two-column heading "Death sentence in bath-tub case – Judge and crucial factor" they reported:

> Sentence of death was passed today at Birmingham Assizes on William Arthur Watkins (aged 49), an enameller, of 6 back 79, Clifton Road, Balsall Heath, Birmingham, after he had been found guilty of murdering his newly-born child at his home on January 21.
>
> The jury were absent for 2½ hours before returning their verdict of Guilty.
>
> It had been alleged that Watkins and the woman with whom he had been living for five years, made no preparations for the birth of the child, and did not report its death to the police. They told neighbours that a doctor and midwife had been called at the birth, but this was later admitted to be untrue.
>
> The baby was found by police officers, head downwards, in a pillow case in a bath tub.
>
> The defence was that the baby was dropped in the bath by accident.
>
> Mr. Justice Finnemore, in his summing up, told the jury that it was clear that Watkins had been anxious to hide the birth of the child.
>
> Turning to the accused's story of bathing the baby, the Judge said: "If this man was washing the baby and it fell into the bath, how would it have got head first into the pillow case?
>
> "If he put the baby into the pillow slip before it went into the water it must throw very grave doubt on to his story that he was washing the child properly at the time of the accident, as he has stated in court.
>
> "This a crucial point to the story."
>
> The jury might feel, the Judge continued, that at the very least Watkins had acted with gross negligence, and, in fact, callousness. If his own story was true the child had fallen into the water and he had taken no steps to rescue it, but had left it in the water. In view of this the jury might think that at the least Watkins was guilty of manslaughter.
>
> "It is an unhappy, sordid story," the Judge added. "In most homes the arrival of a child is an event of rejoicing and happiness. But there is the tragedy of the unwanted child, and the prosecution declare that was so in this case."
>
> Watkins made no reply when the Judge passed sentence.

The *Evening Despatch* managed to find 25 closely printed small type lines for the case and the following morning both the *Birmingham Gazette* and *The Birmingham Post* reported the verdict as a very minor news item. No reporter mentioned the macabre way the sentence had been pronounced, for perhaps they, as others, thought that nothing would come of it, anyway.

To appeal or not was the question, and Fearnley-Whittingstall advised against it taking the view that humanity would step in; and in reality from the prisoner's answers, there was nothing he could in law appeal about. Watkins discussed this with Alderson at the prison and Watkins was quite content to take the advice and continued his daily routine, unperturbed, save and except for periods of his silent sobbing. The prison officers found him so easy. One described him to me as being "a gentleman himself: he did the washing up, he did the cleaning, he was difficult to talk to because he was so deaf but he read a lot and we played games with him, you know, draughts, ludo and snakes and ladders." The officers themselves were convinced there would be a reprieve; to them it was only a matter of time: for this they were thankful for there was no tension, it was only a matter of waiting.

Each day the Governor and the Chaplain came to see him, "Yes, I have everything I want, thank you," he would say to them. He had a special rapport with the Chaplain as they said prayers together.

Easter came and went but on Easter Sunday, 25th March, Bill went to the prison chapel. A special part was set aside so that no one could see him but he could see the Altar and the Chaplain. As always in prison the singing was vigorous and Bill joined in heartily.

The family did not come, and Bill did not ask to see anyone. Doris had been to see Mr. Lovsey to see if anything could be done but his party was not in government and he felt had little influence.

On the morning of 23rd March the following letter arrived at "Help the Poor Struggler" Inn:

OFFICE OF THE SHERIFF OF WARWICKSHIRE

H. M. BLENKINSOP	1 New Street
Undersheriff H/US	Warwick
Telephone No. 7	22nd March 1951

Mr. Albert Pierrepoint
Dear Sir,

William Arthur Watkins

Will you please let me know whether you can undertake to hold yourself available to carry out, should it be necessary at Winson Green Prison, Birmingham, sentence of death passed upon the above named. The date of the execution has been fixed subject to any Appeal, for Tuesday, 3rd. April 1951 at 9.0 a.m.

Will you please acknowledge and reply to this letter by return of post.

Should there be an Appeal or a Reprieve I will immediately inform you of the fact.

Yours faithfully
(Sgd.) H. M. Blenkinsop
Undersheriff of Warwickshire

Pierrepoint had not heard of Watkins and made a note in his diary with a question mark, and duly replied saying that he was available.

The words "should it be necessary" indicated to him that a reprieve was likely. He knew because he had had so many warnings before, and when those words were included his visit was generally cancelled.

On Saturday, 31st March, in the morning, Mr. Brown received a telephone call from the Home Office informing him that there was to be no reprieve and that the execution would take place the following Tuesday, 3rd April, at 9.00 a.m. Mr. Fearnley-Whittingstall had not been inactive: his plaintive request to Sir Frank Newsam had been rejected. At his own expense, in his own time, this great K.C. showed enormous care and courage. Care because it was he who had advised no appeal and courage because it was almost unheard of for an advocate of such eminence to go to the Home Office to plead on behalf of a condemned man.

John Brown immediately had another telephone call, this time from the Undersheriff confirming that he too had heard from Sir Frank Newsam; and adding that Pierrepoint was available.

There was much to be done: the execution chamber next door to the condemned cell had to be prepared, a coffin had to be ordered. It was going to be a terrible week-end.

The Governor and the Chaplain went together to the condemned cell, and when told the news, the prisoner's eyes filled with tears and he nodded. The Governor asked if there was anybody he would like to see. There was silence for a few moments, and then Watkins looked up and said: "Doris; and the kids; and Maisie; and Mr. Lovsey."

Doris was immediately contacted by a plain clothes policeman who told her of the decision and of Bill's request. She had not set eyes upon him since 1946, nor had the children. Arrangements were quickly made and they went to the prison. All now that can be remembered was a walk along a wire mesh corridor, going into a room with a wire mesh barrier and beyond it—"Dad". Two warders stood as if not to listen. It was harrowing, and the meeting suddenly became so poignant when Doris asked Bill if things went O.K. would he come back. He shook his head and said, "We'll have to see . . . we'll have to see." The family were horrified by the way he had aged. By some unexplainable piece of mismanagement, as Doris and the family left the prison, so Maisie entered.

Bill Lovsey, President of the Aston Villa Shareholder's Association, was at Villa Park sitting with Bruce Normansell, whose father, Fred

Normansell was then chairman of the club; to this day, the name Normansell in still associated with the "Villa". It was half-time in the home match against Sheffield Wednesday; the score was 1–1. Dave Walsh, the Villa's Irish International (who was their centre forward) had scored a magnificent goal to put Villa in the lead and then Eric Woodhead had equalized for Sheffield Wednesday. The players were just coming out onto the field for the second half when a policeman tapped Lovsey on the shoulder, "Mr. Lovsey," he said, "Yes?" said Lovsey. "Could you come with me please; I've come from the prison. Billy Watkins wants to see you," said the policeman. They went straight away and when Bill Lovsey learnt later that Tommy Thompson had put the ball in the net for the Villa to win he was past caring. Bruce Normansell, who in 1945 had been driven by Watkins, throughout his election campaign, will never forget that afternoon. After Lovsey had left; the game for him, had no meaning.

At the prison Lovsey was met by the Governor and taken by him to the visitors' room for condemned prisoners, the same room the others had been in. There he saw an old man whom he recognized as Watkins; like the others he had not seen him for five years and the change was remarkable.

"They're going to hang me, Mr. Lovsey," Bill said. Then, after a pause, between his silent tears, he added, "Look after the wife and kids for me." Lovsey nodded; there was nothing he could say but agree—he had scarcely ever had any contact with them and since Bill had left none at all. Bill's enormous eyes for one moment opened in a plea of humanity, then they filled, and Lovsey thought to himself, "they can't hang him".

That same day Mr. Blenkinsop sent a telegram to Pierrepoint and followed it with a letter:

OFFICE OF THE SHERIFF OF WARWICKSHIRE

H. M. BLENKINSOP   1 New Street
Undersheriff   Ref. H/H/US/GEN   Warwick
Telephone 7   31st March, 1951
Mr. Albert Pierrepoint
Dear Sir,

William Arthur Watkins

It is now definite that the Sentence of Death passed upon the above will be carried into effect on Tuesday the 3rd April at Birmingham Prison. I therefore wired you this morning as follows:

14

"The engagement for Tuesday 3rd April definite, please
report Birmingham in good time Monday the 2nd April.
"Undersheriff of Warwickshire.

Yours faithfully

(Sgd.) H. M. Blenkinsop

Undersheriff of Warwickshire

On receipt of the telegram Albert Pierrepoint told Anne that he
had to be in Birmingham for Monday night. Anne knew what that
meant, and as always, asked no questions.

The Editor of the *Evening Despatch* sent a reporter to No. 6 back of
79 Clifton Road and that night published on the front page under the
heading "No reprieve for baby's killer" the following:

> A young woman sat in the fireless front room of a back house in Balsall Heath,
> Birmingham, with her three-year-old son and learned today that his father is to
> hang for murdering her newly-born child.
>
> The Home Secretary has decided not to recommend a reprieve for William
> Arthur Watkins, who was sentenced to death at Birmingham Assizes on March 16.
>
> Since she returned from hospital, where she was taken after Watkins's arrest,
> the woman, Maisie ———, has seen no one except her mother, who stayed only
> a few days.
>
> She is living on 34s. public assistance, and expects to be given notice to quit
> the house at 6/79 Clifton Road, where she lived with Watkins.
>
> "I was sure Bill would be reprieved and I was going to wait for him," she said.
> "But what can I do now?"
>
> *Watkins was told about the no-reprieve decision in the condemned cell at Winson Green
> gaol today. His execution is due to take place next Tuesday.*
>
> *Mr. J. A. Alderson, Birmingham solicitor, said later that Mr. Fearnley-Whittingstall,
> K.C., who defended Watkins, was seeking a further interview with the Home Secretary.*

That night, in Balsall Heath, Percy Shurmer was due to hold his
regular "surgery". He arrived two hours late and was clearly upset.
"I'm so sorry," he said to the constituents, "I was up till 3.00 a.m.
this morning trying to see the Home Secretary about that poor devil
in Clifton Road"—then his voice nearly broke as turning his back
on them and opening the door to the interview room, he said "it was
all to no avail."

That Saturday night the football fans discussed the results, the film
fans the fact that John Mills was ill and the racegoers the fact that
the "wonder boy jockey" Lester Piggott was injured after being
thrown.

Bill asked for pen and paper and wrote to the family; when they
went to him they took letters in case what happened did happen, and
emotion overtook everything. It is not possible to tell exactly when

each letter was written; but clearly all were written during the period 31st March to 2nd April, 1951. He dated two of them 31.3.51 and one he did not date at all. In these letters we find courage and hope and the feeling that he, whatever be the outcome, had found his God: one can imagine the feelings of those that received them. They speak for themselves.

(Each letter is reproduced as Watkins wrote them: the names, of course, except for Doris, have been deleted.)

Goodbye for ever Dad

In replying to this letter, please write on the envelope:—Number 7122 Name Watkins W. BIRMINGHAM Prison 31/3/51

Dear ——— (*This letter is addressed to his youngest daughter*)

I was very pleased you wrote to me such a nice letter. You don't want to worry about being so shy—you will get over that. I have often thought about that game of draughts when you beat me that time and I think I was as pleased as you were. I was so glad you all came up to see me; it cheered me up a lot. Don't worry, I have prayed every day for God's help and He has never let me down yet—a wonderful thing. Even when I wanted a house I prayed for one and got one, so I am confident in God's help always. Well, ———, I am quite well and my hearing is a lot better now than when I came in here first—even in court I couldn't hear a word that was said and it was very awkward for me—still, I am still hoping for the best. Well, ———, you asked me a question and I have often thought how nice it would be to be with you all: remember this, I had nothing against you children. What happened was between your mom and me, you may have heard her side of the story but never heard mine. Still, I shall always love you children and help you all I could like I tried to help ——— [*his eldest living son*], still what is done cannot be undone now, but remember, I am always thinking of you all, wondering how you are getting on. I am very pleased you are married to ——— [*his son-in-law who on the last morning sat in the café*] I didn't know before and I hope you are always happy together. Well, ———, I do hope you write to me again as a letter like your's is a big help to me here and I should always be glad to hear from you, even if I couldn't write back to you straight away. Well, ———, remember me to all my old friends and I am still keeping my chin up hoping for the best. Tell ——— [*the youngest son*] I was glad to see him looking so well and ——— [*the eldest daughter*]. Well I think that is all for now so will close with love to all from your loving Dad

× × × × × × × × × × ×

In replying to this letter, please write on the envelope:—Number 7122 Name Watkins W A BIRMINGHAM Prison 31/3

(*To his wife*)

Dear Doss

I am writing this letter to you as perhaps it may be the last, but please God I am hoping for something to turn up at the last minute. I am still keeping my chin up. I went to Church this morning (Sunday) and I prayed hard. I know you are all doing your best for me. I have arranged visit on Monday. Well, Doss, it is a funny life, please try and don't worry too much: we have both made mistakes, but we had a long time together so try and think of the past when we were happy together. I was very pleased you came up to see me; remember me to all my friends in Victoria Road.

Well, in case, Doss, good bye and God Bless you all. I am sorry things have turned out like this for the children's sake. One thing as they say I was always a good father to them

Good Bye
× × Doss ×

Don't worry too much

(To his eldest son, his daughter-in-law and grandchild)

Well, ———, try and forget things and look after your wife and child like I looked after you, and you will have done your best. I hope you get on alright and I wish you all the best in case of the worst. Goodbye and God Bless. Kiss baby for me. × × × Dad × × × × × × ×

(To his youngest son)

Dear ———

I am very pleased to see you have grown up into such a big boy and your drawings are wonderful. I was very pleased to see you and I wish you all the best. Be a good boy always and always trust in God. Well, ———, I am too full to write much more now so Good Bye and God Bless you always.

Your loving Dad

× × × × × × × × × × ×

I am sending letters back enclosed for you that you sent me

(To his youngest daughter and son-in-law)

I am still hoping that God will help me but I am writing this last Good Bye in case of the worst. Well, I thank you for all you have done for me it doesn't seem real somehow to me at all, still what is to be will be. Well, ———, I wish you both all the best in the world. Don't worry too much. I would like it if you didn't, so buck up and pray for me. Good Bye and God Bless you always.

× × × × × × ×   Your Loving Dad
× × × × × ×

Thank all friends for all help they have given. × × tell Mr. Lovsey I am very grateful for what he has done for me, remember me to all. The last hymn I sang in church was my mother's favourite, "Abide with Me".

Dad.

(To his eldest daughter)

Dear ———

I was pleased to see you all and all looking so well. Well dear, don't worry too much. I know it is very hard but pray to God, and He will help you always. I was very pleased to receive your welcome letter. Well, ———, I can only wish you all the best in the world. I am too full to write any more but I am still hoping

now that something will turn up for me anyway that is in God's hands now, so in case, Good Bye dear and God Bless you. Your loving
Dad.
I shall be seeing you all this afternoon Monday so for now Good Bye All and remember me in your prayers. Please God something turns up for me if not I shall be thinking of you all at the last.
Your Loving
Dad.

In replying to this letter please write on the envelope Number 7122 Name Watkins W BIRMINGHAM Prison

Dear ——— (*to his eldest daughter*)

I am writing to you as I promised yesterday, and I hope you will write back to me as a letter from anyone is always welcome. Well, I was glad you came up to see me. Tell ——— [*the youngest daughter*] to learn not to be so shy. Well, ———, I am glad to say I am feeling very well and my hearing is getting better than it was all the time I was in the court. I couldn't hear a word that was said and it made it very bad for me but I had a lawyer and one of the best K.C's in the country. I may say he is still doing his best for me as I understand he is seeing the Home Secretary about my case, so I am still hoping for the best and I am keeping as cheerful as I can. I have been well looked after here. I came here on my birthday and I was put in a hospital ward. I have plenty of good food, and go outside for fresh air twice a day about half an hour each time. I have about 50 books to read, games, draughts, cards, and jig saw puzzles. Everyone here has been very good to me since I came here. The Governor comes in twice a day to see me, and the Doctor and the Chaplain—he has been very good to me and he stops for half an hour sometimes, talking to me. The Officers and Staff are all good to me as well and I appreciate it very much, so you can see I am alright—in fact I think I have put on a lot of weight in the last week. Tell your mother I was glad she came to see me, and I am looking forward to seeing ——— [*the youngest son*]. I wish you would tell Mrs. Edwards that I am alright and remember me to them all also all my old friends who ask about me. When you write back, put the number on the envelope that is on the top of this letter. If you all write a bit you can make a letter up between you. Tell ——— [*the eldest son*] I wish him many happy returns for his birthday and tell ——— [*the youngest son*] I wish he would write a little letter to me. I went to Church here on Good Friday and last Sunday and we had a lovely service, and I am looking forward to going again next Sunday. Well, ———, I think that is about all for now except don't worry too much about me, I don't like people to worry about me as I always come up smiling as you know. So tell your mom and all at home to hope for the best and keep smiling like me,
so cheerio for now
to all.
DAD.
P.S. Please write back to me.

On Sunday, 1st April, Bill asked the Chaplain if in chapel that morning they could sing "Abide with me". This was readily agreed to and those around him in the prison noticed a change in him; he

had an air of peace and on that Sunday sang with the other prisoners
the hymn he loved so much:

> "Abide with me; fasts falls the eventide:
>   The darkness deepens; Lord, with me abide!
>   When other helpers fail, and comforts flee,
>   Help of the helpless, O abide with me.
>
>   Swift to its close ebbs our life's little day;
>   Earth's joys grow dim, its glories pass away;
>   Change and decay in all around I see;
>   O thou who changest not, abide with me.
>
>   I need thy presence every passing hour;
>   What but thy grace can foil the tempter's power?
>   Who like thyself my guide and stay can be?
>   Through cloud and sunshine, O abide with me.
>
>   I fear no foe with thee at hand to bless;
>   Ills have no weight, and tears no bitterness.
>   Where is death's sting? Where, grave, thy victory?
>   I triumph still, if thou abide with me.
>
>   Hold thou thy cross before my closing eyes;
>   Shine through the gloom, and point me to the skies:
>   Heaven's morning breaks, and earth's vain shadows flee;
>   In life, in death, O Lord, abide with me!"

[*in the letter where he talks of "my mother", I think he is either referring
to Doris or his stepmother: and as he did not think much of her it would seem
to be an obviously, forgiveable, slip of the pen, as of course is the date 31st
March, 1951 when he refers to "today Sunday".*]

The officers flanking him on this Sunday, his last, found his par-
ticipation in the service unnerving. At the end of the service he walked
back with the warders seeing no one, himself unseen.

On the Monday the *Birmingham Gazette* reported that another
attempt by Fearnley-Whittingstall had failed when it printed under
the heading "murderer to hang":

Eleventh-hour attempts have failed to obtain a reprieve for William Arthur
Watkins, aged 49, of Clifton Road, Balsall Heath, due to be hanged at Birmingham
Prison at 9 a.m. tomorrow for the murder of a baby boy, born to a woman with
whom he was said to have been living.

On Saturday, after it had been announced that the Home Secretary had decided
not to recommend a reprieve, it was learned that Mr. W. Fearnley-Whittingstall,
K.C., who defended Watkins at his trial at Birmingham Assizes, intended to
seek a further interview with the Home Secretary.

Today, Mr. J. A. Alderson, a Birmingham solicitor, said: "Mr. Fearnley-Whittingstall has had a further conversation with the Home Secretary, but has been unsuccessful."

Doris and the family came once more to the prison: farewells were said amongst the tears and no one really heard what the others said. The visit was short, emotional and disturbing.

In the early morning, unseen by anyone, a coffin had been brought to the prison and placed in the execution chamber; a grave was dug later that day behind the mat shop.

That same morning Albert Pierrepoint—dapper, wearing his usual trilby hat and smart suit, kissed Anne goodbye and set off to Birmingham carrying his overnight case. He travelled by train and arrived at Birmingham's New Street Station at 12.20 p.m. An Inspector, who Pierrepoint knew from previous visits, was detailed to meet the train. They walked together to the police club and played a game of snooker. The pair then had lunch—Pierrepoint remembers it as being particularly good—and the Inspector drove Pierrepoint to the prison, arranging to pick him up the following morning about 10.30 a.m. He was immediately taken to Mr. Brown's office and they talked about Bill Watkins, the case, the trial and the decision. The Governor asked what length of rope he intended to use but Pierrepoint explained that he would have to see the prisoner first. The Chief Officer was sent for and escorted Pierrepoint to the Judas hole but Watkins was not in view, and after realizing that he was not going to move went back to the Governor's office, from where they went to the execution chamber to make certain that the practical parts of the scaffold were in perfect order. He then tested the scaffold to make certain that all was well. "As we were leaving," Pierrepoint told me, "to go to our room for a meal, I thought I would take another look through the Judas hole into the condemned cell. This time I had a full view, I looked at the slip of paper in my hand which the Governor had given me, which had on it the prisoner's age, height and weight. I found his age was 49 and I looked again to see if I had read his age correctly. I checked again with the Governor and he told me it was correct, but if I had had to give his age I would have put it at 65, if not more. If I remember, correctly, his hair was grey and he looked so dejected and slightly stooped, as though he couldn't care less: suddenly I felt sorry seeing a man looking so sad and just waiting to die. It was not a nice feeling.

window; their coffee getting colder and colder and as their eyes became full, they could not see, but it did not matter: they were there.

Within the condemned cell, things were more peaceful. At 8.00 a.m. the Chaplain arrived and gave Bill communion. Together they said the Lord's Prayer and in the name of the Christ he served, the Chaplain forgave Bill for what he had done. The two prison officers found themselves affected by the scene and wished that time would not linger: the last hour always seemed the longest.

At 8.40 a.m. Mr. Blenkinsop (the Undersheriff) arrived, and was quickly taken to the Governor's Office. Dr. John Humphreys (the prison doctor) was already there. At 8.55 a.m., Pierrepoint and his assistant stood outside the door of the condemned cell and were joined within a minute by the Governor, the doctor and the Chief Prison Officer.

Within the cell Watkins was now seated with his back to the door, and seconds before the door opened, looked up, sobbing, and said to the Chaplain, "I have never met so many kind people in my life as I have met since I have been here. Why did I have to come to prison before people are so kind?" The Chaplain had to turn away for fear of showing his own emotion. Already the Undersheriff had given the signal: it was 30 seconds past 8.59 a.m. The door opened; Pierrepoint was behind Watkins: "Come on, old fellow," he said in his soft Lancastrian voice. He pinioned his arms, and with an officer either side, Bill was escorted through the now opened doors to the scaffold. The assistant was down on his knees pinioning his legs, Pierrepoint put a hand under his drooping chin, placed a white hood over his head and then the noose, stepped back and pulled the lever. Since Pierrepoint had entered the room 12 seconds had passed: justice had been done.

Pierrepoint and Humphreys immediately went down the stairs to the pit where the body of Watkins, dressed in his own old grey suit, gently swung. Humphreys pronounced life extinct after listening with his stethoscope to the dead man's chest. Executioner and doctor then walked up the stairs, closed the door, which was then locked; and went with the Governor, Chaplain and Undersheriff for coffee.

At 9.02 a.m. a notice was affixed outside the prison and the eldest son and the son-in-law put down their coffee they had not touched and walked slowly through the crowd. Their eyes were too full to read what it said: but they knew anyway. There were children in the crowd. Life went on.

At 10.00 a.m. Pierrepoint and his assistant went down to the pit and gently took the body out of the noose and lay it in the coffin. They tidied up, as did the officers in the cell. At 10.30 a.m., as Pierrepoint left the prison, the coffin was placed in the prepared grave. The Chaplain said a prayer for his soul, and the grave was filled in.

Later that day an inquest was held by the City Coroner, Dr. W. H. Davison, and in the evening a photograph of part of the crowd appeared in *The Birmingham Mail*. "Execution at Winson Green" the headline read, "Man's workmates wait at gate" was the subheading. The report read:

> William Arthur Watkins, 49-year-old enameller, of 6/79, Clifton Road, Balsall Heath, was hanged at Winson Green Prison today for the murder of a newly-born child at his home on January 21.
>
> The execution took place at 9 a.m., and two minutes later the formal notice announcing that Watkins had been hanged was placed outside the new teak gates of the prison.
>
> It was signed by Dr. John Humphreys, prison doctor, the governor, Mr. J. W. Brown, Mr. H. M. Blenkinsop, Under-Sheriff, and the Rev. F. Thompson, prison chaplain.
>
> It is understood that Pierrepoint was the executioner.
>
> Two of Watkins's former workmates were in the crowd of about 50 which waited outside the prison. The rest were mainly women and children—the latter on holiday from school.
>
> After reading the notice they dispersed quietly.
>
> Later, the Birmingham City Coroner (Dr. W. H. Davison) sitting with an all-male jury, conducted the inquest at which a verdict was returned of "Death by judicial hanging."
>
> The prison governor, Mr. J. W. Brown, produced a letter which he handed to the Coroner. It was from the Home Secretary saying there were insufficient grounds to interfere with the due course of justice.
>
> Watkins was sentenced to death by Mr. Justice Finnemore at Birmingham Assizes last month. It was stated that after the woman he had been living with gave birth to a child Watkins put it in a pillow case and drowned it in a bath tub.

The death certificate stated the cause of death to be "Fractured dislocation of cervical vertebrae: Execution of sentence of death". On that certificate his occupation was given as "an Enameller", something he had never been. How appropriate it would have been had it said, "Former charabanc driver", but no: like so many things surrounding the life of William Arthur Watkins, people had it wrong.

At 5.30 p.m. that night, Albert Pierrepoint was opening the door of the "Help The Poor Struggler". On drawing the pints that night, no one asked him where he had been; because beyond Birmingham there was no mention of the execution in any newspaper or news bulletin on the radio. Bill Watkins' death had been in keeping with his life; uneventful and un-newsworthy.

Earlier that morning around 9.00 a.m., almost to the second that Pierrepoint pulled the lever, a postman pushed a letter through the letter box at No. 136 Victoria Road, Aston. It was addressed to Bill's youngest daughter: she had gone back home to be with her mum. Whilst her husband and her brother sat in the café, she opened the letter from her dad: written across the top, above his prison number and the letter itself, in much larger, yet bolder writing, without even a quiver, was the last farewell: "Goodbye for ever".

INDEX

The letter-by-letter system is used. For legal issues of trial see under Trial.